D0205312

Time, Tide, and Tempest

DVM CLAVVM RECTVM TENEAM

He, *that his* Courſe *directly Steeres,*
Nor Stormes, *nor* Windy-Cenſures *feares.*

Time
Tide and Tempest

A STUDY OF
SHAKESPEARE'S ROMANCES

by Douglas L. Peterson

THE HUNTINGTON LIBRARY
SAN MARINO, CALIFORNIA
1973

Published with the assistance of the
Union Pacific Railroad Foundation Fund

Copyright © 1973
Huntington Library Publications
San Marino, California
Library of Congress Catalog Card Number 72-94155
Designed by Ward Ritchie
Printed in the United States of America
by Anderson, Ritchie & Simon

FOR
JAN
KRIS
ERIN
AND PETEY

For first, what is this world, but a sea, wherein wee nauigate and are in continuall danger; Nay, the sea is so variable, so inconstant, and so outragious? For if we haue neuer so little respite, peace and rest, (like as when the sea is calme & quiet) presently there arise such violent whirle windes, stormes and furious tempests, as it seemeth oftentimes, that heauen, earth, and all the elements conspire and runne together to worke our ruine. Yea, when this wicked world sheweth vs fairest countenance, and becommeth most calme and gentle, and that it feedeth vs with the fattest morsels, then is it most false vnto vs, and then are we in greatest danger. For when we thinke our selues most sure therein, then are we sodainely tost and carried away, as with violent waues and horrible whirle windes, into the lowest gulfs and deeps of the earth.

PETER DE LA PRIMAUDAYE,
The French Academy
(London, 1618)

Contents

Frontispiece: from *A Collection of Emblemes,*
George Wither, London, 1635

PREFACE

The romances, those enigmatic and strangely remote plays which complete the Shakespeare canon, have not been popular with contemporary audiences and until recently have received relatively little serious attention from the critics. The reasons are not hard to find. The plays disappoint the expectations of audiences who have come to assume that conventions of realism and verisimilitude are essential to the successful representation of human experience in the narrative forms. For the critic they lack the kind of searching exploration and portrayal of character so much admired in the major tragedies. There is also their optimism. Modern skepticism is not amenable to reassuring voices out of the past. Epistemology has been replaced by linguistic analysis; ethical and moral certitudes have gone the way of Christian myth. Lear's violent and apparently indifferent universe seems to us more relevant than Macbeth's. Pericles' world, or Prospero's, seems even further removed than Macbeth's and is at best an entertaining memorial of what was once a comforting illusion.

The questions that the commentators have begun to ask about these enigmatic last plays may lead eventually to a renewed interest in their performance. The puzzling problems of interpretation, the validity of considering them as a group, their relationship to each other and to the rest of Shakespeare's plays, are of immediate interest only to the critic and the scholar. Nevertheless, how those questions are resolved will eventually affect the frequency and quality of the performance of each of the plays. If, for instance, *Pericles* could be shown, as I believe it can, to be concerned with the same problems explored in *Lear* and as carefully (though differently) structured, it might receive the serious attention which has been so long overdue and be performed as something more than a curious antiquarian piece.

My purposes in this book are several. I want to make each of the romances intelligible to an extent they have not been made intelligible before. I hope also to establish their relationship to each other and to Shakespeare's earlier works. Above all, I want to reclaim the romances for the contemporary audience by establishing the mimetic principles that account for the strange worlds they create and by identifying the peculiarly modern epistemological concerns to which each of the plays returns.

The opening section of the first chapter raises the question of why in his last plays Shakespeare turned to the conventions and materials of romance, and proposes as an answer a hypothesis which is tested, and I believe confirmed, by the close examination of individual plays in the chapters following. In the rest of the opening chapter I endeavor to reconstruct the system of ideas which I believe informs what commentators have commonly identified as the "restorative pattern" of the romances. I have been conscious of, and have tried to avoid, the principal dangers involved in the undertaking. J. F. Danby's astute criticism of the "two explaining systems which have been recently applied to the last plays,"—the anthropological and the theological—should serve as a cautionary reminder to anyone who sets out to interpret these plays.[1]

I have tried to stay as close to Shakespeare as possible. I have derived my generalizations about the "restorative pattern" of the romances from the language and action of each of the four plays. I have supported those generalizations with evidence derived from the rest of Shakespeare's works, the sonnets and poems as well as his earlier plays. I have gone outside of Shakespeare to consult his contemporaries and predecessors when it has seemed to me that the evidence of Shakespeare's sharing a common intellectual tradition and its metaphorical configurations is incontrovertible.

The method has had two results which I had not anticipated. It has led me to conclusions about the relationship of the last plays to those immediately preceding them, which, so far as I know, have not been advanced previously. The second result is that I have made, I believe, at least a beginning at establishing the "critical language capable of interpreting the romances" for which Philip Edwardes some years ago cautiously hoped.[2]

The debts incurred in the writing of this book are too numerous to list. At the very least, anyone writing at this date on Shakespeare's last plays must acknowledge a general thanks to such men as G. Wilson Knight, E. M. W. Tillyard, E. C. Pettett, S. L. Bethel, J. F. Danby, Derek Traversi, and Northrop Frye. Whatever my own disagreements with each of these men have been—and they have been substantial—their scholarship and literary intelligence have made my own book possible. They have asked many of the right questions. Bethel, Danby, Frye, and Pettett deserve special mention for calling to our attention intellectual, dramatic, and folk traditions that are contextually important to the plays.

There are several works, however, to which I owe a particular debt. Ernest Schanzer's "The Structural Pattern of *The Winter's Tale*,"[3] and Clifford Leech's "The Structure of the Last Plays,"[4] were extremely helpful in leading me to the theory of cyclical structure that I propose for the romances. Of course neither of these critics is responsible for what errors I may have committed in moving on to my own conclusions. Hallett Smith's "Shakespeare's Romances"[5] and Virgil K. Whitaker's *The Mirror Up to Nature*[6] also deserve special mention. Professor Smith, by calling attention to certain resemblances as well as differences between the romances and the tragedies, raised questions which led me to consider the differences between tragic and romantic modes of mimesis, and thus to the theory I advance as an explanation of Shakespeare's turning in his last plays to the materials of romance. Professor Whitaker's discussion of the tragedies as manifesting a theory of poetry that corresponds closely to the one proposed by Sir Philip Sidney in *The Defence of Poesie* led me to reconsider the similarities between Shakespeare's romances and Sidney's *Arcadia* that J. F. Danby had pointed out in *Poets on Fortune's Hill* and to reconsider the romances in the light of Sidney's notions of poetry as both *poesis* and *mimesis*.

Finally, I am anxious to express my appreciation to those members of the Huntington Library staff who have made the preparation of this book possible and a pleasure to have undertaken; to my wife, Margaret, whose patience is matched only by her eye for cant and folly; to Morton Rosenbaum, who first introduced me to the German art historians and who continues to draw upon his encyclopedic lore to instruct me in iconography; and to Gwendolyn Staniforth, Dolora Cunningham, and Jack Conner for their many helpful suggestions and for their careful reading of earlier versions of the materials that have gone into the making of this book.

November 1971   DOUGLAS PETERSON

Preface

NOTES

[1] "Anthropology does not take us far enough. By its insidious precipitations it tends to silt over the clear and sharp contours of the Renaissance moral world. The second explaining system errs in the opposite direction. It carries us too far and too fast. It particularizes in a field of meaning beyond Shakespeare's intention—though Shakespeare, I have no doubt, would know St. Paul and the burial service, and accepted the New Testament. To theologize the last plays, however, is to distort them. Though patience as Shakespeare conceives it implies St. Paul and the New Testament, patience as Shakespeare realizes it in the Last Plays is a familiar and well-walked parish in a wider diocese. Nor is the parish presided over by the Fisher King, and in it St. Paul is taken for granted but not allegorized in every Whitsun pastoral." John F. Danby, *Poets on Fortune's Hill* (London, 1952), pp. 97-98.

[2] "Shakespeare's Romances: 1900-1957," *Shakespeare Survey*, 11 (1957), 1-18, p. 18.

[3] *Review of English Literature*, 5 (1964), 72-82.

[4] *Shakespeare Survey*, 11 (1958), 19-30.

[5] *The Huntington Library Quarterly*, 27 (1963-64), 279-87.

[6] San Marino, 1965.

Time, Tide, and Tempest

I

Romance Convention
and Modes of Dramatic Illusion

SHAKESPEARE'S ROMANCES, coming as they do in the wake of
the tragedies, suffer an obvious chronological disadvantage.
Even when we realize that beginning with *Pericles*, Shakespeare turned to a new genre, one with different requirements and
with different demands upon his talents, we are still disappointed.
We miss the old intensities. Even *The Winter's Tale* and *The Tempest*, the most widely admired plays of the group, seem pallid when
compared with *Hamlet* or *Lear*.

If we are going to evaluate the romances on their own terms, we
must recognize at the outset that Shakespeare in turning from
tragedy to tragicomedy makes an equally decisive shift in thematic
interests. He turns from the destructive power of evil to the restorative power of good. In so doing, he was not following the example
of Beaumont and Fletcher. He was not retreating into a comfortable
world of pseudo-problems, happy coincidences, and convenient
miracles. He was, rather, seeking more effective ways of dealing with
the metaphysical and epistemological problems with which the

tragedies had begun to involve him. The result was a radically new mode of tragicomedy which, by appropriating the improbable fictions of romance, allowed him to celebrate the restorative power of the good and to affirm, in the face of growing Jacobean skepticism and despite all appearances to the contrary, a morally coherent universe.

The emergence of these concerns is foreshadowed in the late tragedies. In *Richard II, Julius Caesar,* and *Macbeth* a natural and moral order is assumed. Violations of natural law provoke increasingly violent disorder until retribution is visited upon the guilty and order is at least temporarily restored. However shocking the extent of human depravity may be, there is, finally, in each of these plays, the reassuring stability of a universe whose structure and continued existence are contingent upon natural law. The suffering of the innocent is subsumed by the tragic formula. Lady Macduff and her precocious son may fall victim to tyrants; nevertheless, a moral universe is affirmed in the final retribution that is visited upon tyrants. Through violations of natural law they assure their own destruction.

But in *Hamlet* there emerges something that is indicative of the general questioning, at the end of the century, of the old order. This is an epistemological as well as a moral issue: the effect of feeling upon perception. The consequence of Hamlet's inability to reconcile himself to his father's death and his mother's hasty marriage is a pervasive melancholy which colors the way in which he perceives the world. His distorted reading of appearances will be repeated by Othello and, in the romances, by Cymbeline, Posthumus, and Leontes. From his particular situation he draws a general conclusion about the entire world:

> How weary, stale, flat, and unprofitable,
> *Seems to me all the uses of this world!*
> Fie on't! oh fie, fie! 'Tis an unweeded garden,
> That grows to seed; things rank and gross in nature
> Possess it merely.[1]   (I.ii.133-37)

Later, under the weight of his recently acquired knowledge of the circumstances of his father's death, he confesses to Rosencrantz and

Guildenstern that he is no longer able to see the world as he rationally comprehends it. Again the epistemological issue is implicit. Hamlet's misinterpretation of reality comes about through a loss of belief and a subsequent reliance upon *seeming:*

> indeed
> it goes so [heavily] with my disposition that this goodly frame, the earth, *seems* to me a sterile promontory, this most excellent canopy, the air, look you, this brave o'erhanging [firmament], this majestical roof fretted with golden fire, why, *it appears no other thing to me* than a foul and pestilent congregation of vapours. What a piece of work is a man! How noble in reason! How infinite in faculty, in form and moving! How express and admirable in action! How like an angel in apprehension! . . . The paragon of animals! And yet, *to me*, what is this quintessence of dust? (II.ii.308-20)

Under the pale cast of such melancholy reflection Hamlet finds himself, alternately, a slave to ennui and to the passion of revenge. He will free himself only after he recovers his belief in a divinity that "shapes our ends" and comes finally to accept his death on the grounds that there is an unseen reality that gives purpose even to death. Once free, he will submit himself to what is to be, and will finally fulfill the purpose for which he believes he has been born.

A variation of this theme—the consequences of the loss of belief upon perception—occurs in *Timon*. *Timon*, unlike *Hamlet*, does not examine the consequences of the failure to believe in a shaping providence. It explores, instead, the consequences of a loss of belief in *humanitas*. When Timon discovers that the very people on whom he has wasted his fortune refuse to offer him help in his bankruptcy, he succumbs to a skepticism so deep that mankind appears to him to be totally and irredeemably evil. In his self-imposed exile he denies the virtues of *humanitas* on which the idea of community is founded,[2] and calls upon nature to destroy bestial man. His misanthropy begins with his discovery of human imperfection. Like Hamlet he reasons from particular circumstances to a universal condition, allowing his anger and disillusionment to turn every detail of perception into evidence of absolute human depravity.

The fullest exploration among the tragedies of the final dependence of seeing upon belief occurs in *Lear*. The suffering undergone by the innocent raises the question of cosmic justice. How are we to understand Cordelia's death and the additional torment it causes Lear? In posing the question to themselves, Kent, Edgar, and Albany pose for us all the question that has troubled audiences and critics for at least a century.

Albany has interpreted the violent deaths of Goneril and Regan as a "judgement of the heavens, that makes us tremble" (V.iii.231). But the sight of Lear as he enters with the lifeless Cordelia in his arms raises doubts. His response echoes the skepticism of Kent and Edgar.

> *Kent:*   Is this the promis'd end?
> *Edgar:*   Or image of that horror?
> *Albany:*   Fall, and cease!
>
>   (V.iii.263-64)

For these men the notion of cosmic justice is deeply challenged by the scene that confronts them. If such justice exists, it is a terrible justice. The innocent Cordelia has come to the same end as her vicious sisters, and just as violently; and Lear, who would appear already to have more than paid for his folly, must now suffer the loss of his only remaining heir—the daughter whose love for him has never faltered. Hence, the question: Is the figure of Lear with the dead Cordelia in his arms truly an *image* of "the promised end"? Does it truly represent what it seems to represent?

For us these questions have another dimension. We must determine the dramatic intention informing the scene. The matter is further complicated by Lear's,

> This feather stirs; she lives! If it be so,
> It is a chance which does redeem all sorrows
> That ever I have felt;
>
>   (ll. 265-67)

and by his conviction in the moment of his death that she does indeed live. The answer to the question raised by Edgar, Kent, and Albany depends on belief. To believe that "the promised end" for mankind is "fall and cease" is to see Lear and Cordelia as the "image of that horror." To believe as a Christian in a different "promised end" is to see the image differently, perhaps even as a *piéta*. The Christian watches a play cast in a pre-Christian setting, a play from which virtually all traces of the Christian doctrines of *The True Chronicle of King Leir* have been removed. He enjoys the advantage of historical perspective over those virtuous pagans, Edgar, Albany, and Kent; Lear's "If it be so, / It is a chance which does redeem all sorrows / That I ever felt" comes home particularly to him, and he might wonder about a question much debated in the Middle Ages and Renaissance—the fate, or "promised end," for virtuous pagans. He might also wonder about Lear's dying words and how Shakespeare intends them, and thus how the play is finally to be understood. The only thing of which the audience can be certain is that Lear *sees* life in Cordelia and dies happy.

It is possible, as some commentators have argued,[3] that Lear in the moment of his death sees with a more than secular vision and thus that the play concludes with an affirmation of the mercy which perfects divine justice. It may also be that he is fondly deluded. The important point is that our interpretation of what *we* see in these final moments of the play is no less dependent upon what *we* believe than is Albany's or Lear's. Albany might conclude that Lear wants so desperately to believe Cordelia is still alive that he imagines she still lives. The Christian might on the other hand believe that Lear in his final moments acquires a vision which enables him to see beyond the natural boundaries of perception.

Those natural boundaries of perception constitute, it seems to me, the boundaries of dramatic illusion which have become, in *Hamlet* and *Lear*, increasingly strained. The worlds recreated in the tragedies and histories consist of the same particulars that make up the real world in which the audience exists. In a given play they may be arranged to suggest the principles that lie behind phenomenal nature.[4] The audience may also at any given moment enjoy the advantage, over any or all of the inhabitants of the play world, of a fuller awareness of the situation in that world.[5] We know, for instance, that Juliet is alive when Romeo believes she is dead, and that Claudius at prayer is unable to repent. But our understanding of the particulars which make up the play is limited to what sense perception and reason allow us to infer. From the events of the play, events depicted according to principles of probability and derived from a phenomenal world of time, space, and causal relationships, we infer its ultimate design and meaning.

The world of the romances is a different matter. The license of romance allows Shakespeare the freedom to go beyond phenomenal representation. He is able to shift his focus from the physical to the metaphysical, to deal decisively with the question of appearance and reality by representing directly the forces that govern phenomenal nature or which may transcend it.[6]

The differences between these two modes of representation may be briefly indicated by the means used to represent ideas of cosmic justice in *Hamlet* and *Lear* and by those used in *Pericles* and *Cymbeline*. Hamlet is convinced finally of a "divinity that shapes our ends." While at sea he finds heaven "ordinate" in a pattern of events which earlier he would have attributed to chance. Only the denouement of the play and Hamlet's declaration that he has found a pattern in accident confirm his new view. The audience at the play's close is no more fully enlightened than Hamlet. We have no choice other than to believe or deny that the action we have seen is intended to reveal the shaping destiny that Hamlet claims to have found. We are left with the same enigmatic world of appearances, having no alternatives beyond those open to Hamlet. The ghost remains for us a puzzling apparition, evidence indeed of another mode of existence beyond phenomenal nature and of a supernatural interest in the affairs of men; but its identity remains a riddle. We know that it has spoken the truth about Claudius, but only after Claudius' reaction to the play within a play has visually verified its charge. We may believe along with Hamlet that a higher power has been manifest in chance and accident. We may hope along with Horatio that Hamlet will be accompanied to his rest by flights of angels. But the play offers no explicit assurances. All it allows us to conclude without qualification is that in the course of the action Hamlet changes his view of the forces behind events, that in his despair he attributes to fortune the threatening circumstances in which he finds himself, and that only after his discovery of Providence in "chance" is he able to accomplish what has been asked of him.

Similar limitations, as we have already seen, circumscribe the final scene in *Lear*. The audience is left facing the questions asked by those who reflect onstage upon the death of Cordelia. The only reassurance we are given that men are not merely the playthings of the gods, besides the fact that evil has received its due and order has been restored, are the dying words of a tired and demented old man: "Do you see this? Look on her, look, her lips, / Look there, look there!" Lear's perceptions are disordered; the onlookers cannot *see* as he does. But the question remains, What *does* he see? Is he lost in delusion, or does he see beyond the natural boundaries of perception?

Romance convention would have permitted at appropriate points in each play scenes similar to those in *Pericles* and *Cymbeline*, in which Pericles is visited by Diana and Posthumus by Jupiter, if such had been Shakespeare's intention. Romance convention allows Shakespeare in these last plays to affirm through visual representation what in *Hamlet* and *Lear* must be left to inference. Consequently, the audience who watches *Pericles* or *Cymbeline* is not left in doubt about the role that the heavens have played in the lives of the characters. Whatever the follies of men, their depravity and inconstancy, and despite the seeming indifference of nature, the gods protect and finally crown the virtuous with happiness.

The affirmation of the old view of a moral universe is of course not the only concern of the romances; nor are the conventions of romance used in these plays only in the way I have briefly indicated. Their diversity, in modes of representation as well as in the range of experience they explore, is great. The facts that the source of *Cymbeline* is legendary history and that one of the sources of *The Tempest* is in all likelihood a journalistic account of a recent voyage and discovery distinguish them from *A Winter's Tale* and *Pericles*, whose sources are pure fiction. But the "historical" basis of *Cymbeline* does not require of the audience a different kind of involvement from that required by *A Winter's Tale* and *Pericles*. The significant point to be made is that all four plays are to be distinguished from the tragedies on the grounds that they adopt a new mode of imitation, use the freedom of romance to explore the dependencies of perceiving and knowing upon faith, and require, as I expect eventually to show, a kind of ritualistic participation of their audiences.

At the outset of *Pericles*, his first play in the new mode, Shakespeare makes clear his awareness of its novelty. Gower, the Prologue, admits that the play to follow is not in the currently fashionable mode and therefore may not be taken seriously. To those "born in these latter times/ When wit's more ripe" it may seem to be no more than a moldy old tale. But they will be mistaken. Many "lords and ladies in their lives/ Have read it for restoratives." In ages past it has been peculiarly suited to festival occasions, Ember eves and holy days. It will be timely, therefore, so long as the seasons of the year repeat themselves and so long as their annual recurrence is commemorated in man's ritual observances of time. Both ancient and timely, its "purchase is to make men glorious." Furthermore, it is of sufficient merit to cause Gower to reassume "man's infirmities" and make him willing to burn like a taper to provide his audience with light.

Behind Gower's lines, and in fact throughout the entire play, something closely akin to Sidney's theory of imitation is operative. As Gower says, his song may be only a retelling of "what mine authors say"; it may lack the authority of tragedies whose plots are historical. Nevertheless, its very antiquity provides it with an authority of its own; there is something timelessly valuable in it. Gower's "song" proves to be similar in method and purpose to Sidney's *Arcadia*. It consists of "pregnant images of life" in which reside deeper truths than those allowed by historical verisimilitude.[7]

Sidney himself had attacked the current dramatic theory, deriving from the Donatan commentaries on Terence, which insisted that tragedy be based upon history: "And doe they not knowe that a Tragedie is tied to the lawes of Poesie, and not of Historie? not bound to follow the storie, but, having liberty, either to faine a quite newe matter, or to frame the history to the most tragicall conveniencie."[8] As the Poet in *Timon of Athens* observes to the Painter, art may tutor nature (I.i.37). Free of the Donatan requirement that tragedy must be based upon history, and thus free of the necessity of having to confine himself to the imitation of phenomenal nature, Shakespeare as writer of romance is able to imitate ideal nature by creating in Pericles and Marina exemplars of constancy. He is free also to arrange events so as to represent the even-handed working of natural law within the cycles of Pericles' life and thus to reaffirm justice in the natural order. He is free also to replace historical event with moral exemplum, gaining in Sidney's view, and perhaps in his own, in didactic effectiveness.

Such a narrative combines the virtues of painting and speaking, as a kind of "speaking picture," or emblematic narrative, in which the play's several actions provide "moral paintings" of the sort alluded to by the Painter in *Timon* (I.i.90) and which are accompanied by appropriate comments by Gower. There is in fact a good deal of evidence throughout the play to support the suggestion that the narrative is to be viewed and interpreted emblematically. There is, first of all, the figure of Gower, who tells us what to look for in the action to come and what we should have seen in the action just completed. There is also the fact that Pericles and Marina draw attention to the play's symbolic mode by often interpreting emblematically the situations in which they find themselves. Pericles, for instance, as he sits at the banquet given in his honor by Simonides, detaches himself from the immediate action and reflects upon the image of the king, generalizing upon time and transience. Setting and verse strongly suggest the emblem:

> Yon king's to me like to my father's picture,
> Which tells me in that glory once he was;
> Had princes sit like stars about his throne,
> And he the sun for them to reverence;
> None that beheld him but, like lesser lights,
> Did vail their crowns to his supremacy;
> Where now his [son's] like a glow-worm in the night,
> The which hath fire in darkness, none in light;
> Whereby I see that Time's the king of men:

He's both their parent, and he is their grave,
And gives them what he will, not what they crave.

(II.iii.37-47)

Similarly, Marina, as she wanders along the ocean's shore casting
flowers upon the water's surface, reflects upon her plight, interpreting it emblematically:

Ay me! poor maid,
Born in a tempest when my mother died,
This world to me is [like] a lasting storm,
Whirring me from my friends.[9]

(IV.i.18-21)

The involvement that such a narrative requires of its audience is
fundamentally different from that required by tragedy. In the tragedies Shakespeare sets up at the very outset a certain kind of perspective, and with it certain expectations that determine the kind of audience involvement he seeks to initiate and sustain. Perspective in the
tragedies is always retrospective. For the sophisticated member of
the audience, as well as for the dramatist himself, the plots of tragedy
are the "given" and have the authority of accomplished fact. But
whether the members of the audience are aware of the historical
truth or not, they know from the title of the play they are about to
see that it will end with the protagonist's death. In either instance, the
audience enjoys from the beginning of the play an advantage in
awareness over the characters; and from the vantage point of its foreknowledge it awaits the depiction of the chain of events which will
lead up to and in some way account for the tragic fact they know
will conclude the play's action.

What kind of involvement proceeds from such expectations? Obviously, audience involvement varies with its members. One member
may become absorbed in rough humor and bawdiness, another in the
surfaces of the play as spectacle, and still another in its rhetoric. But
the question I have raised is best approached by considering an ideal
audience, one which is the most fully prepared to experience *Hamlet*
or *Lear* on Shakespeare's terms. The matter is complicated, and I

shall confine myself only to what seems to me to be necessary to the distinction I want to make.

In tragedy we must be convinced of the causal logic of the plot. Given the protagonist as the dramatist has conceived him, the situation in which he finds himself, and the choices open to him, we must be convinced that the choices he makes are probable and their consequences inevitable. In brief, we expect the world of the play to mirror the real world more or less as we perceive and interpret it. Our involvement, our suspension of disbelief, depends upon versimilitude and dramatic probability. So long as events in the world of the play do not violate our sense of the phenomenal world, our feelings and minds are engaged by the illusion of the play we watch.

In *Pericles* verisimilitude and dramatic probability are no longer conditions of involvement. The suspension of disbelief that makes it possible to witness a play as if it were not simply illusion is no longer requisite. In fact, a "distance" must be maintained between audience and play, for the effectiveness of the narrative depends upon the audience's awareness of themselves as spectators.[10] Our involvement as spectators is conditional, it seems to me, upon two things. We must exercise "the judgment," as Gower puts it (I. Prol. 41) of our eyes and discover the moral truths represented in the "speaking pictures" invented by the poet; and we must be favorably disposed to the truths and beliefs the play celebrates.

The latter is analogous to a requirement of ritual. Unless we, as members of the audience, are able to accept the vision of the world affirmed by the play, our involvement can only be partial. We may enjoy discovering what the play means and be entertained by incidental felicities. We may even be ready to participate in the celebration of parts of the vision—for instance, the act of trust which in *Pericles* is affirmed as the necessary condition of love and community, or the play's celebration of constancy—but, finally, unless we are ready to believe in the play's vision of an ordered universe presided over by gods who are just and merciful, our involvement cannot be complete.

What is true of *Pericles* is equally true of each of the later romances. Each requires that the audience be continuously aware of the fact that it is watching a play, and to guarantee such audience awareness each contains devices which call attention to the play itself as a contrived work of art. Each also requires, finally, the same ritualistic participation—an initial acceptance on the part of the audience of the truths it celebrates.

GENERATIVE LOVE AND METAPHORICAL TIME

Gower in the epilogue to *Pericles* reminds us of the truths his "song" has celebrated. Helicanus has been "A figure of truth, of faith, of loyalty" and Cerimon has represented "the worth that learned charity aye wears"; but the play's major concern has been the celebration of cosmic justice. Retribution has been exacted upon the evil doers. The "monstrous lust" of Antiochus and his daughter has been punished suddenly and directly by the heavens. Cleon and Dionyza have been burned to death by the citizens of Tarsus. On the other hand, virtue, though violently threatened by evil and mischance, has been "led on by Heaven" and finally "crown'd with joy."

The conflict between good and evil that Gower has summarized and out of which the virtuous have emerged victorious is depicted in the play itself as between natural and unnatural love. The former is the means by which man may "outbrave" the destructive forces of nature and depraved man, and cooperate with the creative energies in nature that sustain being. It is represented in the play as the generative force in the mutable order. It sustains Pericles, Thaisa, and Marina in the midst of present adversity; it restores to each what seems to have been irrevocably lost in the past; and at the play's close it promises the continuation of Pericles' family line and future kings for the throne of Tyre. This vindication of natural love is threatened throughout the play by unnatural love. Incest, maternal jealousy, uxoriousness, and lust are conceived as manifestations of the destructive forces in both the micro- and macrocosms. Whatever its express form, unnatural love is generative love's opposite: barren and feeding upon itself, it contains the cause of its own destruction. The point is twice underscored in the play: first by the fiery deaths of the incestuous Antiochus and his daughter, and again by the executions of Cleon and the jealous Dionyza.

These contraries center in what was an abiding concern of Shakespeare: the power of love to shape and even to transcend the processes of mutability. From the earliest sonnets on, he represents love as a powerful restorative, vitally affecting not only the lives of men and the human community but even the subjective quality of time itself. The young man addressed in the marriage sonnets is urged to outbrave time by begetting children. In Sonnets 29, 30, and 65 love for a friend restores all losses and renews hope in times of despair. In *As You Like It* a brother's readiness to love and thus to forgive an enemy provides Oliver with the opportunity to renew his life through repentance.

What emerges as new in Shakespeare's treatment of love in *Pericles* and in each of the later romances, is a matter of focus, emphasis, and dramatic conception. Each of these last plays focuses almost exclusively upon the renewing and destructive forces of nature as they affect the continuity of family lines and the harmony of domestic and public institutions. The action in each play arises out of a conflict between generative and destructive love. In *Pericles* the conflict is between protagonists and antagonists who are emblematic exemplars of the two forces. In the later plays the conflict is represented more subtly. But in every instance generative and destructive love are contraries in a dialectic that works itself out in the action. The resolution of that dialectic in each play's conclusion is an affirmation of the sustaining, restoring, and renewing powers of human love in a precarious world of sudden and violent natural catastrophes and nearly overwhelming human depravity.

Generative and destructive love are the means by which the principal characters in the last plays decisively influence, within the spheres of their own lives, the processes of growth and decay. As the unalterable condition upon which human existence depends, mutability demands simple resignation from Pericles, Leontes, Polixenes, and Prospero. Nevertheless, under certain conditions and within certain limitations—when the time is ripe—each has the opportunity to renew the future for himself, for his successors, and for his country. Or each may, through acts of unnatural love, initiate an action which may eventually destroy him and his family line. Leontes in his jealousy unleashes the forces of nature which destroy Mamillius and threaten to leave Sicilia without an heir. Prospero, by rejecting revenge and choosing forgiveness, not only decisively shapes his own future, but the future of those over whom in the closing minutes of the play he has the power of life and death. By forgiving he becomes an agent of renewing love. Pericles, too, although less obviously, becomes an agent of renewing love by meeting adversity as he does, bringing food, for instance, to the starving inhabitants of Tarsus, and at the play's close by obeying Diana's instructions instead of seeking revenge upon Dionyza and Cleon.

It is, in fact, a distinguishing characteristic of the romances that the choices their characters make are depicted—even the choices of an Autolycus—as expressions of either natural or unnatural love, and that the consequences of those choices decisively affect the processes of growth and decay. In each play characters confront circumstances which may or may not be the consequences of their own folly, but in which the decisions they make unleash either the destructive or creative energies of nature.

Such choices are construed in terms of time. To choose is to choose how to use time. How Cymbeline and Leontes use the past as well as the present determines the shape of future time. The way in which Leontes remembers the past gives rise to a passion which shatters the pastoral serenity of Sicilia and very nearly destroys his family line. Cymbeline's folly, first in believing the charges levelled against Belarius and again in denying Posthumus' nobility, very nearly destroys his lineage and the sovereignty of Britain. Each king in his folly abuses time and faces retribution at the hand of Time the Destroyer. The prudent man, on the other hand—a Prospero, a penitent Leontes, or a Gonzalo—has learned how to use time. By calling upon the resources of the past, in the form of either history or personal memory, and by making the right choice at the right time, he converts impending destruction into potential renewal.

Shakespeare's source in these matters appears to have been a long-standing and well-known tradition. Primaudaye, citing Cicero, writes:

> Moral Philosophers attributed three Eies to this vertue of Prudence, namely, Memory, Understanding, and Providence. . . . a prudent and wise man, by the consideration of things past, and of that which hath followed since, judgeth of that, which in the like case may fall out in the time following. And after long deliberation, he inspecteth the times, weigheth the dangers, and knoweth the occasions: and then, yeelding now and then to the times, but alwaies to necessity, so it be not against duty, he boldly setteth his hand to the works.[11]

Thomas Wilson offers the same definition of prudence to the readers of *The Arte of Rhetorique, 1560*.[12] Prudence is an exercising of memory, understanding, and foresight:

> The memorie, calleth to accompt those things that were done heretofore, and by a former remembraunce getteth an after wit, and learneth to auoyde deceipt.
> Vnderstanding, seeth thinges presently done, and perceiveth what is in them, weighing and debating them, vntill his minde be fully contented.
> Foresight, is a gathering by coniectures, what shall happen, and an euident perceiuing of thinges to come, before they doe come.
>
> (pp. 31-32)

The prudent man knows when, as well as how, to act. He knows that a foolish choice, a choice made at a wrong time, or a failure to make any choice at all when occasion demands it, may turn time destructive.

To depict choice and its consequences in terms of time is to adopt the language of metaphor, for time in the Renaissance cosmology is only the measure of motion, a condition rather than an agent. As Richard Hooker observes, time "neither causeth things nor opportunities of things, although it comprise and contain both."[13] George Hakewill provides a fuller statement:

> that which Poets faigne of *Time*, that it eates out and devoures all things, is in truth but a poetical fiction, since *Time* is a branch of *Quan-*

tity, it being the measure of motion, and *Quantity* in it selfe in no way *active*, but meerely passive, as being an accident flowing from the matter. And thereupon *Contarenus* . . . having touched of the passage of the Poet, *Tempus edax rerum*, Time eates out all things; presently adds, *Quae sententia ut propius ad vulgus accedat, ita est remotior a veritate.* . . . It is then either some inward conflict, or outward assault which is wrought in *Time*, that eates them out; Time itself without these is toothlesse, and can never doe it.[14]

One finds throughout Shakespeare, and especially in the romances, the metaphorical figures which represent time in its various dimensions—as Revealer, Destroyer, Renewer, and Occasion. Shakespeare, however, avoids the causal error described by Hakewill. Whatever force time as Destroyer or Renewer may have in the romances is a consequence of human choice, the result of such "outward assault" as Dionyza's against Marina or of such "inward conflict" as one finds in the uxorious Cleon and the insanely jealous Leontes.

Behind these metaphorical figures there is a twofold conception of time that is new in the Renaissance: time as duration and time as occasion.

There is the space of time, and there is the opportunity of time. *Tempus longum*, and *tempus commodum;* Time and opportunity differ, time is the duration or succession of so many minutes, hours, days or years one after the other, from the beginning of a mans life, to the end thereof. . . . Opportunity is the time apted and fitted in order to this or that work of business, *viz.* a meeting of time and means together, to effect the end. This is called the season or tempestivity of time, when time, tide, and wind meet and clasp together.[15]

The notion of time as duration and as occasion is not only the basis for Shakespeare's metaphorical use of time throughout his work, it is also the conceptual basis of the restorative pattern of the romances. Since it differs in important respects from the old Augustinian view of time as merely the measure of transience, it requires careful elucidation.

DURATIVE TIME

Durative time is cyclical, bringing life out of death as inevitably as spring emerges out of winter. It is no longer Augustine's Destroyer, but the measure of the process which sustains genera and species. Individual life is utterly dependent upon process, but in the continuum of time in which the living emerge out of and replace the dying, genera and species subsist eternally. George Hakewill makes the point when discussing the human "species" in book four of his *Apologie*:

> With mankind then or any other *species* it fares as with a river, which varies every moment one part driving out another, yet it is still the same river which it was in hundred years since, though in that compasse of time it hath perchaunce emptied every dropp of water above a thousand times. . . .
>
> Such a fugative face hath every man and mankind itself, but with this difference that the face of mankind is daily decayed and daily renewed but the face of individual men decayes daily without any compensative renewing and in respect of this renovation by degrees chaining one part as it were link to another the *species* is still the same, and hath still the same existance.

> (pp. 12-13)

In this view durative time is no longer only the agent of death and measurer of decay; for in its cyclical movement it promises endless renewal. Mutability and time are therefore agents of permanence; they are subordinate, as Spenser in the Mutability Cantos makes clear, to the sustaining powers of divinity.

These notions of time, mutability, and permanence are emblematically represented by Hakewill on the Frontispiece of his *Apologie* and summarized by the accompanying "Argument of the Front and of the Work."

> Although the Creator and Disposer of all things hath left all Particulars and Individualls, under the circle of the *Moone*, to the stroake of *Time* and *Death*; yet by His powerfull Hand He holdeth backe the

Sythe of *Time* from destroying or impayring the Vniverse: Though the same Hand shall at last destroy the Whole by Fire.

In the meane time, he hath so ordained, that the Elements, of which all sub-lunary bodies are composed, doe so beget one the other, and are againe so begotten, each from other; that while they seeme to dye, they become immortall. For as *Earth* is resolved into *Water*, the *Water* rarefied into *Ayre*, and the *Ayre* into *Fire*, in the way of their ascension; So in their descending down-ward, by a mutuall Compensation, the *Fire* becometh *Ayre*, the *Ayre* thickeneth into *Water*, and the *Water* againe into *Earth*.

And as a *Ship* which rideth at Anchor is tossed to and fro by the Windes and Waves, and yet cannot move beyond the length of his Cable, but is carried about in a Round, still moving yet never re-mooved.

Or as a *Wheele*, at every turne, bringeth about all his Spoakes to the same places, observing a constancy even in turning.

So though there be many changes and variations in the World, yet all things come about one time or another to the same points againe.

And there is nothing new under the *Sunne*.

While such a conception may have profoundly altered man's appraisal of the value of things existing in time and of time itself,[16] it seems to offer little, at least directly, in the way of consolation to man faced with his own mortality. The fact that the human species is sempiternal is little consolation to the individual who faces in death the destruction of his identity and awareness of self; and yet the continuation of one's name and family line, as we shall eventually see, is a consolation as well as an obligation both to the Shakespeare of the sonnets and the fathers of his last plays.

The new conception of durative time is also responsible for a sharper awareness of the minute variations of process and of the degree of man's implication in them. It subtly but deeply alters the way in which the future is regarded. Institutions, estates, titles, even one's name, have a substantiality which the old Augustinian view of time as absolutely distinct from eternity had denied.[17] For in the new view all temporal things actively participate in the eternal. On the other hand, to be more sharply aware of process is to be more sharply aware of its remorselessness and of the precariousness and dependency of one's existence upon it.[18]

Another consequence of the new view of time is a complication of the problem of perception. The Augustinian dichotomy between the eternal and the temporal no longer separates this world from eternity, but is now manifest in things. Thus man can no longer simply dismiss temporality for the sake of contemplation. He must discover his role in process itself. He must discover in transience what is permanent, sifting out the real from the illusory.

This process of sifting out the real from the seeming—a central concern in each of Shakespeare's romances—begins with a recognition of the absolute determinacy of the laws governing process. From one point of view the only constant in the "changefull world" is the circular pattern of time itself. Louis Le Roi's representation of that view is typical:[19]

> We see euery yeare at the springtime, and beginning of Summer, how being watered with small rayne, caused by soft windes, and moderately heated, it openeth the seeded of all things which before were shut vp, and putteth some of them into herbes, stalkes, and eares, others into stems and husks, others into budds, others into tender topps: the garden trees yeeld buds, flowers, leaues, and fruits; the trees clothed greene, bearing on their branches and boughes, the birdes pricked with a desire of engendring, which record by themselues their melodious songs: The fishes leape; and the beasts amidst the greene pastures skip vp and down, being inflamed with loue. In briefe euery thing springeth, groweth embellisheth, florisheth, and fructifieth: all things are renewed. On the contrarie, when Autumn and Winter do returne, all is full of horror, and of sadnes, cold, raine, dirt, sleete, hayle, snow, frost, yce, foggy mists, long nights, and almost continual dampnes.

Man, according to Le Roi, is even more subject than the rest of the organic world to the minute and unceasing variability of process:

> But the varietie, and alteration is greater in man, than in any other thing; as soone as he is borne he beginneth to dye, and his end dependeth of his beginning. During the time while he liueth from his infancy, euen til his old age, he hath neuer the same things in him, neither is he

the same: but is stil renewed, subiect to change as well as in his body, his heare, flesh, bloud, & bones; as in his minde: changing his maneers, customes, opinions, appetites, pleasures, sorrowes, feares, and hopes. We learne, forget, and remember the sciences. Wee receaue into our bodies, and cast out the excrement by the ways. . . .

(p. 11)

Man's freedom, his ability to transcend in some measure those continual and various influences, is limited by his understanding of natural necessity. When considered exclusively in terms of mutability, human existence is wholly contingent upon process, and it is with the acceptance of such contingency that man can begin to free himself from the claims of time. He must appreciate the truth of the commonplace of which Vincentio reminds Claudio in *Measure for Measure* when urging him to prepare himself for death:

> A breath thou art,
> Servile to all the skyey influences,
> That dost this habitation where thou keep'st
> Hourly afflict. Merely, thou are Death's fool;
> . . . .
> Thou are not thyself;
> For thou exist'st on many a thousand grains
> That issue out of dust. Happy thou are not;
> For what thou hast not, still thou striv'st to get,
> And what thou hast, forget'st. Thou are not certain,
> For thy complexion shifts to strange effects
> After the moon.   (III.i.8-11, 19-25)

Freedom requires that man break with time by exercising reason and thereby controlling the appetites and claims of the humors which are servile to "skyey influences."[20] To fail to exercise reason or to surrender reason to the claims of the humors or appetites is, as the Duke suggests, to remain Death's fool and a slave to process.

But reason is at best only a means of acquiring a limited freedom. Although it may afford man a means of resisting and ordering the rain of influences which "hourly afflict" him and thus free him from the deterministic claims of passion, it will take him no further. It cannot reveal to him a purpose in process beyond the general one of sustaining the sublunary world. Within the narrow perspective of unaided reason he remains servile to time.

Authentic freedom within time is contingent upon a belief in a purposeful and benevolent universe. The lives and deaths of individual members of the human species are purposeful only to those who believe, as Hamlet comes finally to believe, in a final cause which shapes the course of man's history.

In the absence of that belief man can only await his own death with stoic resignation. He may accept Time as Renewer as well as Destroyer; but, seeing no purpose in time's cyclicity beyond the mere perpetuation of being, he is prisoner to his resignation. He confronts the future without hope, for it contains only the promise of his own death. For him, the meaning of time is merely the process of ripening and rotting which it measures. On the other hand, the man who, like Pericles, believes in a divinity that shapes man's ends, accepts time as purposeful. For him, time unfolds to an ultimate purpose which gives his own life meaning. Constant in that belief, he accepts with equanimity both the destructive and renewing aspects of time. He is resigned to his own mortality; and yet he views the future hopefully.

In this view there are, then, two orders of existence within the mutable order between which man is free to choose. Within the one, he remains finally servile to time; within the other, he is free. In either instance what he believes determines what and how he perceives. To see reality as merely process is to take upon oneself the limitations that circumscribe process. Life, so construed, becomes no more than the "stuff" of which dreams are made and history, an "unsubstantial pageant." On the other hand, to see reality in terms of purpose, and purpose as determined by a just and benevolent deity, is to see purpose, justice, and benevolence in what on the level of appearances seems random, indifferent, or unjust. Viewed in terms of purpose, Time remains a Destroyer and Renewer, but in both roles he permits man authentic freedom. As Destroyer he exacts retribution from all men for the wages of sin, but leaves each man free to decide how he will endure his retribution. As Renewer he presents man with the opportunity to participate in the generative process.[21]

The two orders of existence between which man has the freedom to choose—the one in which he remains servile to time and to circumstance or "fortune"; the other in which he may achieve constancy and shape time—are variously represented in the Renaissance. In a frontispiece to Bovillus' *De Sapiente* (1511) they are represented by the figures of Fortuna and Sapientia.[22] Fortuna is blindfolded and seated on a chair that balances precariously on a sphere. On her knee she balances her wheel, which is apparently revolving. A king, attired in the regalia of his office, is perched on it. Other figures are struggling to climb toward the top of the wheel. Sapientia is seated opposite Fortuna on a throne that rests on a solid rectangular base. She gazes into a mirror. On the mirror's circumferences one can make out the several spheres of the Ptolemaic system. Sapientia contemplates her own image which is at the center of the mirror and of the universe it represents. The moral is clear: in knowing onself as an inhabitant of the sublunary and mutable order, one escapes Fortuna and the enslaving claims of her domain.

In another emblematic representation, the frontispiece to Sir John Davies' *Scourge of Folly*,[23] the general opposition between wisdom and folly is represented by the figure of Wit whipping Folly. Folly, wearing a cockscomb and with his backside bared to Wit's scourge, is held captive on the back of a figure who has hooves for feet and a single lock of hair protruding from his forehead and who is identified as Time. Wit punishes those who in their folly have surrendered their freedom to time.

The alternatives represented by the figures of Sapientia and Fortuna, and by Wit and Time, are unmistakably present in the world of Shakespeare's plays. Romeo, for instance, in choosing a course of "sudden haste" surrenders himself to the circumstances and accidents that are seemingly ruled by Fortune. The folly of his surrender is repeatedly driven home. Ignoring Escalus' edict against further fighting in the streets, he avenges Mercutio's death and then complains that he is Fortune's fool. The irony is clear. His observation is correct—but not in the sense he intends. He blames Fortune while failing to realize that by giving in to his thirst for revenge he has surrendered himself to consequences over which he has no control. Again, when he is later told that Juliet is dead he ignores Balthazar's advice to be patient, rushes out to buy poison, and then returns immediately to Verona. Any pause for reflection between receipt of that report and his suicide might have led to the discovery of its error. By rejecting deliberation he allows himself to become a victim of time and circumstance. By following his passions he becomes Time's fool and victim.[24] The point is brilliantly underscored throughout the latter half of the play, in which the rush of time is evoked and sustained by repeated allusions to clock time.

Macbeth is another of Time's victims by choice. Frustrated by Macduff's escape, he surrenders to sheer impulse in an attempt to foil Time:

> Time, thou anticipat'st my dread exploits:
> The flighty purpose never is o'ertook
> Unless the deed go with it. From this moment
> The very firstlings of my heart shall be
> The firstlings of my hand.
>
> (IV.ii.144-48)

The result, as he eventually discovers, is that he has destroyed for himself the meaning of time. The past has merely "lighted fools/The way to dusty death"; the future is now but a tedious succession of tomorrows; and life itself is no more than an idiot's tale. Hotspur, too, in his dying words to Hal discloses that he has made himself a fool of time by having mistaken fame for honor.

> O, Harry, thou hast robb'd me of my youth!
> I better brook the loss of brittle life
> Than those proud titles thou hast won of me.
> They wound my thoughts worse than thy sword my flesh.
> But thoughts, the slaves of life, and life, time's fool,
> And time, that takes survey of all the world,
> Must have a stop.   (V.iv.77-83)

His thoughts have been only of fame, and fame is utterly dependent upon the recollection of others and thus contingent upon time.

In each of the above instances time is conceived as a destroyer by men who are unable to find any meaning in time beyond existence itself. Their view is symptomatic of ennui and despair. Other characters in Shakespeare's plays view time in the same way but eventually recover from their spiritual malady and discover the other dimension of durative time. Prospero, for example, while enjoying the idyllic and timeless future that he conceives for Miranda and Ferdinand in the illusion he has created for their entertainment, suddenly remembers Caliban and the conspiracy and lapses into a melancholy reflection upon time as the destroyer. In that mood all existence appears to him as no more than the insubstantial stuff of dreams; but his act of forgiving and of thus restoring the future to all those who are in his power is proof of his recovery. It is an act grounded in a belief in the future and in the substantiality of the sublunary pageant.

Among all the plays written before *Pericles, As You Like It* contains the fullest and most illuminating exploration of durative time and the two orders of existence, represented metaphorically by Fortuna and Sapientia.[25] The two orders are introduced in I.ii.34-58 when Rosalind and Celia playfully ask whether Fortuna or Nature is sovereign in the lives of men.

> *Celia:* Let us sit and mock the good housewife Fortune from her wheel, that her gifts may henceforth be bestowed equally.
> *Rosalind:* I would we could do so; for her benefits are mightily misplaced, and the bountiful blind woman doth most mistake in her gifts to women.
> *Celia:* 'Tis true; for those that she makes fair she scarce makes honest, and those that she makes honest she makes very ill-favouredly.

Up to this point their debate is little more than an exchange of courtly commonplaces; but Rosalind's next remark contains the distinction between fortune and nature that I have discussed above and which proves to be crucial to the play's emergent concern with time.

> *Rosalind:* Nay, now thou goest from Fortune's office to Nature's. Fortune reigns in gifts of the world, not in the lineaments of Nature.

Physical charms are "gifts of the world," seemingly a matter of circumstance and accident. Therefore they may be figuratively asscribed to Fortune. Honesty, however, is a matter of nature, specifically, of human nature. Fortune may reign, or seem to reign, in "gifts of the world," but Nature is sovereign in matters of virtue.

The playful banter which follows does not detract from the rightness of Rosalind's distinction. When Touchstone enters, Celia sees her opportunity to gain the advantage:

Celia: No? When Nature hath made a fair creature, may she not by Fortune fall into the fire? Though Nature hath given us wit to flout at Fortune, hath not Fortune sent in this fool to cut off the argument?

Rosalind accedes:

Indeed, there is Fortune too hard for Nature, when Fortune makes Nature's natural the cutter-off of Nature's wit.

But Celia changes sides, suggesting that the fool as "Nature's natural" may in fact serve the ends of nature.

Celia: Peradventure this is not Fortune's work neither, but Nature's; who, [perceiving] our natural wits too dull to reason of such goddesses, hath sent this natural for our whetstone; for always the dullness of the fool is the whetstone of the wits. How now wit! whither wander you?

Her suggestion underlines what proves to be the play's central concern and instructs the audience in how to understand the function of Touchstone's role in the exploration of that concern. The Fool's entrance has interrupted the exchange of wit; and since fools are under the guidance of Fortune and are bound by their folly to do her bidding, the goddess has seemingly been responsible for the interruption and thus proved her superiority to Nature. But Celia suggests that Touchstone is a *natural* fool and therefore in the service of Nature. He may be serving Nature's purpose as a whetstone on whom others may sharpen their wits in order to withstand the misfortunes they are bound to encounter in the world.

Wit, then, is necessary if one is to "flout at Fortune"; and throughout the rest of the play we find that Fortune's only real power over men is a consequence of their own folly and that Fortuna is merely a

"God of fooles" whose only existence is in the eyes of foolish men.[26] Circumstance, chance, and the misdeeds of others may impose physical necessity and suffering upon the world's unfortunates. Orlando, Rosalind, and Duke Senior have no alternatives but to seek the safety of Arden, and once there they must find food and shelter. Nevertheless they remain free to choose how they will endure their misfortune. Through the right use of wit—that is, through reason illuminated by a faith in a just divinity—they may, like the banished Duke, "translate the stubbornness of fortune" (II.1.19) into the sweet and quiet style of patience and preserve their freedom.

Touchstone's function in the dramatization of these ideas is the one suggested by Celia. His folly provides the whetstone on which others may sharpen their wit and thus better their chances of defeating Fortune. He also proves to be the touchstone for testing the quality of the wit of others. Thus he provides for the audience a norm of folly—just as Duke Senior provides a norm of wisdom—against which it may measure the wit or folly of the other characters.

Unlike Feste, a wise fool who uses his license deliberately to expose the folly of others, Touchstone is unaware of the function he performs; for he is "Nature's natural," a natural fool and an unwitting foil. His folly is revealed generally by his discontent; for him "the stubbornness of fortune" is untranslatable.

Together, then, Duke Senior and Touchstone represent the extreme options available to man as he faces misfortune. The patient man retains his freedom even in the face of necessity by accepting as purposeful whatever time bestows. The foolish man surrenders his freedom to the flow of external events and blames Fortune for his troubles.

With this distinction between Fortuna and Sapientia in mind, the ways in which the play's unfortunates respond to misfortune reveals a new logic. Their responses are depicted in terms of time. Touchstone's moralizing upon time, as reported by Jaques, is proof of his discontent and folly:

> "It is ten o'clock.
> Thus we may see," quoth he, "how the world wags.
> 'Tis but an hour ago since it was nine;

28

And after one hour more 'twill be eleven;
And so, from hour to hour, we ripe, and ripe,
And then, from hour to hour, we rot and rot;
And thereby hangs a tale."

(II.vii.22-28)

He sees existence as wholly servile to time, and time only as the measure of a process which ends in death. The fact that Jaques approves of what he has heard identifies him also as a fool, an identification which is reinforced when he invites Orlando to join him and "rail against our mistress the world, and all our misery" (III.ii.295-96) and again by his "seven ages of man" speech in which he reiterates the moral drawn from time by Touchstone. Both men in their folly are fools of time and fortune.

Other characters arrive in Arden assuming that time is only to be wasted, or that its inhabitants, as rumor has it, "fleet the time carelessly" (I.i.124). Orlando, for instance, on first meeting the banished Duke and his followers assumes that they merely "lose and neglect the creeping hours of time" (II.vii.112); and later when asked the time by Rosalind, he protests, "There's no clock in the forest" (III.ii.319). What he has yet to learn is that the Duke, for one, has put time to use and that there are means other than clocks for keeping time in Arden. The only wasters of time in Arden are those who, like Jaques and Touchstone, find no meaning in it. Orlando himself will be instructed by Rosalind in the use of time and will eventually prove how to use it properly when he saves Oliver from the lioness. In that moment when he sees his enemy asleep under the giant oak the choice he makes determines for him as well as for his brother the course of future events, or, metaphorically, the course of future time. The opportunity for revenge is ripe. All he need do is leave his brother to his fate.

But kindness, nobler ever than revenge,
And nature, stronger than his just occasion,
Made him give battle to the lioness,
Who quickly fell before him; . . .

(IV.iii.129-32)

By forgiving his brother and risking his own life he seizes the occasion and turns time to renewal.

Durative time demands acquiescence rather than surrender—an acceptance of present adversity and of death that is qualified by a belief in a reality beyond process which makes time purposeful. The difference between surrender and acceptance is the difference between Touchstone's "from hour to hour, we ripe and ripe, / and then, from hour to hour we rot and rot," or Jaques' "seven ages of man" speech, and Hamlet's "the readiness is all." Whereas Touchstone and, until the final moments of the play, Jaques find time only the measure of process,[27] Hamlet, having convinced himself of a "divinity that shapes our ends," awaits coming events, confident that beneath their surfaces are a reality and design in which all men participate. In terms of that design even the fall of a sparrow is purposeful.

Touchstone and Jaques, in finding no purpose in time beyond growth, decay, and death, have surrendered to time. They are time's fools. Thus, although each in his way discloses a kind of wit, it is a wit that is controlled by folly, entertaining perhaps, but dissonant and sterile. For "Nature's natural" there appears to be little chance that he will ever be purged of folly. His motive for marrying Audrey, along with her ambition to be "a woman of the world," promises that his marriage will be vulnerable to change because subservient to time. As Jaques indicates, Touchstone's "loving voyage / Is but for two months victuall'd" (V.iv.197-98). For Jaques himself there is distinct hope. The possibility that he may free himself from time by purging his wit of folly is introduced in the play's final moments. He refuses the Duke's invitation to return with him to court and announces his intention to seek out the holy man who has converted Celia's father. He may put time and wit to use and eventually discover the "uses of adversity"; he may finally, like the Duke, discover how to translate "the stubbornness of fortune" into the Duke's own harmonious style.[28]

Orlando and Rosalind come early and by different means to regard time hopefully. In circumstances that are desperate for Orlando, and will shortly be for Rosalind, they meet and fall immediately in love.

It is the hope of love's eventual fulfillment which sustains them in the bleak moments before and during their exile in Arden. Time for them holds the promise of eventual fulfillment, remote and wavering though it may initially be.

Another equally important, though less immediately apparent, aspect of renewing love is manifest in Celia's devotion to Rosalind and in Adam's service to Orlando. Celia is willing to give up all the comforts at court in order to accompany her friend into exile; and Adam is willing to share with his young master the small sum he has managed to save for the day when he is too old to work, and to accompany him into exile. Dramatically, the significance of these actions is barely stressed, especially Celia's. The audience is inclined to dismiss them as plot exigencies. Rosalind needs a companion and confidante in Arden and eventually there must be someone around for the repentant Oliver to marry. Furthermore, the prospects of Arden do not seem ominous. It has the atmosphere of a spacious and well-kept park. Nevertheless, we must appreciate Celia's readiness to leave the security of court, to share her possessions, and to risk travail in the forest as something more than a mere gesture. Adam's action is dramatically more convincing. It provides Orlando with an alternative to remaining at home and facing the threat of his brother's violence or fleeing and living as a thief. His pledge to continue to serve despite his age, and to risk the future for the sake of his old master's son, is a model statement of a constancy grounded in the conviction that Providence will provide:

> I have five hundred crowns,
> The thrifty hire I sav'd under your father,
>
> . . . .
>
> Take that, and He that doth the ravens feed,
> Yea, providently caters for the sparrow,
> Be comfort to my age!
>
> (II.iii.38-39, 43-45)

The self-sacrificing love manifest in the constancy of Adam and Celia serves a function no less important than that of romantic love. It offers hope and practical aid in the face of immediate adversity and helps to make possible the eventual restoration of the social order and the renewal of time in Duke Senior's duchy. Romantic love gives direction and purpose to the lives of the young outcasts and thus, subjectively, to time, once they meet in Arden; but it is the constancy of Adam and Celia that makes possible the fulfillment of that romantic love.

It is in its treatment of durative time, nature and fortune, and love that *As You Like It* anticipates the romances. In both *Pericles* and *The Tempest* the acceptance of durative time as purposeful, of a belief that beneath the shifting surfaces of transience there is a reality in which man may participate, is a dominant thematic concern. The ways in which this belief, in turn, affects reason and the senses is variously explored; and in each play the reality beneath appearances is represented as being finally beyond the reach of both. It is, in fact, the deluding surfaces of the sensible world which in each of the romances challenge the existence of any such reality and the principal characters' belief in it. Further, by refusing to surrender to the view that events are random and therefore under the absolute domination of fortune, or that life is merely a matter of ripening and rotting, Pericles, Marina, Imogen, and Prospero retain their freedom from the deterministic claims of nature. And, finally, love's role in giving time a subjective meaning—in sustaining hope in the presence of overwhelming adversity—is fundamental to the restorative pattern. In each play hope is contingent upon love, upon a conviction, sorely tried in various ways, that through love the past may be redeemed and the future renewed.

As I have observed earlier, love's power to save man from time's claims, and even to renew time, is an early and persistent concern throughout Shakespeare's works. The Sonnets celebrate love as the only means of meeting the depredations of time. To marry and beget children is to renew time. The aging father finds in his children the hope that time will in some sense be redeemed:

> This were to be new made when thou are old,
> And see thy blood warm when thou feel'st it cold.

> (No. 2)

In the continuity of succession there is the reassuring fact that one's self lives on and is remembered (Nos. 3, 5, 6). In the mutable order

> . . . nothing 'gainst Time's scythe can make defence
> Save breed, to brave him when he takes thee hence.
>
> (No. 12)

At one time I dismissed such arguments as merely a form of polite compliment.[29] I am now convinced that they are offered quite seriously.

In the romances, in *King Lear*, and even in *Romeo and Juliet*, Shakespeare represents succession as a restorative for men of winter in exactly the ways described in the marriage sonnets, but within a considerably more complex view. In that view man does not, as the fertility-myth critics have mistakenly assumed, simply reproduce himself. He is subject to reason and to natural, civil, and divine law. The romances make clear the nature of the obligations that human generation must fulfill if love is to be fully and truly generative, and they celebrate a far richer kind of renewal than is suggested in the marriage sonnets.

"Breeding" is the means by which all organic nature renews itself. But human nature is subject to nurture, and this brings us to art, the second of Shakespeare's preservatives against time. Man may learn the various arts through which he may direct and exercise reason to fruitful ends. In the Sonnets the value of art in the war against destructive time is confined to poetry as a means of preserving the memory of the beloved. In Sonnet 18 the poet assures the young man a kind of immortality in the "eternal lines" of verse:

> Nor shall Death brag thou wand'rest in his shade,
> When in eternal lines to time thou grow'st;
> So long as men can breathe or eyes can see,
> So long lives this, and this gives life to thee.

Sonnet 19 goes even further, promising the young man eternal youth. Sonnet 55 argues that verse is a more effective memorial than "marble" and "gilded monuments," and Sonnets 63, 65, and 100 offer similar assurances.

Art in the romances is also conceived as a means of combating Time the Destroyer. Monuments serve as memorials in *Pericles* and *The Winter's Tale*. But art in these plays is taken more broadly to include not only the theatrical art of pretending to be what one is not, but all of the various skills by which man perfects and directs his life.

We shall see in the romances that the importance of art in the generative process is various and complex, but, finally, insufficient. Generation and renewal are vitally dependent upon it, but fulfillment requires something more. Marina's skill in mimetic art rivals Nature's:

> She sings like one immortal, and she dances
> As goddess-like to her admired lays.
> Deep clerks she dumbs; and with her neeld composes
> Nature's own shape of bud, bird, branch, or berry,
> That even her art sisters the natural roses.
> Her inkle, silk, [twin] with the rubied cherry,
> That pupils lacks she none of noble race, . . .
>
> (V.i.3-9)

But something beyond nurture and skill will be required of her when she confronts the silent king who proves to be her father. Prospero's art, too, is limited. Though he has used it well during the years of his exile and during the time spanned by the play, he must finally acknowledge its limits. He must accept the persistence of evil in the world and the fact that man's attempts to eradicate it through nurture are futile. He must finally give up his magic, the art which isolates him from the community of man, and resume his obligation to govern; and finally, he must affirm his humanity by forgiving the guilty, trusting that they are able and ready to live good lives. In *The Winter's Tale* the art of the pilot Camillo is instrumental to the happy resolution of the action, but it is productive only after he persuades the lovers to trust in his counsel. Love and trust in each instance are the necessary conditions under which art contributes to reconciliation, recovery, and renewal.

The limits of art's efficacy are further illustrated in the final scene of *The Winter's Tale*. The best that art seems to have accomplished is the preservation of Hermione's memory in the life-like statue supposedly created by Julio Romano. Furthermore, a life-like image is the best that an artisan could have provided—the young man as memorialized by Shakespeare in the sonnets, Hermione as preserved by the art of Romano. The art which has in fact contributed to the restoration of Hermione is the art of memory as rigorously exercised by Leontes under Paulina's scrupulous supervision. Through the right use of memory he has preserved along with the image of Hermione not only the extent of his own guilt for her death but also the exact words of the oracle and the obligation it has imposed upon him. But something beyond art is required to restore Hermione. Paulina identifies it for us. All that is required, she says, to "make the statue move, indeed descend," is that "you do awake your faith."

It is clear, then, that art's effectiveness as a means of furthering the generative process is real but limited. Through the creation of an image, either as artifact or, as in *The Winter's Tale*, simply in the memory, it may preserve what otherwise would be lost. It may also provide the means of directing the natural appetites to their proper ends. Art may even prove to be a genuine restorative. Cerimon's learned art, for instance, revives Thaisa, and Prospero's art is a powerful aid to the recovery of what has been lost. But a power that is higher than art is necessary for the kind of recovery that Pericles eventually experiences and for the ultimate success of Prospero's efforts.

The triumph over destructive time that concludes each of the romances is, finally, effected by love grounded in trust. It is precisely the kind of love which Shakespeare summarily describes in Sonnet 116:

> Let me not to the marriage of true minds
> Admit impediments. Love is not love
> Which alters when it alteration finds,
> Or bends with the remover to remove.
> O, no! it is an ever-fixed mark
> That looks on tempests and is never shaken;

It is the star to every wand'ring bark,
Whose worth's unknown, although his height be taken.
Love's not Time's fool, though rosy lips and cheeks
Within his bending sickle's compass come;
Love alters not with his brief hours and weeks,
But bears it out even to the edge of doom.
　　If this be error and upon me proved,
　　I never writ, nor no man ever loved.

It is the one constant in a shifting world of process. In time and yet inviolate to time, its constancy is as firm as the trust on which it is founded and is proved by nothing other than the fact of its endurance. The strength of its constancy can only be known in retrospect, for always the future holds the possibility, unforeseen and unpredictable, of its failure. Neither a king's authority, a father's generosity, nor a wife's fidelity can assure it. Posthumus' love for Imogen, Leontes' love for Hermione, and Lear's love for Cordelia exemplify the point. What is often taken as a weakness of dramatic plotting in the opening acts of *Lear* and *The Winter's Tale* may in fact be Shakespeare's conscious effort to emphasize the very unpredictability of human love. Finally, its reality even for the poet is a matter of trust. He has no alternative at the close of his definition but to affirm, in a couplet which so many have found disappointing, his belief in love as he has described it.

Although man must accept the consequences of mutability, he may, if his conviction in the purposefulness of time is constant, participate in the renewing process of great creating Nature. By remaining firm in that conviction he preserves his own freedom, even when he is absolutely confined by physical necessity. The alternative, as I have shown earlier, is to become a fool of time and fortune.

OCCASION

If time demands of man resignation to its consequences, it nevertheless provides man with moments of decisive choice. This brings us to the second important aspect of time: time as *tempus commodum* or, metaphorically, Occasion, the Daughter of Time. As represented in the emblem books she is a woman who is bald, save for a single lock of hair just above her forehead. Occasionally in the emblem books *tempus commodum* is identified with Fortuna and called Opportunity.[30] In either instance the significance of the allegory is that the moment must be seized.

But there is also a difference between occasion and opportunity—a difference which Shakespeare consistently observes. How a character construes *tempus commodum*—whether he construes it as occasion or as opportunity—indicates whether he believes in a shaping Providence or in a random universe presided over by chance.

To recognize Occasion as the Daughter of Time is to recognize time's orderly progression as a manifestation of cosmic order and purpose. In this view the right use of occasion is a moral obligation. On the other hand, to view occasion as opportunity and a gift of fortune that is to be seized and used to one's own selfish ends is to assume a universe of random chance. Before he discovers at sea a pattern in coincidence, Hamlet views occasion as opportunity. Falstaff, Cloten, Malvolio, and Autolycus are also "time servers" and opportunists. They are indifferent to man's obligations to time. They view time narrowly and erroneously in terms of the opportunities it offers for the selfish gratification of personal desires.

Occasion as the Daughter of Time provides man with the chance to determine how he will use present time and thus to determine for himself in some measure the course of future time. Cassius refers to occasion when urging Brutus to take action against Caesar:

> Men at some time are masters of their fates;
> The fault, dear Brutus, is not in our stars,
> But in ourselves, that we are underlings.

(I.ii.139-41)

But Cassius and Brutus mistake the moment, and in slaying Caesar initiate the action which finally destroys them. Perhaps, as the play strongly suggests, Caesar might eventually have become a tyrant and thus given Brutus just cause; but he bases his decision to act on what the future *may* prove:

> since the quarrel
> Will bear no colour for the thing he is,
> Fashion it thus: that what he is, augmented,
> Would run to these and these extremities;
> And therefore think him as a serpent's egg
> Which, hatch'd, would, as his kind, grow mischievous,
> And kill him in the shell.
>
> (II.i.28-34)

He is aware of the danger of failing to seize occasion when it presents itself, but he fatally mistakes the time.[31] The misconstruing of occasion is what finally proves fatal to the rebel forces. Advised by Cassius, a seasoned military campaigner, not to advance on Philippi, Brutus insists that "our cause is ripe" and orders his forces to advance:

> We, at the height, are ready to decline.
> There is a tide in the affairs of men
> Which, taken at the flood, leads on to fortune;
> Omitted, all the voyage of their life
> Is bound in shallows and in miseries.
> On such a full sea are we now afloat,
> And we must take the current when it serves
> Or lose our ventures.   (IV.iii.217-24)

On the other hand, the right use of occasion may lead, as *The Tempest* demonstrates, to the recovery of what has been lost. Prospero recognizes occasion and appreciates its urgency. In I.ii.36-37, he tells Miranda "The hour's now come;/The very minute bids thee ope thine ear." Later in the scene he again stresses the urgency of the time, in lines echoing Brutus':

> ... by my prescience
> I find my zenith doth depend upon
> A most auspicious star, whose influence
> If now I court not but omit, my fortunes
> Will ever after droop.   (I.ii.180-84)[32]

Not to act when time provides the occasion for it is no less serious than the mistaking of occasion. Richard II recognizes occasion and what his office demands of him in the way of action, but in his cowardice he is unable to seize it. From the beginning of the play until moments before his death Richard abuses time by failing to act as his office dictates. He is in charge of what William Perkins refers to as "Civill Time";[33] but Richard neglects his charge in pursuit of profligate pleasures; and when, to finance a necessary expedition against the Irish, he seizes Lancaster's estate, he "violates time's charter," the law of primogeniture, the very law by which he has succeeded to the throne. Later, it is his delay in returning from Ireland that leads to the dissipation of the formidable military force that grew tired of waiting for his return. He again misses occasion at Flint Castle. In that moment when he appears upon the castle wall, there is the suggestion that all of the powerful nobles below, even Bolingbroke, are ready to receive him as king; if in that moment he had asserted his royal prerogatives, he might have regained the allegiance of the nobility.[34] He realizes only too late, after he has been imprisoned and has struggled unsuccessfully through the "study" of meditation to resign himself to prison, that time now wastes him because he formerly had wasted it. He accurately sees that he is now little more than a timepiece passively measuring out mere progression.

> I wasted time, and now doth Time waste me;
> For now hath Time made me his numb'ring clock.
> My thoughts are minutes; and with sighs they jar
> Their watches on unto mine eyes, the outward watch,
> Whereto my finger, like a dial's point,
> Is pointing still, in cleasing them from tears.
> Now sir, the sound that tells what hour it is
> Are clamorous groans, which strike upon my heart,
> Which is the bell. So sighs and tears and groans
> Show minutes, times, and hours; But my time
> Runs posting on in Bolingbroke's proud joy,
> While I stand fooling here, his Jack o' th' clock.
>
> (V.v.49-60)

Other examples in Shakespeare of the failure to seize occasion are easily cited. Hamlet finds that the time is out of joint and deplores his duty to set it right. The one clear and unmistakable opportunity he has to kill Claudius he rejects, because to kill him at prayer and send him to heaven will not satisfy his desire for revenge. The folly of his passion causes him to miss the occasion. Ironically, if Hamlet had been concerned only with justice, he could have slain Claudius then and there and sent him straight to hell. But his desire for vengeance makes of him a fool of fortune; moments later he sees the arras move and without pausing to find out who is behind it, he acts on impulse and kills the wrong man.

Both aspects of time, duration and occasion, are dominant concerns in *1 Henry IV* and are introduced in the opening dialogue between Falstaff and Hal.

> *Falstaff:* Now Hal, what time of day is it, lad?
> *Prince:* Thou art so fat-witted, with drinking of old sack and unbuttoning thee after supper and sleeping upon benches after noon, that thou hast forgotten to demand that truly which thou wouldest truly know. What a devil hast thou to do with the time of the day? Unless hours were cups of sack, and minutes capons, and clocks the tongues of bawds, and dials the signs of leaping-houses, and the blessed sun himself a fair hot wench in flame-coloured taffeta, I see no reason why thou shouldest be so superfluous to demand the time of the day.
>
> (I.ii.1-13)

The Prince's response to Falstaff leaves no doubt about the extent of his awareness of what it means to keep time. He sees clearly in Falstaff's dissoluteness a complete subservience to time that makes him time's fool. The Prince, who has seemed to a number of critics to be allowing time to waste him, is actually constantly "redeeming time," as Paul Jorgenson has shown,[35] by learning the ways of those over whom he will eventually rule. When time provides the Prince with the occasion to redeem public time, he is ready for it. He also provides Falstaff with the opportunity to redeem time by giving him a company of soldiers.

Durative time and occasion demand acceptance and readiness. Their acceptance follows the realization that there are times that can only be endured, times during which, as the youthful Milton concludes, one serves by standing and waiting; but that there are other times when one must act decisively and without delay. Finally, then, the readiness which is all is the readiness for whatever future time may bring—whether it be adversity or death, or occasion and prosperity.

RECURRENT OCCASION

We are now ready to consider how these notions of time affect structure in the romances.

Durative time dominates *Pericles* as the revolving years measure out Pericles' life and try his endurance. Occasion is represented in the play by Shakespeare's choice of events in that life, and, in the latter parts of the play, in Marina's as well. Each episode represents a critical time, an occasion, in which Pericles and later Marina must make a choice. Certain occasions permit them the freedom of positive action. Pericles is free, for instance, to disregard or follow Helicanus' advice to leave Tyre in order to avoid its invasion by Antiochus, or to disregard Diana's instruction in V.i. More often they are free only to choose how they will endure necessity. Nevertheless the choices they make on every occasion decisively affect the future.

In *Cymbeline*, on the other hand, occasion is dominant. The play focuses upon a critical interval of several months during Cymbeline's reign. It is a time during which the king's folly runs its course and the future of Britain, as well as his own, depends precariously upon the decisions his own children and Posthumus make. Durative time is also present, though less conspicuously than in *Pericles*. *Pericles* creates its own past as the action moves through the years. *Cymbeline* reconstructs the past through exposition.

The Winter's Tale combines the techniques used in the two earlier plays, introducing past time at the outset through exposition and then creating past time for the latter half of the play by focusing upon the occasion of Leontes' jealousy and its nearly tragic consequences. In the final action the focus is upon occasion. In the opening action time runs a destructive course. In the final action the principal characters redeem time through the prudent use of occasion. Thus the play's two actions cover the full course of cyclical time.

In *The Tempest* occasion again dominates, although again, as in each of the preceding plays durative time is conceptually and structurally important.

The cyclical progression of time provides the basis for a pattern of recurrent occasions which in each of these plays complicates narrative structure. If the course of time is cyclical, it follows that time repeats itself. According to Richard Hooker, "forasmuch as that motion is circular whereby we make our divisions of time, and the compass of that circuit such, that the heavens which be therein continually moved and keep in their motions uniform celerity must needs touch often the same points, they cannot choose but bring unto us by equal distances frequent returns of the same times."[36] It follows from the notion of cyclical recurrence that just as the seasons of the year repeat themselves, so the seasons of man repeat themselves in the lives of successive generations, presenting men of every generation with the same temptations and difficulties that are peculiar to each of the seasons or ages of life.

It is on the premise of cyclical recurrence that history is regarded in the Renaissance as a mirror in which "each man may . . . see things past whereby to judge justly of things present and wisely of things to come."[37] The patterns in the lives of nations as well as in the lives of individual men are ever recurrent and they are preserved in history. As Samuel Daniel writes in the Dedicatory Epistle to *Philotas*,

> These ancient representments of times past
> Tell vs that men haue, doe, and alwayes runne
> The selfe same line of action, and doe cast
> Their course alike, and nothing can be done,
> Whilst they, their ends, and nature are the same:
> But will be wrought vpon the selfe same frame.[38]
>
> (ll. 26-31)

What a father encounters, his sons and daughters will also encounter. Circumstances may differ—Pericles is threatened by an incestuous father; Marina, by a queen whose love for her daughter begets a murderous envy—but the strength of their virtue is challenged equally. In short, although everything *specific* happens for the first time, *generically*, there is nothing new under the sun.

Time may also repeat itself within a single lifetime. Dionyza and Cleon experience two complete revolutions of time, falling from prosperity to adversity, rising again to prosperity through the charity of Pericles, and then falling again, because of their failure to honor their pledge to Pericles, into the final adversity of death. Pericles, Leontes, Prospero, and Cymbeline discover that time repeats itself within the circumference of their own lives. Cymbeline, for instance, finds the Romans threatening Britain as they had years earlier when his sons were but children. He is also given the opportunity to make the same mistake he had then made. He denies the nobility of Posthumus as he had refused the nobility of Belarius. On both occasions he is punished by the loss of children.

If recursive time allows man the opportunity to repeat an earlier error, it also offers him the chance to redeem earlier failures. The possibility is elaborated in one of George Wither's emblems:

> Occasions-past *are sought in vaine;*
> *But, oft, they* wheele-about *againe.*

> Unwise are they that spend their youthful *Prime*
> In Vanities; as if they did suppose
> That men, at pleasure, might redeeme the *Time;*
> For, they a faire advantage fondly lose.
> As ill-advis'd be those, who having lost
> The first *Occasions,* to *Despairing* runne:
> For, *Time* hath *Revolutions;* and, the most,
> For their Affaires, have *Seasons* more, than one.
> Nor is their Folly small who much depend
> On *Transitorie things,* as if their Powre
> Could bring to passe what should not have an *End;*
> Or compasse that, which *Time* will not devoure.
> The first Occasions, therefore, see thou take
> (Which offred are) to bring thy hopes about;
> And, minde thou, still, what *Haste* away they make,
> Before thy swift-pac't houres are quite runne out.

Yet, if an *Opportunity* be past,
Despaire not thou, as they that hopelesse be;
Since, *Time* may so revolve againe, at last,
That *New-Occasions* may be offred thee.
And see, thou trust not on those fading things,
Which by thine owne *Endeavours* thou acquir'st:
For, *Time* (which her owne *Births* to ruine brings)
Will spare, nor *thee*, nor ought which thou desir'st.
His *Properties*, and *Vses*, what they are,
In vaine observ'd will be, when he is fled:
That, they in season, therefore, may appeare,
Our *Emblem*, thus, hath him deciphered;
    Balde save before, and standing on a Wheele;
    A Razor in his Hand, a Winged Heele.[39]

The cyclical progression of time provides man, therefore, with grounds for hope. Time's cyclicity is in itself evidence of the mercy which even within the natural order tempers justice, for it offers the man who has missed occasion, or abused time, the opportunity for future redemption. Such opportunities are depicted by Shakespeare as recurring moments.[40] Belarius, Cymbeline, Leontes, and Prospero after failing initiallly to use time properly, discover years later that time has "wheeled about again" and provided them with the opportunity to "redeem time" and to regain what has been long lost.

TIME, SEA, AND TEMPEST

The system of time figuratively represented by Occasion and by Time as Destroyer and Renewer provides an instructive context in which to consider the sea and the tempests which figure so prominently in the action of *Pericles*, *The Tempest*, and *The Winter's Tale*.

The tempests which frequently occur throughout Shakespeare's plays seem, initially, to have no consistent meaning. The violent storm in *Julius Caesar* seems prophetic, a warning to the conspirators as well as to Caesar; although Cicero, whose one appearance is only to comment on the storm, reminds the audience that even storms so violent and unusual as the one of the preceding night are in all probability natural, and that the meanings attributed to them are subjective:[41]

> Indeed, it is a strange-disposed time;
> But men may construe things after their fashion
> Clean from the purpose of the things themselves.
>
> (I.iii.33-35)

In *Macbeth* and *Lear* storms appear to be evidence of the belief that disruptions of the social order, as Virgil Whitaker proposes,[42] have their reverberations in the natural order. The tempests in *King Lear* and *The Winter's Tale* seem to be retributive, although the innocent as well as the guilty suffer their violence. In *Twelfth Night* and *Pericles* the storms at sea which wreck ships and isolate lone survivors on the shores of strange lands strongly suggest Fortuna and her domain of random chance. Nevertheless, Knight's observation that a consistency underlies the apparent diversity of the tempest's meaning seems to me correct.[43] After noticing that it is "always the same tempest" that recurs in play after play, he concludes that it symbolically embodies Shakespeare's "intuition of discord at the heart of existence." At this point, however, one must disagree with a critic from whom many of us have learned so much. Symbolic Shakespeare's tempests may sometimes be, but they are not born of intuition; nor are they Shakespeare's invention.

Tempests have a well-establlished emblematic meaning throughout the Renaissance; that meaning is an extension of the meaning that tempests as natural phenomena have within the Renaissance time system and the more inclusive system of mutability.

Throughout the Renaissance tempests are frequently symbolic of temporality under both aspects of time, duration and occasion. According to the Christian myth, literal tempests, as well as "the tempestivity at the heart of existence" which they come figuratively to represent, originate with The Fall, when the earth was tilted on its axis and the seasons began. Tempestuousness pertains to the persistent dissonances that reverberate in the micro- and macrocosm as a consequence of the disruption of the once harmonious union of reason and the appetites, and to the endless flux in which man exists in

45

the world of time. Tempests therefore become symbolic of time as duration. Time itself is tempestuous; the world is "a lasting storm."

Tempests are as inevitable as the seasons and are thus to be accepted on the same grounds that durative time and the natural order are to be accepted. Threnot makes the point in the February Eclogue of *The Shepheardes Calender* when he scolds Cuddy for complaining against the "bitter blasts of winter."[44]

> Lewdly complainest thou laesie ladde,
> Of Winters wrack, for making thee sadde.
> Must not the world wend in his commun course
> From good to badd, and from badde to worse,
> From worse vnto that is worst of all,
> And then returne to his former fall?
> Who will not suffer the stormy time,
> Where will he liue tyll the lusty prime?
> Selfe haue I worne out thrise threttie yeares,
> Some in much ioy, many in many teares:
> Yet neuer complained of cold nor heate,
> Of Sommers flame, nor of Winters threat:
> Ne euer was to Fortune foeman,
> But gently tooke, that ungently came.
>
> (ll. 9-22)

Cuddy has foolishly ignored the cyclical pattern of time. The seasoned man "gently" takes what "ungently" comes. Moreover, the violence of the seasons—winter weather and sudden tempests or, figuratively, adversity in all its various manifestations—have a value if man will but recognize it. It may lead, as the banished Duke in *As You Like It* discovers, to knowledge of self.

> Here feel we not the penalty of Adam,
> The season's difference, as the icy fang
> And churlish chiding of the winter's wind,
> Which, when it bites and blows upon my body
> Even till I shrink with cold, I smile and say,
> "This is no flattery: these are counsellors
> That feelingly persuade me what I am."
>
> (II.i.5-11)

The Duke is no "foeman to fortune." His gentle acceptance of "the season's difference" is proof of his acceptance of "the penalty of Adam" as just. His use of tempestuous time to achieve knowledge of self demonstrates that the answer to the question raised earlier in the play by Celia and Rosalind as to whether nature or fortune reigns over the affairs of men depends upon man himself. Fortune is victorious only when man loses his faith in the purposefulness of time and surrenders to chance and circumstance.

Inasmuch as tempests may unexpectedly and violently disrupt temperate time, they come also to be symbolic of sudden crisis. As such, tempests, literal or metaphorical, provide one with the opportunity to prove the strength of his constancy. According to Philip du Vair, "The sailor groweth to be a Pilote amongst tempests and stormes: and man becomes not a man indeed, that is constant and courageous, but in adversity. It is affliction makes him know his strength. . . ."[45] Samuel Daniel offers the same advice to Henry Wriothesly:

> He who hath never warrid with misery,
> Nor ever tugged with Fortune and Distresse,
> Hath had n' occasion nor no field to trie
> The strength and forces of his worthinesse.
>
> . . . .
> It is not but the Tempest that doth shew
> The Sea-mans cunning: but the field that tries
> The Captaines courage.[46]

Nestor adopts the same argument in *Troilus and Cressida* when endeavoring to persuade the Greeks to take heart. Agamemnon has just explained to his followers that the obstacles they have encountered during the seven-year siege have been "But the protractive trials of great Jove / To find persistive constancy in men" (I.iii.20-21). Nestor, enlarging upon the point, develops the familiar analogy between men caught in sudden adversity and the sailor suddenly beset by a tempest:

> In the reproof of chance
> Lies the true proof of men. The sea being smooth,

How many shallow bauble boats dare sail
Upon her patient breast, making their way
With those of nobler bulk!
But let the ruffian Boreas once enrage
The gentle Thetis, and anon behold
The strong-ribb'd bark through liquid mountains cut.
. . . .
                     where's then the saucy boat
Whose weak untimber'd sides but even now
Co-rivall'd greatness? . . .
                       Even so
Doth valour's show and valour's worth divide
In storms of fortune; . . .   (I.iii.33-47)

Whether tempests are finally destructive will be decided by those whom they afflict. The constant man is unshaken even at that moment when the tempest is about to capsize his ship. Gonzalo, who in *The Tempest* will represent the norm of constancy whenever he appears in the later action, accepts shipwreck as willed by the heavens: "The wills above be done!" (I.i.71).[47] The figure of the constant man also appears in I.ii. of *Twelfth Night*—in the Captain's description of the tempest-tossed Sebastian, courageously managing to stay afloat after the ship has broken up. "I saw your brother," he tells Viola,

Most provident in peril, bind himself,
Courage and hope both teaching him the practice,
To a strong mast that liv'd upon the sea;
Where, like [Arion] on the dolphin's back,
I saw him hold acquaintance with the waves
So long as I could see.   (ll. 11-17)

To the constant man shipwreck may even prove to be a blessing in disguise. The storm which shipwrecks Pericles on the shore of Pentapolis, for instance, provides him with the opportunity to meet and win Thaisa. As he emerges from the sea, alone and cut off from all connections with his past, the Prince is resigned even to death. He has "gently" accepted what "ungently" came; but there is a readiness in his resignation. When the sea casts up his father's armor and the fishermen extend their charity, he initiates the action which confirms his right to a noble title and wins him Thaisa's love. He is ready for the opportunity that *occasio* provides. He recovers what the tempest seemed to have destroyed, his name and noble lineage, and he wins a wife who promises to bear him heirs to perpetuate his name. Like the constant voyager in the verses which accompany Geoffrey Whitney's emblem, *Constantia comes victoriae*, Pericles finally wins "That wished porte, where lastinge ioye beginnes."

> *Boni gubernatoris est, ventoru se flatibus*
> *accomodare: viri autem sapientis, animi affectibus.*
>
> The shippe, that longe vppon the sea doth saile,
> And here, and there with warriing windes is toste
> On rockes, and sandes, in daunger ofte to quaile,
> Yet at the lengthe, obtaines the wished coaste:
> Which beinge wonne, the trompetts ratlings blaste,
> Doth teare the skie, for ioye of perills paste.
> Though master reste, thoughe Pilotte take his ease,
> Yet nighte, and day, the ship her course dothe keepe;
> So, whilst that man doth saile theise worldlie seas
> His voyage shortes: althoughe he wake, or sleepe.
> And if he keepe his course directe, he winnes
> That wished porte, where lastinge ioye beginnes.[48]

Romeo, on the other hand, believing that Juliet is dead, finds his loss too much to endure. He expresses his despair metaphorically: "now at once run on / The dashing rocks thy sea-sick weary bark!" (V.iii.117-18). He is one of those men who, according to George Wither, finding themselves in the midst of a tempest, curse destiny and ignore their own folly.

> He, that his Course directly Steeres,
> Nor Stormes, nor Windy-Censures feares.
>
> We to the Sea, this World may well compare
> For every Man which liveth in the same,
> Is as a Pilot to some Vessell there,
> Of little size, or else of larger frame.

Some, have the Boats of their owne Life to guide
. . . .
Some others, rule great Provinces, and they
Resemble Captaines of huge Argosies;
But, when of Kingdomes, any gayne the Sway,
To Generalls of Fleets, we liken these,
Each hath his proper Course to him assign'd,
His Card, his Compasse, his due Tacklings, too;
And, if their businesse, as they ought, they mind,
They may accomplish all they have to doe.
But, most Men leave the Care of their owne Course,
To judge or follow others, in their wayes;
And, when their Follies make their Fortunes worse,
They curse the Destiny, which they should prayse.
For, Waves, and Windes, and that oft-changing Weather
Which many blame, as cause of all their Losses,
(Though they observe it not) helpes bring together
Those Hopes, which their owne Wisedome,
    often crosses.[49]

It is easy to understand how tempests, especially tempests at sea, come to symbolize the general turbulence and affliction of man's lot. It is a short step from the emblematic reading of literal storms at sea to the use of such storms as emblematic of the adversity that man encounters on his voyage through life. The sea's appropriateness as a symbol of nature itself has been noticed by Kathleen Williams. Although she is writing of the Florimell-Marinell narrative in *The Faerie Queene*, her remarks are equally appropriate to Shakespeare's romances and especially to *Pericles*. The sea is

> the remotest of all things from man, home of hydras and "sea-shouldering whales," and yet it is the most perfect of all symbols for the whole multiple, changing, but unified world, "eterne in mutabilitie." The sea can symbolize the character and meaning of the universe and so embodies truth beyond itself, but it stands also, in its own right, for nature at its least formed and nearly chaotic. It can show the thoughtless, blameless cruelty of nature, its blind suffering, and also the justice which works through it as through all creation.[50]

One need only add to Miss Williams' eloquent description that beneath the sea's ceaselessly shifting surfaces, sudden calms, and violent storms there is the periodic ebb and flow of its tides, controlled by the revolving heavens and thus, like process and time, manifesting the cyclic pattern. In its surface unpredictability it suggests the randomness of fortune, but the periodic regularity concealed beneath its surfaces is a manifestation of the general law which governs all existence in the mutable order. Its rhythms are the rhythms of process itself. As all must ebb so must all rise and return.

If the movement of the sea demands the same kind of resignation that time demands, it also offers the same hopes of restoration, recurrent occasion, and renewal that the cyclical movement of time offers. It is precisely that rhythm of the sea which dominates the narrative of *Pericles*. Although sea, time, and the tempest have seemed indifferent and cruel to Pericles, the story of his life viewed retrospectively from the point of view provided by Gower's epilogue indicates otherwise. Tempests and the sea have figured as actively in providing and restoring as they have in destroying and separating. For example, the first tempest that Pericles encounters leaves him isolated and destitute; but the sea delivers up his father's armor and, together with the winds, has brought him to Pentapolis where he finds Thaisa. Again, years later when Pericles floats aimlessly on the sea after being told that Marina is dead, it is the ocean's tides, winds, and currents that carry him to Mytilene and reunion with Marina.

PILOTS AND HELMSMEN

The sea's action of bringing Pericles to Mytilene brings us to a final nautical figure within the general metaphorical configuration of the time system which I believe to be the basis for the restorative pattern of the romances. It is the figure of the Pilot or Helmsman.[51]

Gower tells us that Pericles changes pilots after he has returned to Tarsus and been told that Marina is dead. The journey to Tarsus has been charted by reason: "think [his] pilot thought" (IV.iv.18); but the voyage which carries him finally to Mytilene is charted by Lady Fortune:

Let Pericles believe his daughter's dead,
And bear his courses to be ordered
By Lady Fortune; . . .   (IV.iv.46-48)

The change of pilots suggests on a first reading that Pericles has found this latest "tempest" too much to endure and that in his despair he surrenders himself to the blind goddess of chance. But his surrender is not to be mistaken for despair. Gower's exposition and dumb show stress that Pericles' sorrow while all-consuming, is nevertheless informed by patience. He "gently" accepts Marina's death as, years earlier, he had accepted shipwreck and Thaisa's death—as another instance of the adversity under which sinning man must labor to satisfy divine justice.

The proof of Pericles' patience in this latest adversity is his purpose in once again putting to sea:

He swears
Never to wash his face, nor cut his hairs.
He puts on sackcloth, and to sea. He bears
A tempest, which his mortal vessel tears,
And yet he rides it out.   (IV.iv.27-31)

There is no indication here of desperation or defiance. Like the familiar ship in Renaissance emblems of patience, Pericles "bears/A tempest, which his mortal vessel tears, / And yet he rides it out." He abdicates his power to direct his own actions in order to withdraw completely from the world of men and society for a purpose which is visibly identified by sackcloth and monkish vows.

Pericles' relinquishing of his future to Fortune is to be understood as an ultimate act of faith and obedience. Deprived by Marina's death of his last worldly hope, he surrenders his future to chance, on the grounds that whatever happens in the future will happen because the heavens have willed it.

In this context *fortune* is not the blind goddess who presides over a random universe. *Fortune* here represents what Thomas Browne identifies as one of the two ways in which Providence realizes its ends. The "ordinary and open way" consists of the operation of the laws of nature. "The obscure way" is commonly known as *fortune*:

This [*i.e.* the operation of natural law] is the ordinary and open way of His providence which Art and Industry have in a good part discovered; whose effects we may fortel without an Oracle: to foreshow these, is not Prophesie, but Prognostication. There is another way, full of Meanders and Labyrinths . . . and that is a more particular and obscure method of His Providence, directing the operations and single Essences: this we call *Fortune,* that serpentine and crooked line, whereby He draws those actions His Wisdom intends, in a more unknown and secret way. This cryptick and involved method of His Providence have I ever admired . . . Surely there are in every man's life certain rubbings, doublings and wrenches which pass a while under the effects of chance, but at the last well examined, prove the meer hand of God.[52]

Patient and impatient men sometimes reveal themselves in Shakespeare's plays by their interpretations of Fortune and adversity. As we have seen, an impatient man—Romeo, for instance—may recklessly surrender reason to passion and protest that all is fortune. On the other hand, the patient man who finds himself in a situation in which all of his worldly hopes are frustrated, never loses his faith in a purposeful universe. Like Pericles, he never doubts the divine purpose of those "rubbings, doublings and wrenches which pass a while under the effects of chance." When he alludes to Fortune he alludes to the "meer hand of God."

Cymbeline provides an instructive analogy.When the loyal Pisanio has done all that he can on behalf of Imogen and Posthumus, he reaffirms (in terms of time and fortune) his faith in the powers above man:

> The heavens still must work.
> Wherein I am false I am honest; not true, to be true.
> These present wars shall find I love my country,
> Even to the note o' the King, or I'll fall in them.
> All other doubts, by time let them be clear'd;
> Fortune brings in some boats that are not steer'd.
>
> (IV.iii.41-46)

Pisanio at this point in the action is convinced he has done all that is humanly possible. He is "perplex'd in all"; but he does not despair.

"The heavens still must work," and they will work through "time" and "fortune." Time will eventually resolve all doubts by revealing the truth; and in that eventual clarification the victims of the present confusion may even reach a safe harbor; for the heavens work in unforeseeable and wondrous ways—in ways which are sometimes referred to even by the faithful as the ways of Fortune.

The action which brings Pericles to Mytilene affirms the view expressed by Browne. The "rubbings, doublings and wrenches" in Pericles' life, which seemed to be "the effects of chance," prove to be the "obscure method" of providence. The pilot that finally brings Pericles to Mytilene is identified by Gower as Dame Fortune; but as Sir Walter Ralegh observes, "Whom the Poets call Fortune, we know to be God."

The metaphorical pilot to whom Pericles entrusts his ship is a part of the general metaphorical system I have been discussing throughout this chapter. In man's voyage through the tempestuous seas of this world the choice of helmsman is crucial. The most reliable helmsmen include Sapientia, Virtue, Prudence, and God. According to Spenser in *The Teares of the Muses*, Sapientia

> armes the brest with constant patience,
> Against the bitter throwes of doulours darts
> She solaceth with rules of Sapience
> The gentle minds, in midst of worldly smarts.
>
> (ll. 133-36)

Without her "skill" man

> Is like a ship in midst of tempest left,
> Withouten helme or Pilot her to stay,
> Full sad and dredfull is that ship's euent.
>
> (ll. 141-43)

Primaudaye recommends that Prudence be given the helm.

> It is by her that man is alwaies clothed with a mild and setlet disposition, whereof he standeth no less in need, than a ship floating on the sea doth of the presense of a pilot, that he may prudentlie undertake, and wisely execute whatsoever he knoweth to be good, after mature deliberation, and consideration of all the Circumstance of the fact.[53]

According to George Herbert, man must resign the helm to God, whether his voyage, as in "Obedience," is that of the Christian poet—

> O let thy sacred will
> All thy delight in me fulfill!
> Let me not think an action mine own way,
> But as thy love shall sway,
> Resigning up the rudder to thy skill.—
>
> (ll. 16-20)

or, as in "The Bag," that of the penitent whose sense of guilt threatens to become despair:

> Away despair; my gracious Lord doth heare.
> Though windes and waves assault my keel.
> He doth preserve it: he doth steer,
> Ev'n when the boat seems most to reel.
> Storms are the triumph of his art:
> Well may he close his eyes, but not his heart.
>
> (ll. 1-6)

The helmsmen to avoid include Affection and Cupid. The man who abandons all hope in the midst of a tempest is not merely a coward; in his despair he surrenders his ship to the brute forces of nature. The lover, likewise, who allows Eros, Cupid, or Passion to pilot his ship commits himself to a course of unreason and thus, in a view that is traceable to Boethius, makes himself vulnerable to the winds and tides of chance. Like Wyatt's lover in "My galy charged with forgetfulness," he finds Eros a lord who "sterith with cruelnes," that "reason is drowned" and, more often than not, that he remains "despairing of the port." Tarquin in *The Rape of Lucrece* entrusts his course to Desire—"Desire my pilot is, beauty my prize:/Then who fears sinking where such treasure lies?" (ll. 279-80), and reaffirms his commitment several stanzas later: "Then Love and Fortune be my gods, my guide!" (l. 351). The Chorus in *Samson Agonistes*, commenting on Samson's fall, identifies Samson as a pilot but designates Dalila as the helmsman who wrecked his ship: "What Pilot so expert but needs must wreck/Embarked with such a steers-mate at the helm" (ll. 1044-45).[54]

An anonymous contributor to *The Phoenix Nest* (1593)[55] develops the figure of Eros as helmsman in a way that is of particular interest to the commentator who would like to make sense of the nautical metaphors in *Romeo and Juliet* and *The Winter's Tale.*

> My fraile and earthly barke by reasons guide
> (Which holds the helme, whilst will doth wield the sail)
> By my desires the windes of bad betide,
> Hath saild these worldly seas with small avail,
> Vaine obiects serve for dreadfull rocks to quaile,
> My brittle boate, from haven of life that flies,
> To haunt the Sea of Mundane miseries.
> My soule that drawes impressions from above,
> And viewes my course, and sees the windes aspire,
> Bids reason watch to scape the shoales of Love,
> But lawles will enflamed with endles ire,
> Doth steer in poope whilst reason doth retire:
> The storms increase, my barke loves billowes fill:
> Thus are they wrakt, that guide their course by will.[56]

Romeo in the opening scenes is Cupid's victim, desperately infatuated with a woman who ignores him. His melancholia, although expressed in terms so conventional that commentators are inclined to dismiss it as a merely fashionable pose, is taken quite seriously by his father: "Black and portentous must this humour prove/Unless good counsel may the cause remove" (I.i.147-48). Despite his father's efforts to provide him with such counsel, Romeo remains "his own affections' counsellor" (I.i.153). Mercutio and Benvolio also attempt to advise him when in the second scene of the opening act they urge him to go with them to the Capulet ball. There he will have the chance to compare Rosaline "with all the admired beauties of Verona," and thus come to see that there are other women at least as lovely as she. Romeo agrees to go, but not for the reason urged by his friends. He will go "no such sight to be shown, / But to rejoice in splendour of mine own" (I.ii.105-06). When we next see him he is on his way to the ball. His melancholy remains obvious. He is "not for this ambling" (I.iv.11); his "soul of lead / So stakes me to the ground I cannot move" (I.iv.15-16); and when Mercutio urges him to "borrow Cupid's wings," he protests:

> I am too sore enpierced with his shaft
> To soar with his light feathers, and so bound
> I cannot bound a pitch above dull woe.
> Under love's heavy burden do I sink.
>
> (I.iv.19-21)

The audience presently discovers that Romeo has also received counsel from another quarter. He has had a dream in which he was warned not to attend the ball; but the warning has no effect. He remains "his own affections' counsellor." Mercutio teases him for taking the dream seriously, but Romeo remains convinced of its seriousness; for when Benvolio urges the group to proceed immediately or be late for the festivities, Romeo remarks:

> I fear, too early; for my mind misgives
> Some consequence yet hanging in the stars
> Shall bitterly begin his fearful date
> With this night's revels, and expire the term
> Of a despised life clos'd in my breast
> By some vile forfeit of untimely death.
>
> (I.iv.106-11)

But he ignores the warning and agrees to proceed:

> But He that hath the steerage of my course
> Direct my [sail]! On, lusty gentlemen!
>
> (I.iv.112-13)

The pilot's identity is obvious, although it has not seemed so to the critics. It is Cupid, who from the very beginning of the play has been charting his course. It is still Cupid who directs his course when he climbs the Capulet's orchard walls and finds Juliet at her window. When Juliet asks, "By whose direction found'st thou out this place?" Romeo replies:

> By Love, that first did prompt me to inquire;
> He lent me counsel and I lent him eyes.

> I am no pilot; yet, wert thou as far
> As that vast shore [wash'd] with the farthest sea,
> I should adventure for such merchandise.
>
> (II.ii.80-84)

Cupid not only continues to chart Romeo's course throughout the action leading to the secret marriage; he is also the "desperate pilot" who at Romeo's command fatally wrecks the young lover's "sea-sick weary bark" (V.iii.118). The final line of the poem from *The Phoenix Nest* provides an appropriate epitaph for such impetuous lovers: "Thus are they wrakt, that guide their course by will."

The counselor on whom so much depends in *The Winter's Tale* is Camillo. He enables Polixenes in the opening action to escape Leontes' madness; and years later he designs the plan which brings Perdita and Florizel to Sicilia. In each instance he is called a pilot. After Polixenes has heard of Leontes' plan to have him assassinated and of the means of escape Camillo has proposed, he entrusts his future to him and the course he has charted: "Give me thy hand" and "be pilot to me." The situation years later in which Camillo urges Florizel first to listen to and then to follow his advice unmistakably suggests the emblematic representation of that moment of critical choice when man may either entrust his future to Sapientia or surrender to despair. Florizel, his love for Perdita denied him by his father, is about to commit his destiny recklessly to "the winds of chance"; he refuses to listen to Camillo. "Be advised," Camillo urges, and Florizel replies,

> I am, and by my fancy. If my reason
> Will thereto be obedient, I have reason;
> If not, my senses, better pleas'd with madness,
> Do bid it welcome. (IV.iv.492-95)

When Camillo warns him of the folly of what he has been expressing, the young prince tells him to counsel his father instead of him:

> —cast your good counsels
> Upon his passion; let myself and Fortune
> Tug for the time to come. This you may know

> And so deliver: I am put to sea
> With her who here I cannot hold on shore.
>
> (504-08)

Having neither helmsman nor destination, he is ready to surrender his future to fortune:

> ... as th' unthought-on accident is guilty
> To what we wildly do, so we profess
> Ourselves to be the slaves of chance, and flies
> Of every wind that blows.   (548-51)

Camillo persists, however, offering him hope in

> A course more promising
> Than a wild dedication of yourselves
> To unpath'd waters, undream'd shores,
>
> (575-77)

and Florizel finally acquiesces. He accepts Camillo as his "pilot," allowing him to chart a course back to Sicilia and a happy ending of the play.

The episode in which Camillo wins Florizel's trust returns us to the subject introduced at the outset of this chapter—the modes of representation which distinguish the romances as a group. Pericles, standing shipwrecked on the shore of Pentapolis, or in the midst of a violent tempest at sea, and Florizel, responding to the tempestuous rage of his father by impulsively surrendering his freedom to choose, are equally indebted to the emblems of the sea and the tempest which I have been discussing in the final section of this chapter. Similar examples of indebtedness come to mind: Pericles, disconsolate and brooding aboard a ship whose course he has surrendered to wind and tide; Marina, alone on the shores of Tarsus, reflecting on her life and finding the world "a lasting storm"; in *The Winter's Tale* the Shepherd's discovery of the infant Perdita in the midst of a tempest which sinks the boat that has brought her to Bohemia. Each of these episodes is an *exemplum*, an episode invented to represent a moral commonplace, and as such is typical of the kind of representation

59

that is peculiar to the romances. If Shakespeare's purpose in the tragedies—and I realize that I am risking an over-simplification—is to discover meaning in the historically given, his purpose in the romances is to invent fictions which will "figure forth" meaning.

But between the emblematic episodes in *Pericles* and the Camillo-Florizel episode in *The Winter's Tale* there is also a difference. It is indicative of a significant difference between the techniques of imitation used in *Pericles* and the three succeeding plays. In each of the emblematic episodes mentioned above Shakespeare began with a commonplace and a general image often used to represent it; but whereas the emblematic scenes in *Pericles* remain close to the commonplaces they are intended to figure forth, the Camillo-Florizel episode is closer to what we may call the imitation of phenomenal reality. It is particularized by the setting and flow of action which provide its context. It climaxes a sequence of actions, carefully plotted and involving characters who, although they lack the fullness of a Hamlet or a Desdemona, or even an Ophelia, nevertheless, have a substantiality which is lacking in Pericles and Marina. There is also throughout the action leading up to the episode an interaction among the characters—the Shepherd, Polixenes, Camillo, and the young lovers—which adds to the illusion of realistic representation. Perdita's ironic awareness that she, a maiden whose love will never be consummated, must play the role of Flora, Polixenes' suspicions, the Shepherd's simple, unquestioning innocence, the ambiguity of Florizel's motives—all contribute to the irreducible particularity of the events leading up to the climactic episode. Finally, there are the naturalistic details that particularize the setting, partly provided by the rural, festive action and partly by the bits of realistic descriptive detail and the homely allusions which occur in the speeches of Autolycus, the Shepherd, and Perdita. The illusion is of a real festival in an imaginary Bohemia.

The emblematic scenes in *Pericles* of course also exist in a context of action and setting. But the details depicting settings are much sparser, and the action, while not merely naive chronology, is nevertheless essentially episodic. Such scenes as those in which we encounter the shipwrecked Pericles or Marina reflecting on the world appear as tableaux, as static, but speaking, moral pictures in loose sequence rather than as parts of a continuing and consecutive action; and that effect is strengthened by the minimum of localizing detail they contain and the way in which they are introduced and commented on by their purveyor, Gower.

The effect is surely deliberate. For instance, by leaving the localizing detail to be provided by Gower, Shakespeare is able to make of Pericles' soliloquy on the shores of Pentapolis an exemplary statement of the quality of resignation that a world of affliction and unforeseen adversity demands of fallen man:

> Yet cease your ire, you angry stars of heaven!
> Wind, rain, and thunder, remember earthly man
> Is but a substance that must yield to you;
> And I, as fits my nature, do obey you.
> Alas, the seas hath cast me on the rocks,
> Wash'd me from shore to shore, and left me breath
> Nothing to think on but ensuing death.
> Let it suffice the greatness of your powers
> To have bereft a prince of all his fortunes;
> And having thrown him from your watery grave,
> Here to have death in peace is all he'll crave.
>
> (II.i.1-11)

The soliloquy expands the moral commonplace,

> When thou are shipwrakt in Estate
> Submit with patience, unto Fate.

Its visual and emblematic particularization is provided by the figure of Pericles as he stands, weak and alone, on the bare stage before us.

In each of the later romances the mode of imitation is more like the mode represented by the Camillo-Florizel episode. The closest resemblances to *Pericles* in the matter of representation are in fact to be found in *Timon of Athens*, in which episodic and tableau-like scenes are also present, and in which the action of the entire play seems to be a dramatic "figuring forth" of what the Painter and the Poet have, within the narrower limits of their respective arts, less effectively represented. And yet, each of the later plays adapts what is essentially the mimetic mode of *Pericles*. They may in some ways be more "realistic" than *Pericles*; nevertheless, each is devoted to the representation of the principles and laws that lie beneath the surfaces of the phenomenal world.

Whatever their differences, then, the romances disclose a common purpose and method. They are fictions conceived to figure forth a reality that is only inferentially revealed to the observer of phenomenal nature. They frequently ignore dramatic probability and, occasionally, even the natural boundaries of sense perception. Gods appear on stage to affirm the perfect justice that is manifest in the laws of mutability; and the wildly improbable stuff of romance is made to figure forth the ways in which errant man may recover what he has lost, if his trust in the heavens remains unshaken.

In these plays Shakespeare focuses the mirror of his art specifically upon the forces of generation and decay which sustain the natural order and define the condition of human existence. In that mirror, in which the invisible is made visible through the dramatist's invented fiction, man's position within the natural order is depicted metaphorically in terms of time. Through the right use of time fathers and their children may participate in the generative process by which the social and natural orders are sustained. By enduring tempestuous time patiently they prove their trust in a purposeful and just universe. By knowing when as well as how to act, and by acting promptly when occasion presents itself, they defeat Time the Destroyer.

Even those characters who have initially missed occasion, or who have wasted or abused time—Leontes, Posthumus, Alonso, and Prospero—have the opportunity to redeem themselves. For time's course is cyclical, and provides the patient man with recurrent occasions. The patient man seizes the recurring occasion, redeeming himself and the past and completing the restorative pattern. He also transforms a potentially tragic action into a comic one: through a love which redeems and renews he restores to public and private time a harmony which in the tragedies is accomplished only through death. The restorative, love, replaces the purgative, retributive justice; and apparent tragedy is transformed into authentic comedy.

NOTES

[1]All quotations from Shakespeare are taken from *The Complete Plays and Poems of William Shakespeare*, ed. William Allan Neilson and Charles Jarvis Hill (Cambridge, 1942). Italics, unless otherwise noted, are mine.

[2]In *The Book Named the Governor*, ed. with an Introduction by S. E. Lehmberg (London, 1962), pp. 120-21, *humanitas* is defined by Thomas Elyot as "a general name to those virtues in whom seemeth to be a mutual concord and love in the nature of man." The principal virtues of which "humanity is chiefly compact" are "benevolence, beneficence, and liberality."

[3]See, for instance, Virgil K. Whitaker, *A Mirror up to Nature* (San Marino, 1965), p. 228.

[4]See Virgil K. Whitaker's discussion in *A Mirror up to Nature*, pp. 76-93, of Shakespeare's theory of imitation and its possible indebtedness to Sidney's *An Apologie for Poetrie*.

[5]The most extensive consideration of Shakespeare's control of audience awareness is Bertrand Evans' *Shakespeare's Comedies* (Oxford, 1960). Although sometimes tedious in the singleness of its concern, it is an intelligent book rich in insight.

[6]I am indebted in the following pages to the discussion by Whitaker, cited above, of Shakespearean tragedy as imitations in which the general principles or laws governing nature are revealed through fictions invented by the poet. Whitaker confines himself to a consideration of the tragedies. It seems to me that the romances are more convincing evidence than the tragedies of Whitaker's thesis.

[7]*The Life of Sidney* in *The Works of Fulke Greville*, ed. Alexander B. Grosart, 1870, 4 vols. (reprinted New York, 1966), IV, 19.

[8]*An Apologie for Poetrie* in *Elizabethan Critical Essays*, ed. with an Introduction by G. Gregory Smith (London, 1904), I, 150-207.

[9]The fishermen whom Pericles encounters after he has been shipwrecked on the coast of Pentapolis also speak in the language of emblematic symbol (II.i.32-38). The point is not lost on Pericles, and in his remarking it we are once again reminded of the kind of interpretation that the "speaking picture" of which he is a part requires:

> How from the finny subject of the sea
> These fishers tell the infirmities of men;
> And from their wat'ry empire recollect
> All that may men approve or men detect!

> (II.i.52-55)

[10]The notion that Shakespeare is working with non-representational modes of mimesis in the romances is advanced by E. M. W. Tillyard in *Shakespeare's Last Plays* (London, 1938). S. L. Bethel in *"The Winter's Tale": A Study* (London, 1946), pp. 35-44, demonstrates how Shakespeare in *The Winter's Tale* achieves a "distance" between audience and play by freeing dramatic action from specific time and place. See also Bethel's *Shakespeare and the Popular Dramatic Tradition* (London, 1944), especially the chapter entitled "Planes of Reality" in which he discusses the kind of

"double consciousness" that is created in an audience which watches a play that calls attention to its own artificiality. According to Bethel, this "double-consciousness of playworld and real world has the solid advantage of 'distancing' a play, so that the words and deeds of which it consists may be critically weighed in the course of its performance" (pp. 31-39). Norman Rabkin also discusses Shakespeare's cultivation in the romances of devices which call attention to the plays as merely illusion. "Shakespeare's game," he suggests, "is to engage us in the naïve artifice of the piece, to make us believe in its reality, and then to make us recognize the game he is playing. If everything comes out happily, we must be aware in the end that it does so because the playwright has made it do so by tricks which he has made us acknowledge as tricks even while we believe in them." *Shakespeare and the Common Understanding* (New York, 1967), p. 210.

[11]Peter de la Primaudaye, *The French Academy* (London, 1618), p. 43.

[12]Ed. G. H. Mair (Oxford, 1909). The same definition occurs in Sir Walter Ralegh: "[Divine] Providence ... is divided into Memorie, Knowledge, and Care: Memorie of the past, Knowledge of the present, and Care of the future: and wee our selues account such a man for prouident, as remembering things past and obseruing things present, can by judgement and comparing the one with the other, prouide for the future and times succeeding." *The Historie of the World* (London, 1614), p. 15. Joseph Hall in "Character of a Wise Man" writes: "His Free discourse runs back to the ages past, and recovers euents out of memory, and then preuenteth Time in flying forward to future things; and comparing one with the other, can give a verdict welneere propheticall: wherein his conjectures are better than anothers judgements," *Heaven upon Earth and Characters of Virtues and Vices*, edited by Rudolph Kirk (New Brunswick, New Jersey, 1948), p. 148. William Wrednot provides another example: "A man endued with wisdome ought to ranke his actions into three partes, ordering well his actions present, forecasting for those that are to ensue, and calling to minde those that are passed: for he that neuer thinketh of his deeds passed destroyeth his owne life, and he that foreseeth not those to come, falleth all vnawares into many dangers, and inconveniences." *Palladis Palatium, or the fourth part of Wits Commonwealth* (London, 1604), p. 138.

[13]*Laws of Ecclesiastical Polity*, ed. John Keble (London, 1888), II, 383.

[14]*An Apologie or Declaration of the Power and Providence of God in the Gouernment of the World* (London, 1635), 3rd ed., pp. 32-33.

[15]John Fox, *Time and The End of Time* (London, 1664), pp. 1, 2.

[16]Ernest Kantorowicz discusses the impact of the Averroists upon the medieval and essentially Augustinian notion of time. Under the influence of Augustine "Time, *tempus*, was the exponent of transitoriness; it signified the frailty of this present world and all things temporal, and bore the stigma of the perishable. Time, rigorously severed from Eternity, was of an inferior rank." The new conception of time, and the new conception is clearly manifest in Hakewell's Frontispiece, "asserted that there was neither Creation nor Last Day, that by corruption and generation the dispositions of the world might change but that the present world itself was permanent by the laws of nature, and that Time was infinite, a continuum of successive events rolling forth perpetually from endlessness to endlessness." One consequence is evident in the way time is conceived symbolically. It is no longer only a "symbol of Caducity, of Death"; it becomes "a symbol of endless duration, of Life"—of "the eternal continuity and immortality of the great collective called the human race, of the species of man, of the seminal powers, of the forces of Creation." *The King's Two Bodies* (Princeton, 1959), pp. 275-77.

64

[17]Ibid. pp. 277-78, 284-91.

[18]Notice, for instance, the intense awareness in Shakespeare's Sonnets of the minute but relentless encroachments of time.

[19]*Of the Interchangeable Course, or Variety of Things in the Whole World*, trans. R. A. (London, 1594), p. 5.

[20]The prevailing view in the sixteenth century concerning the extent of the influences of the heavens in the lives of men is that they were pervasive though not absolute. The basic position appears to derive from Aquinas. Sir Christopher Heydon in *A Defence of Iudicial Astrologie* (London, 1603) cities Aquinas: ". . . as *Aquinas* noteth, as man consisteth of a bodie, he is subiect to the heavenly bodies, as he is indued with vnderstanding, to the angels: but lastly as he vseth will, he is gouerned by God: the heauens therefore doe but incline, as we are induced by passion, to elect, either for loue, hatred, anger, profit, pleasure, or the like," p. 213. Ralegh's position is identical: ". . . that the Starres and other celestiall bodies incline the will by mediation of the sensitive appetites, which is al so stirred by the constitution and complexion it cannot be doubted . . . for the bodie . . . hath vndoubtedly a kind of drawing after it the affections of the minde, especially bodies strong in humour and weake in uertues; for those of choléricke complexion are subiect to anger, and the furious effects thereof; by which they suffer themselues to bee transported, where the minde hath not reason to remember, that passions ought to be her Vassals, not her Masters. And that they wholly direct the resonlesse mind I am resolued." *Historie of the World*, p. 13.

[21]These two levels of existence, distinguished as they are by two ways of seeing, appear to be identical with the levels commonly alluded to in the Renaissance as the order of nature and the order of grace. Viewed in the light of reason alone, the mutable order appears to be governed by mere change. Viewed in the light of grace (that is, in the light of Right Reason) mutability discloses beneath its surfaces of seeming an underlying reality and an ultimate purpose. See Kathleen Williams' discussion of Spenser's Mutability Cantos, *Spenser's World of Glass* (Berkeley and Los Angeles, Calif., 1966), pp. 225-34. See also A. S. P. Woodhouse, "Nature and Grace in *The Faerie Queene*," *English Literary History*, 16 (1949), 194-228.

[22]The woodcut is reprinted by Eugene Rice in *The Renaissance Idea of Wisdom* (Cambridge, Mass., 1958), following p. 128.

[23] *Collected Works*, ed. Alexander Grosart (Edinburgh, 1878), 2 vols., Vol. II.

[24]See Douglas L. Peterson, "*Romeo and Juliet* and the Art of Moral Navigation," in *Pacific Coast Studies in Shakespeare*, ed. Thelma Greenfield and Waldo F. McNeir (Eugene, Oregon, 1966), pp. 33-46. Studies of the time element in the play have not taken due consideration of the fact that Romeo's refusal to deliberate and his dedication to a course of "sudden haste" are responsible for the rush of time that seems to consume the lovers. See, for instance, Tom Driver, "Shakespearean Clock: Time and the Vision of Reality in *Romeo and Juliet* and *The Tempest*," *Shakespeare Quarterly*, 15 (1964), 364-70; and Thomas G. Tansélle, "Time in *Romeo and Juliet*," *Shakespeare Quarterly*, 15 (1964), 348-61.

[25]John Shaw's "Fortune and Nature in *As You Like It*," *Shakespeare Quarterly*, 6 (1955), 45-50, is the first attempt of which I am aware to isolate and account for the serious philosophical concerns of this deceptively simple play. He sees that Nature and Fortune are the conflicting forces represented in the action of the play.

[26]According to Ralegh, Fortune "is nothing else but a power imaginarie, to which the success of humane actions and endeavors were for their varietie ascribed; for

when a manifest cause could not be given, then was it attributed to fortune, as if there were no cause of these things, of which most men are ignorant. . . . Whom the Poets call Fortune, we know to be God," *Historie of the World*, p. 17. According to Guillaume du Vair, Fortune is born of human ignorance. Men, deeming "all to happen by Chance" have "made themselves a Goddesse, which they call Fortune, and paint her out blind-fold, turning with a wheele worldly affaires, casting al at randome, and throwing her presents and favours by Chance." *A Buckler Against Aduersitie*, trans. Thomas James (London, 1598), p. 75.

[27]Kathleen Williams has shown in the Mutability Cantos that Mutability makes the same error when arguing her supremacy in the natural order: Mutability "misinterprets her proper function, as we are tempted to misinterpret it while we are carried on the wheel of change, but she performs it none the less. For the wheel where Fortune's victims desperately cling can also be seen as Hakewill was to see it, 'observing a constancy even in turning,' and as the circle through which the creatures work their own perfection: a movement made under control. Mutability, caught in her own nature, cannot see herself so; fallen with us she shares our blindness, and like us she will not accept as true what she cannot see. 'But what we see not, who shall us perswade?' she answers Jove; and the words typify her situation and ours, unless 'grace and goodnesse' give us the vision to recognize great Nature, 'unseene of any, yet of all beheld.' " *Spenser's World of Glass*, p. 228.

[28]Throughout the play Jacques' "style" is that of a "dissonant" malcontent. The "verse" he contributes to the forester's song in II.vi. is harshly out of keeping with the spirit of gentle acceptance of life in Arden that is expressed in Amiens' opening verse. In the scene immediately following, the banished Duke conjectures that if Jacques' "compact of jars, grow musical, we shall shortly have discord in the spheres" (ll. 5, 6).

[29]Douglas L. Peterson, *The English Lyric from Wyatt to Donne* (Princeton, 1967), p. 218.

[30]See R. W. Patch's *The Goddess Fortuna in Medieval Literature* (Cambridge, Mass., 1927). The following verses from Geoffrey Whitney's *A Choice of Emblems*, ed. Henry Green (London, 1866) p. 181, describe the figure of Occasion as the Daughter of Time:

> What creature thou? *Occasion I doe showe*
> On whirling wheele declare why doste thou stande?
> *Bicause, I still am tossed too, and froe.*
> Why doest thuu houlde a rasor in thy hande?
> *That men maie know I cut on euerie side,*
> *And when I come, I armies can deuide.*
> But wherefore hast thou winges vppon thy feete?
> *To showe, how lighte I flie with little winde.*
> What meanes longe lockes before? *that suche as meete,*
> *Maye houlde at firste, when they occasion finde.*
> Thy head behinde all balde, what telles it more?
> *That none shoulde houlde, that let me slippe before.*
> Why doest thou stande within a open place?
> *That I maye warne all people not to staye,*
> *But at the firste, occasion to imbrace,*
> *And when shee comes, to meete her by the waye.*
> *Lysippus so did thinke it best to bee,*
> *Who did deuise mine image, as you see.*

(p. 181)

[31]The following stanzas from a poem by Robert Southwell on the importance of seizing occasion when it presents itself are from *The Book of Robert Southwell*, ed. Christobel M. Hood (Oxford, 1926). They contain both of the figures used by Brutus to justify acting without delay; in the lines cited and again in his "There is a tide in the affairs of men" speech:

> 1. Shunne delayes, they breede remorse
>   Take thy time while time doth serve thee;
>   Creeping snayles have weakest force,
>   Fly their fault lest thou repent thee.
>   Good is best when soonest wroughte,
>   Lingred labours come to nought.
>
> 2. Hoyse upp sale while gale doth last,
>   Tyde and winde stay no man's pleasure;
>   Seeke not tyme when tyme is paste,
>   Sober speede is wisdom's leysure
>   After-wittes are deerely boughte,
>   Lett thy *forewytt* guide thy thoughte.
>
>   . . . .
>
> 4. Crush the serpent in the head,
>   Breake ill egges ere they be hatched;
>   Kill bad chekins in the tredd,
>   Fligg they hardly can be catched.
>   In the rising stifle ill,
>   Lest it growe against thy will.

[32]A letter from Marsilio Ficino to Giovanni Rucellai provides an illuminating context in which to consider Prospero's speech. The contents of the letter are summarized by Edgar Wind in "Platonic Tyranny and the Renaissance Fortune," *Essays in Honor of Edwin Panofsky*, ed. Millard Meiss (New York, 1961), 1, 491: ". . . Ficino explained to that seasoned merchant-prince and politician how human foresight can conspire with chance, despite their obvious conflicts. *Chance and foresight*, he argued, *have their source in God, who mysteriously provides for their final agreement*. The prudent man should therefore take the divine hint, and not conceive of chance as merely capricious or of the relation of foresight to chance as one of enmity only. To oppose the whims of chance may be noble and to evade them may be wise; but *by far the best and most prudent course is to conspire with the forces of chance through skill*" (italics are mine). Prospero takes "the best and most prudent course" by conspiring "with the forces of chance through skill."

The letter provides an equally illuminating context in which to consider the feeling about Hamlet's heart and the "rashness" ("Ere I could make a prologue to my brains, / They had begun the play" [V.ii.30-31]) which leads him to the discovery that Providence and not Fortune is ordinate in chance. Even the fact that Hamlet has taken with him his father's signet, the "model" of the "Danish Seal" (l. 50), and thus can seal the "new commision" which sends its bearers to their death, is proof to Hamlet that "chance and foresight have their source in God"; for, as he says to Horatio, "Why, even in that was Heaven ordinant" (l. 48).

[33]Human Time, according to Perkins, "is three-fold, *Naturall, Ciuill, Ecclesiasti- call. Naturall* is, the obseruing of the motion of the Sun, the Moone, and the Starres, whose reuolutions make times and seasons. . . . *Ciuill* is, when times are obserued in regard of pollicie, or of the good of the commonwealth. . . . *Ecclesiasticall*, when set

times are obserued in the Church for order sake. . . . Amongst Christians, festiuall daies: as the feast of the Natiuitie, of Circumcision, of the resurrection, and ascension of Christ." *Works* (London, 1613), II, 406.

[34] Boling......
The rage be his, whilst on the earth I rain
My waters—on the earth, and not on him.
March on, and mark King Richard how he looks.

. . . .

See, see, King Richard doth himself appear,
As doth the blushing discontented sun
From out the fiery portal of the east,
When he perceives the envious clouds are bent
To dim his glory and to stain the track
Of his bright passage to the occident.
York. Yet looks he like a king! Behold, his eye,
As bright as is the eagle's, lightens forth
Controlling majesty.   (III.iii.59-70)

[35]"Redeeming Time in Henry IV," in *Redeeming Shakespeare's Words* (Berkeley and Los Angeles, 1962), pp. 52-69. Of the several studies devoted to Shakespeare's conceptions and use of time in the Sonnets and plays that have appeared in recent years, Professor Jorgenson's has been the most useful to me. Two other studies deserve special mention: Tom Driver's *The Sense of History in Greek and Shakespearean Drama* (New York, 1960); and L. C. Knight's "Time's Subjects: The Sonnets and *King Henry IV, Part II*" in *Some Shakespearean Themes* (London, 1959), Chapter 3. Other studies of time in Shakespeare include Richard J. Quinones, "Views of Time in Shakespeare," *Journal of the History of Ideas*, 26 (1965), 327-52, and Harold E. Toliver, "Shakespeare and the Abyss of Time," *Journal of English and Germanic Philology*, 64 (1965), 234-54.

[36]*In Laws of Ecclesiastical Polity*, II, 382. Augustine attacks the notion of cyclical recurrence: "Would to God that people could avoid these round-about aberrations, discovered by false and deceiving philosophers, and stick to the straight path of sound doctrine! Why, there are some people who want to twist even a famous passage in the book of Solomon, called Ecclesiastes, into a defense of these recurring cycles of universal dissolution and re-evocation of the past. . . .
"Far be it from us Christians, however, to believe that these words of Solomon refer to those cycles by which, as these philosophers suppose, the same periods of time and sequence will be repeated. . . ." *The City of God*, XX, Ch. 7, in *The Fathers of the Church*, trans. Gerald G. Walsh, S.J. and Daniel J. Honan (New York, 1954), XXVII, 276-77.

[37]Thomas Norton, "A Commendatory Epistle to Grafton" in Richard Grafton, *An Abridgement of the Chronicles of England* (1563), as quoted by William Haller in *The Elect Nation* (New York and Evanston, 1963), p. 145.

[38]*The Complete Works of Samuel Daniel*, ed. Alexander Grosart (London, 1885), III, 100.

[39]*A Collection of Emblemes* (London, 1635), p. 4.

[40]I am indebted to Ernest Schanzer's "The Structural Pattern of *The Winter's Tale*," *Review of English Literature*, 5 (1964), 72-82. Professor Schanzer is the first to notice, as far as I am aware, the series of parallels and contrasts between the two halves of the play. His view of their function differs considerably from my own.

[41]See Douglas L. Peterson, "Wisdom Consumed in Confidence: An Interpretation of Shakespeare's *Julius Caesar,*" *Shakespeare Quarterly,* 15 (Winter, 1965), 19-28.

[42]*Shakespeare's Use of Learning* (San Marino, 1953), pp. 298, 301-03.

[43]G. Wilson Knight, *The Shakespearean Tempest* (London, 3rd ed., 1953), p. 16.

[44]*Poetical Works,* ed. with Critical Notes by J. C. Smith and E. de Selincourt (London, New York, and Toronto, 1912).

[45]*A Buckler Against Aduersitie,* p. 91.

[46]"Epistle To Henry Wriothesly, Earl of Southhampton," in *Samuel Daniel, Poems and a Defence of Ryme,* ed. A. C. Sprague (Cambridge, Mass., 1830), pp. 122-23.

[47]The following verses from George Wither's *A Collection of Emblemes,* (London, 1635) p. 221, together with the illustration they accompany, serve to suggest the emblematic nature of *The Tempest's* opening scene.

> When thou art shipwrackt in Estate,
> Submit with patience, unto *Fate.*
>
> When I beheld this Picture of a *Boat,*
> (Which on the raging *Waves* doth seeme to float)
> Forc'd onward, by the current of the Tide,
> Without the helpe of *Anchor, Oare* or *Guide,*
> And, saw the *Motto* there, which doth imply,
> That shee commits her selfe to *Destinie;*
> Methinks, this *Emblem* sets out their estate,
> Who have ascribed ev'ry thing to *Fate;*
> And dreame, that howsoe're the businesse goe,
> Their *Worke,* nor hinders, neither helpes thereto.
> The leaking *Ship,* they value as the sound:
> Hee that's to hanging borne, shall ne're bee drown'd;
> And, men to happinesse ordain'd (say these)
> May set their *Ship* to float, as *Fate* shall please.
>   This *Fancie,* springing from a mis-believing
> Of God's *Decrees;* and, many men deceiving,
> With shewes of *Truth,* both causeth much offence
> Against God's *Mercies,* and his *Providence;*
> And brings to passe, that some to ruine runne,
> By their neglect of what they might have done,
> For, *Meanes* is to bee us'd, (if wee desire,
> The blessing of our safetie to acquire)
> Whose naturall effects, if God deny,
> Vpon his *Providence* wee must relye,
> Still practicing what naturall aydes may bee,
> Vntill no likely ayd untride wee see.
> And, when this *Non plus* wee are forc'd unto,
> Stand still, wee may, and wayt what God will do.
>   Hee that shall thus to *Fate,* his fortunes leave,
>   Let mee bee ruin'd, if Shee him deceive.

[48]*A Choice of Emblems,* ed. Henry Green (London, 1866), p. 137.

[49]*A Collection of Emblemes,* p. 37.

[50]"'Eterne in Mutabilitie,'" *English Literary History,* 19 (1952), 115-30; 123.

[51]H. R. Patch, in *The Goddess Fortuna in Medieval Literature*, cites numerous examples of the pilot figure in Medieval and Renaissance art and literature.

[52]*Religio Medici*, ed. Halliday Sutherland (London, 1906), pp. 19-20.

[53]*The French Academy*, p. 99. John Davies of Herford in *Mirum in Modum*, in *The Complete Poems*, ed. Alexander B. Grosart (Edinburgh, 1878), I, 11, identifies Reason as the desirable pilot:

> For Reas'n (th' effect of the *Intelligence*)
> Winde-driu'n from the Sterne that rules the Minde,
> What shall direct the faculties of *Sense*
> In their right course, but bold affections blind,
> Which headlong runnes into all foule offence,
> As they are moou'd by their corrupt Kind?
>   For eu'ry *Sensuall* man in sensuall sort,
>   Of *Sensualitie* makes but a sport.

[54]Samson also uses the figure to castigate himself:

> How could I once look up, or heave the head,
> Who like a foolish Pilot have shipwreckt
> My Vessel trusted to me from above,
> Gloriously rigg'd . . .   (ll. 197-200)

[55]Ed. Hugh Macdonald (London, 1926), p. 52.

[56]See Peterson, "*Romeo and Juliet* and the Art of Moral Navigation," in *Pacific Coast Studies in Shakespeare*, pp. 348-61.

II

Pericles: The World as
"a Lasting Storm"

PERICLES is a dramatic elaboration of the tempest emblem and its variants.[1] The world of the play represents life as "a lasting storm" of adversity into which all men are born.[2] The sudden and unexpected tempests (real and metaphorical) which beset Pericles and Marina in that world represent the mischance that puts constancy to the test.

The lasting storm introduces old and enduring questions about appearance and reality and cosmic justice. In the absence of belief the lasting adversity of the world appears to be evidence of divine indifference. Sudden and seemingly capricious mischance (Pericles' shipwreck, the untimely death of Thaisa, the loss of Marina) and evil which seems to flourish unnoticed by the heavens (incest at Antioch, jealousy and murderous intent in the Court of Tarsus) appear to confirm that view and, further, to suggest that Fortuna is the prevailing goddess in the lives of men. Thus through their long association with "the winds of chance," tempests throughout the play represent the seemingly random mischances that try man's faith in a just and merciful deity.

Pericles encounters four such trials: (1) the threat to himself and his subjects which the superior military power of Antiochus represents and which Pericles forestalls by putting "himself unto the shipman's toil, / With whom each minute threatens life or death" (I.iii. 24-25); (2) the tempest which wrecks his ship and washes him ashore in Pentapolis; (3) the tempest during which Thaisa apparently dies and Marina is born; (4) the occasion in Tarsus when Pericles is told that Marina is dead. Considered in their sequence, they disclose a symbolic progression of crises in Pericles' life. Each of the four ages of his life that are represented in the play—as a youthful and unmarried prince, as a son cut off from his noble inheritance, as a husband and new father, and as an aging father and king who faces the future without heirs—is threatened by a tempest. Each poses a peculiar threat to his "lines of life," and in each instance those lines are sustained by fortitude and by a love which works through a combination of human and natural agencies.[3]

When the play is over and we have reflected upon those four tempestuous times, we should be able to perceive that the play itself is a complex emblem. As a sequence of "speaking pictures," it has celebrated love's restorative power in a fallen world. Beset by mischance and by human depravity, Pericles never relinquishes his faith in a purposeful universe. What had seemed for a time to be the work of the blind goddess, or to be evidence of divine indifference, is finally confirmed for him (and revealed to us) to be proof that the heavens are just.

To make sure that we do not miss the moral content of his sequence of "speaking pictures," Shakespeare provides us with a guide in the person of Gower. He is Shakespeare's means of controlling audience perspective. By providing us with a partial foreknowledge, Gower focuses our attention and sets up in us certain expectations.[4] Sometimes this foreknowledge gives us an advantage over the characters in the play. We know, for instance, what the real situation at Antioch is before the action there begins, and it is not long after the action is under way that we realize that we are watching an idealistic young prince discovering in Antioch what we already know about Antioch and the world in general: there are often ugly discrepancies between things as they seem to be and as they in fact are. On other occasions we are given only general and sometimes apparently misleading hints. The opening chorus furnishes an excellent example. Gower, risen from the grave, stands before a façade adorned with skulls and announces that he has come to "glad" our ears and "please" our eyes with an ancient song that down through time has often been read as a "restorative." As the exposition proceeds we learn that the death's-heads are the grotesque relics of a love that feeds on itself—a strange beginning for a festive restorative whose "purchase is to make men glorious." Nevertheless, when the play is over we realize that Gower's return from the grave and the depravity in Antioch to which he introduces us were foreshadowings of things to come. We see, finally, that the play he has brought us has celebrated as a "restorative" a love which is the exact antithesis of the incest of Antiochus. Incest, feeding upon itself, bred death rather than successors; love, realizing the generative potentialities of natural affection, has made possible the restoration of what has been lost.

About one thing we are always kept fully informed, either through Gower or through shifts of dramatic focus. We always know within the world of the play the differences between the way things appear and the way they are. We know that Marina and Thaisa are alive when Pericles believes they are dead. We also know when characters are misled by appearances, either inadvertently, as Cleon and Dionyza are by Pericles' fleet as it sails into their harbor, or deliberately, as Pericles is misled by Simonides at the victory banquet, and, years later, by Cleon and the monument he has raised in memory of Marina.

This foreknowledge is essential to the kind of involvement the play requires of its audience. Our attention is focused upon the ways in which the characters respond to misfortune and to the discovery that they have been deceived. Knowing as we do that final reconciliation will occur, and being kept fully apprised of the discrepancies between appearances and the true state of things, we are made to notice and to appreciate those attributes of character which are identified in the play as the only means of coping in a world of beguiling and discouraging illusions.

As the opening action gets under way we watch the Prince of Tyre confidently accepting the conditions of the wager. From the moment he solves the riddle until he is shipwrecked upon the coast of Pentapolis our attention is focused on his response to his disillusioning discovery and on the way in which he meets the threat of death to which it has given rise.

Pericles had gone to Antioch seeking "the purchase of a glorious beauty, / From whence an issue I might propagate," such an "issue" as would "bring joys to subjects" (I.ii.72-74). When he arrives he finds a princess who is

> apparell'd like the spring,
> Graces her subjects, and her thoughts the king
> Of every virtue gives renown to men!
>
> (I.i.12-14)

—only to discover that she is engaged in a love whose sterility and self-destruction could not be farther removed from the bountiful fertility her springlike appearance seems to promise. His resulting disillusionment and revulsion are evident in his questioning not only of courtesy but even of the powers of heaven who have seemingly not seen, or who have chosen to ignore, the ugly depravity he has uncovered. Courtesy seems only a covering of sin (I.i.121-23). To the gods he says:

> O you powers
> That give heaven countless eyes to view men's acts.
> Why cloud they not their sights perpetually
> If this be true which makes me pale to read it?
>
> (I.i.72-75)

The princess is

> a fair viol, and your sense the strings;
> Who, finger'd to make man his lawful music,
> Would draw heaven down and all the gods to harken;

But being play'd upon before your time,
Hell only danceth at so harsh a chime.

(I.i.81-85)

The play thus begins with the discovery of a violation of the natural familial relationship from which generation and succession ordinarily proceed. Though physically more abhorrent, that violation is
analogous to Lear's rejection of Cordelia, to Cymbeline's refusal to
accept Posthumus as a son-in-law, and to Leontes' rejection of Hermione and their newborn daughter. Each of these fathers, Lear ir-
reparably, frustrates the generative process of time. Each, then, becomes an agent of disorder and the abettor of destructive time. In
Pericles the incestuous king and his daughter are exemplars of the
destructive forces of unnatural love. After their deaths those forces
will be represented by Dionyza and Cleon, and, in the later action in
Mytilene, by Boult, the Pandar, and the Bawd. Dionyza becomes another parent whose improper love for a daughter proves to be self-
destructive. Cleon's sin is an excessive love for Dionyza. Although
shocked to learn of the Queen's apparently successful conspiracy to
murder Marina, he implicates himself by keeping her ugly secret.

Until Antiochus and his daughter are destroyed by a bolt of fire
from the heavens, their depravity is the dominating force in the action. It allows Pericles only the option of retreating before it; but
even in retreat—and this is a point that has gone unnoticed by those
who have studied the play—Pericles has a vital freedom.[5] He is free
to choose the way in which he responds to his disillusioning discovery; and he is also free to choose the way in which to avoid the
overwhelming power of Antiochus that threatens to destroy him.

The manner in which Pericles exercises those freedoms establishes
him as an exemplar of constancy and the agent of a love that sustains
and renews. He refuses to succumb, as the result of his discovery in
the court of Antioch, to the utter cynicism of a Timon. He shows
that he is still able to trust by accepting the advice of Helicanus. He
elects exile as the only means of removing Tyre from the threat of
bloody invasion—of stopping "this tempest ere it come" (I.ii.98).
It is a choice born of "princely charity" and "a love for all" (I.ii.100,
93).[6] Furthermore, he elects as his destination a country whose in-

habitants are starving; and in return for the help he brings them he asks only "love, / And harbourage for ourself, our ships and men" (I.iv.99-100).

By the time Pericles sets sail from Tarsus, again under the threat of a pursuing Antiochus, and the play's opening action is completed, the fundamental opposition between generative and destructive love, in terms of which the play's entire action is conceived, has been firmly established. Pericles has met the destructive threat of Antiochus with two acts of charity and thus identified himself in the eyes of the audience with a love that sustains, renews, and replenishes.

It is also evident that the view held by the majority of critics of Pericles as a passive hero and of the play's structure as loosely episodic is simply not borne out by the opening act.[7] Even in flight Pericles has the opportunity to make choices. The sequence of action in the first act cannot, therefore, be said to be ordered by naïve chronology. It is shaped in part by the choices Pericles makes in the face of necessity; and we shall see that what is true of the opening act is equally true of the entire play. Choice will continue to shape the action, determining, within the limits of circumstance, the sequence of events.

The role of choice in *Pericles* has been all but totally ignored,[8] because we are accustomed to and prefer the way in which Shakespeare depicts choice in the tragedies. It is a comforting illusion that we have the opportunity to make choices which decisively shape the personal future or directly alter the circumstances in which we live, and that wise choices are rewarded and foolish or evil choices receive their just due. We are reassured, for instance, when we see finally in *Macbeth* that the wages of sin is death. But we are inclined to ignore, partly because they receive little attention in the play and partly because of our preference for comfortable illusions, the injustice and futility that prevail in the lives of the innocent and the good who suffer and die under the tyranny of Macbeth. We prefer also the illusion that with the aid of reason we may fathom appearances and choose the good over the seemingly good and in turn be duly rewarded. All we need do is exercise reason and, like Bassanio, choose the proper casket.

It seems to me that the representation of choice in *Pericles* is more persuasive. Focusing on the afflictions that a Macbeth or an Antiochus impose upon those who have the misfortune to come under their malevolence, the play depicts choice as essentially a matter of responding to circumstances that are, at least temporarily, unalterable and affirms those choices which are grounded in trust and love. The world of *Pericles*, with the kinds of choices it depicts, seems to me to be a good deal closer to our own contemporary world in which choices are preponderantly between ways of meeting and enduring unalterable and threatening necessity.

Choice and character are not, however, the only determinants of the structure of action in *Pericles*. As I have said, they determine, within the limits of circumstance, the sequence of events. But a pattern in that sequence is established through a technique of correspondences and inverted parallels which provides the play with a unity that has gone largely unnoticed.[9]

The technique emerges in the opening dialogue of Act II. Cleon recounts the miseries suffered by his country during recent years, finding in them proof that the heavens do not ignore the moral lapses of man. They have inflicted on the people of Tarsus poverty and all its accompanying miseries as a punishment for their pride and ingratitude during an earlier time of richness and plenty:

> This Tarsus, o'er which I have the government,
> A city on whom Plenty held full hand,
> For Riches strew'd herself even in the streets;
> Whose towers bore heads so high they kiss'd the clouds,
> And strangers ne'er beheld but wond'red at;
> Whose men and dames so jetted and adorn'd,
> Like one another's glass to trim them by.
> Their tables were stor'd full, to glad the sight,
> And not so much to feed on as delight.
> All poverty was scorn'd, and pride so great,
> The name of help grew odious to repeat.
>
> (I.iv.21-31)

The misery of Tarsus, he continues, might well serve as a moral reminder to other cities now enjoying prosperity:

> O, let those cities that of Plenty's cup
> And her prosperities so largely taste
> With their superfluous riots, hear these tears!
> The misery of Tarsus may be theirs.
>
> (I.iv.52-55)

But now the heavens seem indifferent. Although they have exacted justice, they seem disinclined to extend mercy:

> Our tongues and sorrows [do] sound deep
> Our woes into the air; our eyes [do] weep
> Till tongues fetch breath that may proclaim them louder;
> That, if heaven slumber while their creatures want,
> They may awake their [helps] to comfort them.
>
> (I.iv.13-17)

Pericles in Antioch had hinted that the gods leave evil unpunished because they do not *see* it. Perhaps they even "cloud . . . their sights perpetually." Now Cleon hints that the heavens do not *hear* because they sleep. The correspondence and its inversion are exact: Pericles wondered about the justice of the gods and their readiness to see; Cleon wonders about their mercy and their readiness to hear.

Two more inverted parallels emerge in the scene. Cleon's description of "those mothers" who "are ready now / To eat those little darlings whom they lov'd" (I.iv.43-44), echoes the opening lines of Antioch's riddle, "I am no viper, yet I feed / On mother's flesh which did me breed" (I.i.64-65); and Cleon's discovery that Pericles' fleet has not come, as he had initially feared, "like the Trojan horse" furnishes a parallel to Pericles' discovery of corruption concealed by apparent courtesy.

On one level these correspondences serve a rhetorical purpose. Cleon's allusion to mothers who are ready to eat their children serves to keep alive in the minds of the audience the fundamental conflict between destructive and renewing love that the play depicts. Fierce affliction no less than incest may threaten the natural function of generative love in the lives of men. Furthermore, as the play progresses we discover that these mothers of Tarsus, together with the incestuous Antiochus and the jealous Dionyza of Act IV, furnish

78

contrasts in the final action for the renewing and sustaining love of Pericles and Marina.

The other parallels also serve to remind the audience of the major questions about appearance and reality and of the role which the heavens play in the lives of men.[10] But they have another function as well. They are the means by which the play's initial statement about belief and trust, truth and seeming, and the role of the gods in the affairs of men is dramatically realized. Through them we discover a purpose in the gods' seeming indifference to incest. In allowing Antiochus to go unpunished, they have permitted the situation to occur in which Pericles finds himself at Antioch. They have made it necessary for him to flee and thus narrowed the range of choices that he can make at that particular point in his life. He must flee or surely die; and by choosing to sail to Tarsus, rather than to endanger his subjects, he fulfills the gods' design.

The audience sees from its vantage point that Pericles has become, through his own benevolence, the agent through which the heavens answer Cleon's prayers. It also realizes that the action it has just witnessed affirms the justness and mercy of the gods, and that they seem indifferent only in the limited perspective of men. They are neither blind to evil nor deaf to the prayers of the afflicted.

Finally, these parallels are the means by which the audience is to understand the ultimate statement made by the play: love and trust provide the only certain grounds on which to act. Actions in the play affirm and reaffirm that man, limited as his perspective is by space and time and his own sense perception, can only trust that the heavens are ultimately just and benevolent, despite appearances to the contrary. He must base his own actions on that trust.

Later actions in the play will also sorely try Pericles' readiness to trust in other men as well as in the heavens. He will have to be ready to trust in others, even after he discovers that he has been cruelly betrayed. Since reason and the senses can no more determine the motives of others than they can the purpose of the gods, the only source of constancy is an unswerving belief in the justness of the gods and the potential goodness of men.

We shall also see that the technique of drawing inverted parallels between past and present action continues to be the principal means by which the play's controlling ideas are dramatically realized. As the play moves through the years of Pericles' life, the technique becomes the means of depicting the cyclical course of cosmic time within the linear dimension of dramatic time—the means of marking off alternate periods of prosperity and adversity and of underscoring the return of time to "the same times."

Before proceeding to a consideration of the next act, one dramatic effect of the episodic structure of the opening action remains to be accounted for. The frequent interruptions of the flow of action strengthen the impression that the play we watch consists of discrete episodes loosely ordered by chronology and thus create an illusion of apparent randomness in the life of man. Life itself, the play seems to imply, is mainly episodic, a record of intentions frustrated by natural accidents and the unpredictable actions of others. The only constant is seemingly the continuing consciousness of the self in the flow of time.

We never lose the sense of the episodic and random in the life of Pericles. Nor are we expected to, for that is the sense of life that the play sustains as true about the phenomenal world. What we are expected eventually to see, however—and we will if we are alert to Gower's hints—are the deeper continuities that provide coherence to Pericles' life and structural unity to the play. We should be able to see, for instance, when Pericles and Thaisa sail off to Tyre at the end of the second act, that the completed action of Acts I and II are now two parts of a single and complete action, that the same principles of order that united the two episodes of the opening action now bring into a simple unity all of the individual episodes of the first two acts, and that Pericles' constancy has made that unity possible.

The unity of that action reveals the paradigm of "the just circle."[11] The play began with Pericles' voyage to Antioch in quest of a bride who would bear him noble heirs; in the interval between the close of the second act and the resumption of the action in the third, Pericles sets sail for Tyre with Thaisa, who has already conceived his child. This pattern of "the just circle" will eventually emerge as the pattern which informs the entire play. Beginning with Pericles' discovery, in a seemingly noble princess, of a daughter's incestuous love, the play will conclude with his discovery of a truly noble daughter's restorative love. The Wheele of Time comes full circle; and the firmness of Pericles' love and trust has made the circle "just." Like the ship riding at anchor in Hakewill's Frontispiece, Pericles has been "carried about in a Round, still moving yet never removed." With hope as his anchor he has ridden out tempests and calms and found confirmation of the gods' justice and love in the circular progression of time itself.

At the outset of Act II Gower introduces us to the next action in his entertainment and reminds us of what we ought to have seen in the action just completed. The "better prince and benign lord" of the opening action, who has endured necessity quietly as men should, will eventually "prove awful both in deed and word" (II.i.4). In the meantime we are to see how "those in troubles reign, / Losing a mite, a mountain gain" (II.i.7-8). In focusing our attention upon the general truth that will provide the ensuing action with significance, Gower has reminded us of the moral purpose of the song he has come to sing and of the exemplary nature of the dramatic entertainment he is providing. In the action to come Pericles will lose a ship with all its men and be isolated completely from his past; but he will gain a wife and beget an heir. Knowing in advance that Pericles will suffer losses for which he will somehow be doubly recompensed, we await the opening of the new action with our attention focused on the means by which losses are recovered or restored.

Pericles, cast up on a strange seacoast by the storm, has lost all of his followers and whatever visible tokens he may once have had of his royal birth—those surface signs of virtue and courtesy which when worn by Antiochus had concealed depravity. Stripped of all but his identity as "unaccomodated man," he stands on the strange shore, "a poor naked wretch" clothed only in common mortality and, in his helplessness, resigned to death. His situation here is in certain ways similar to that of the exposed infant Perdita at the close of the third act of *The Winter's Tale*. Perdita's only visible connections with her past are a chest of gold and a "bearing-cloth for a squire's child," vague signs of gentle birth. Her future, whether she lives or dies, depends in that critical interval upon the charity of the lowborn rustics who discover her. Pericles, too, is saved from death by charitable men of low birth. The only visible token of his lineage is his father's rusty suit of armor which the sea will fortuitously deliver up. Both Perdita and Pericles will visibly confirm through appropriate action the legacy of a noble birth; Perdita, by successfully meeting a trial of her innocence in the pastoral action of the fourth act; Pericles, by successfully meeting a series of tests which begin with the tempest itself and which eventually prove that he is a suitor worthy of a king's daughter.

As the new action gets under way correspondences begin to emerge between situations in the present and preceding actions. When Pericles had accepted the conditions laid down by Antiochus, and had seen the tombs of previous suitors, he had been forced to reflect upon precarious mortality, and in his innocence he had thanked the incestuous king for teaching

> My frail mortality to know itself,
> And by those fearful objects to prepare
> This body, like to them, to what I must;
> For death remembered should be like a mirror,
> Who tells us life's but breath, to trust it error.
>
> (I.i.42-46)

Now the elemental forces of nature drive that lesson home. What he had learned originally through meditation he has now experienced. His opening speech has occasionally been likened to Lear's apostrophes to the elements (*Lear*, III.ii.1-9, 14-24),[12] but is similar to them only in its consideration of the tempestuous elements as agencies of retributive justice. Whereas Lear's cries are those of a man who would have the heavens rain vengeance on "ingrateful man" and who refuses to see that he, too, deserves that retribution, Pericles' speech accepts what tempestuous time has bestowed.

Pericles has been able, like Duke Senior in *As You Like It*, to "translate the stubborness of fortune" into the sweet style of quiet resignation and to use adversity as a means of acquiring the essential knowledge of what it means to be a man. His humility is not, as one critic has assumed, feigned.[13] In suffering "what wretches feel" he accepts the common mark of *humanitas* and is able to yield with dignity to the common destiny that he shares with all men.

As the new action progresses other correspondences emerge. Pericles had sailed to Antioch by choice. The present action, which will conclude with the fulfillment of the very concerns which had taken him to Antioch, is initiated by the gods' delay in punishing Antiochus and by the tempest. At the outset of the former action the grace and beauty of the incestuous princess seemed to indicate that she was favored of the gods. Furthermore, the gods, in appearing to ignore incest, had seemed to Pericles indifferent to evil. Now, the tempest seems to him to be evidence of heavenly wrath to be obeyed (to the audience, evidence of a wrath visited upon a man who is not only innocent but who up to now has been the play's principal agent of benevolence and charity).

Another parallel emerges following Pericles' opening speech. The Prince who left Tyre to save his subjects from a "tempest" and who brought aid to the impoverished inhabitants of Tarsus, now must depend on charity. He is taken in, fed, and clothed by the poor fishermen (whose colloquy on the selfishness and greed of mankind serves to emphasize their own unselfishness in offering help to the tempest's victim);[14] and then the sea itself, which has just cut him off so cruelly from his past, yields up his father's armor. The fishermen save his life; the sea, by restoring to him a vestige of his noble patrimony, allows him the opportunity to "show the virtue I have borne in arms" (II.i.151) and thus through action to renew the lines of his father's life and confirm his own noble name.

More parallels emerge as the action moves toward Pericles' marriage to Thaisa. The idealistic young prince who discovered in Antioch that surface tokens of courtesy and nobility may be utterly misleading must now prove to others that the rust on the armor he wears is equally deceiving. Once again he will be tested by a dissembling king who threatens him with death and will discover in a princess that appearances may mislead. Again the action will be completed when truth has been sifted from seeming; on this occasion, however, it will prove to be unattractive appearances which have been misleading. Rusty armor, a father's ire and threat, and a princess's seeming indifference conceal honorable intentions, genuine grace, and love.

The action at Pentapolis consists of three trials: the tournament, the banquet, and Simonides' charge on the day after the banquet that Pericles has bewitched Thaisa. Each of the trials will provide him with the opportunity to regain a portion of his lost legacy, the dignities that are his birthright but which are mere tokens until they have been earned. The order in which he encounters them leads him from mean and obscure knighthood, to status as a gracious and skilled courtier, and finally to his titled identity as king of Tyre. Dramatic focus in each instance centers on disparities between truth and appearances.

The tournament proves simply that rustiness of armor is no indication of physical prowess and thus confirms Simonides' observation to the attendant lords during the tournament procession that

> Opinion's but a fool, that makes us scan
> The outward habit by the inward man.
>
> (II.ii.56-57)

It is also a victory for the one knight whose actions, of which entry in the tournament is only one, are inspired by the memory and obligations of a noble name. The other knights who passed in procession before Simonides and Thaisa revealed through the heraldic devices on their shields various motives for their entry into the tournament, including fame and courtly service to a lady. Pericles presented "a withered branch, that's only green at top" together with the motto, " '*In hac spe vivo*' " (II.ii.43-44). The meaning of the symbol and its accompanying moral were misread by Simonides:

> A pretty moral.
> From the dejected state wherein he is,
> He hopes by you his fortunes yet may flourish.
>
> (II.ii.45-47)

The hope in which Pericles "lives," and which leads to eventual victory, is in the living though seemingly dead branch that represents the family of whom he is the only survivor.[15]

If rusty armor is no indication of physical skill and valor, neither are they, in turn, proof of the "inward man." Pericles' inner qualities will be discovered at the banquet. Simonides' welcoming speech to his guests introduces the thematic concern on which the banquet scene focuses:

> To say you're welcome were superfluous.
> [To] place upon the volume of your deeds,
> As in a title-page, your worth in arms,
> Were more than you expect, or more than's fit,
> Since every worth in show commends itself.
>
> (II.iii.2-6)

External tokens, the robes of royalty and the elegant symbols of rank and birth, are merely tokens of earned worth. They are, at best —in moments when truth has been sifted from seeming, and nobility and worth are visibly revealed for all to see—only symbolic.[16]

The progression of the scene is toward such a moment—that moment at the close of Act II when Pericles, his actions having clarified all discrepancies between truth and seeming, stands before King Simonides as the noble prince of Tyre. From the beginning of the scene Simonides is impressed by the grace and modesty with which the stranger responds to the praise and honors offered him: "By Jove, I wonder, that is king of thoughts, / These cates resist me, he not thought upon" (II.iii.28-29). It may be, as Bertrand Evans suggests, that Simonides intuitively perceives "the hidden royalty, known to us" that "shines through the patched apparel of 'the mean knight.' "[17] In any event, he is skeptical of the strength of his admiration, and when Thaisa observes that their guest is surely "a gallant gentleman," he replies that he is "but a country gentleman" who "Has done no more than other knights have done, / Has broken a staff or so" (II.iii.33-35). Pericles has yet to prove that he possesses courtly and civil graces.

Simonides continues to misconstrue appearances by assuming that his guest's grave and even sorrowful countenance is expressive of a dissatisfaction with the evening's entertainment. The audience knows, however, from Pericles' aside on Time, "the king of men" (ll. 37-47), that it is a sign of the same humble resignation with which he had accepted his shipwreck. The humility with which he accepts prosperity rounds out his portrayal as exemplar of constancy. The constant man "gently" accepts whatever time bestows.

By the time Pericles responds to Simonides' request for more information about his "name and parentage," the scene is as obviously emblematic as the scene in which the shipwrecked Pericles contemplates common mortality. But the failure to recognize its emblematic mode has led astray even so careful a reader of the play as Bertrand Evans. He finds "the Prince's motive in posing as a 'mean knight' and an obscure 'gentleman of Tyre' . . . inexplicable."[18] If the scene is read with representational expectations, the question of Pericles' motives naturally arises. Why should he not reveal immediately that he is a king? Or, earlier, why did he not tell the fishermen of his royal birth? But if we recognize that the purpose of the scene is to illustrate the process by which an Exemplar of Constancy, who has been stripped of all but his legacy of mortality, regains his royal name, we realize that Pericles is not merely posing. When Pericles identifies himself as a "gentleman of Tyre" who has been educated in "arts" as well as "arms" (II.iii.81-82), the audience is to understand that through his victories in the tournament and his modest response to praise he has regained exactly that portion of his noble name to which he now admits.

Following his acknowledgment that he is a gentleman of Tyre, Pericles demonstrates his skill at dancing with such grace that on the following morning Simonides invites him to be Thaisa's music instructor. But such accomplishments are not sufficient to qualify him as a proper suitor for a princess. As the scene ends Pericles has yet to confirm his royalty.

The final trial, in which he confirms his right to his father's royal title and thus wins the right to marry Thaisa, is delayed by what seems initially to be crude dramatic exigency. A sudden change of

scene takes the audience back to Tyre. The dramatist seems suddenly to have remembered that the audience may be in danger of forgetting the situation that Pericles' long absence from Tyre has created.
But the interruption is thematically appropriate and, within the
structure of inverted parallels which unifies the first two actions of
the play, dramatically effective.

The opening announcement that the gods have suddenly exacted
terrible vengeance upon Antiochus and his daughter is carefully
timed to be thematically significant. In this destruction of incestuous
love one action in the play has been completed just as a new action is
about to begin with a marriage and the conceiving of an heir. Incestuous love has run its course. It has been destroyed by an act of
the heavens at just that moment in dramatic time when a benevolent
prince is about to win a wife and conceive a daughter whose own
benevolence and grace will one day prove the means of his re-
juvenation. But the parallels extend further. Incest became a
threatening and moving force in the play when Pericles as a suitor
discovered the hypocrisy of the Princess of Antioch's springlike appearance and her father's thin veneer of courtesy. The new action
will begin after Pericles has given the lie to his own shabby appearance by demonstrating that he is a king in deed and name. In that
action the love he shares with Thaisa will prove to be, in contrast to
the barrenness of incest, natural and fruitful. In spite of the severity
of its trials, it will prove constant and, ultimately, restoring and renewing.

The remainder of the scene is also carefully timed. Here, moments
before we see Pericles verify his royalty in the eyes of Simonides and,
in the dumb show immediately following, see his royal person fully
confirmed, we discover in Pericles' palace at Tyre a movement
among his lords to replace him with Helicanus. At the moment he
regains his royal inheritance in Pentapolis he is in danger of losing it
at home. The lords of Tyre interpret his long absence as evidence of
his death at virtually the moment in dramatic time when he visibly
confirms his own royalty and enters into a marriage which will provide for Tyre a successor.

The audience thus sees in yet another dimension the discrepancies between truth and appearances which in this play so deeply try constancy and trust. It recognizes also in Helicanus' constancy and in the obedience of his peers an exemplary faith in the face of challenging appearances.

The fifth scene, in which Simonides dissembles,[19] presenting a façade of disapproval in a dramatically perfunctory testing of Pericles, completes the pattern of the "just circle." The test confirms that Pericles is ready to take actions that are as noble as his thoughts and, at the same time, provides Thaisa with the opportunity to prove what Pericles demands of her:

> Then, as you are virtuous as fair,
> Resolve your angry father if my tongue
> Did e'er solicit, or my hand subscribe
> To any syllable that made love to you.

> (II.v.67-70)

The final parallels to emerge in Act II—between the dissembling fathers, Antiochus and Simonides, and the tests they impose upon Pericles, between the princesses who variously dissemble, and between the discoveries Pericles makes about appearances and reality in the courts of Antiochus and Pentapolis—are further evidence of what in the opening moments of the second act has already emerged as the play's major principle of order and progression.

The specific pattern is a way of representing generic truths about the nature of human existence in the mutable order. As such, it is consistent with what I have described earlier as the play's emblematic mode of mimesis. We have seen that the dialectical terms of process—a love that sustains, restores, and renews and a love that corrupts and destroys—are represented throughout the play by characters who are simple exemplars. Pericles and Antiochus, and Marina and the Princess of Antioch, are closer to the abstractions they represent than they are to the phenomenal world of concrete particulars. The same thing is true of the actions in which they are involved and of the sequences of action which comprise the play. The representational significance of action in *Pericles* is manifest in what it reveals about the reality behind the phenomenal world.

In temporal terms, the chronology of events in the play mirrors the cyclical pattern of mutability as that pattern is affected by human choice. Caught in the succession of events, man is, nevertheless, free to determine whether the creative and sustaining energies of love or the sterile and self-destroying forces of perverse love will complete the circle of his own life. Time in the lives of Antiochus and his daughter has proved destructive and barren. An incestuous king has destroyed "the lines of life that life repair." Pericles, through his own benevolence and trust, completes a cycle of his life by marrying and conceiving an heir. He has renewed time and may now look toward returning to Tyre, confident in the expectation that his "lines of life" will continue. We see therefore, in the parallel but contrasting lives of Antiochus and the youthful Pericles, the triumph of generative love over incest and natural calamity. We see also how, in the language of metaphor, Time has been made a Destroyer by Antiochus and a Renewer by Pericles.

The structure of inverted parallels is also a means of affirming the justice of the laws of nature. Time, sea, and tempest may destroy, but the constant man, whose actions are grounded in trust and directed by benevolence, discovers in retrospect that they also restore and provide. The sea and the tempest may destroy Pericles' ship and all of his connections with his past; but by casting him up on the shores of Pentapolis and then delivering up his father's armor, they provide him with the opportunity and means to meet and win Thaisa.

The inverted parallel is also the means of depicting what time inevitably bestows upon the constant man. Remaining constant in the flow of process, he may expect things to reverse themselves. As the wheel of time revolves, prosperity gives way to adversity, which, in turn, gives way to prosperity:

> Thus doth the euer-changing course of things
> Runne a perpetuall circle, euer turning:
> And that same day that hiest glory brings,
> Brings vs vnto the point of backe-returning.[20]

Finally, the structure of parallels is the means of indicating the pattern in chronological time of recurrent occasion. In the next major action of the play, time will repeat itself in the lives of both Pericles and Marina. What has happened to Pericles in the opening action will be repeated in some form; and what Pericles had been forced to undergo in his youth, Marina will also have to endure.[21] For instance, in the action which proceeds from Dionyza's jealousy and in which Marina is saved from death by pirates only to be sold into a brothel, the pattern of time repeating itself is unmistakable. What happened to her father also happens to Marina. Her ordeal is initiated, as was her father's, by a parent's twisted love for a daughter. Isolated from her past, she successfully proves her noble lineage in the brothel at Mytilene as her father had confirmed his royal identity in Pentapolis. Pericles won a wife and conceived a successor to his throne; Marina wins a prospective husband and the reputation which accounts for her being called in to cure the brooding, silent king who turns out to be her father. Pericles brought food to the starving inhabitants of Tarsus and restored a sick kingdom to health. Marina restores to health a city that is morally diseased and, finally, her own father.

The tempest dominates the latter half of the play. In its untimeliness—it interrupts Pericles' return to Tyre with his expectant queen and thus forestalls what promises to be a happy ending to the action —it suggests an indifferent universe and thus serves in the play the same symbolic purpose it serves in the emblematic literature. It is representative of the affliction that tries man's faith and makes him know himself. Later in the action the tempest is used metaphorically in exactly the sense that it is used in the emblems: by Gower to describe Pericles' reaction to the report of Marina's death:

> He bears
> A tempest, which his mortal vessel tears,
> And yet he rides it out. (IV.iv.29-31)

and by Marina, as she wanders along the sea's edge, reflecting on the life she has led:

> Ay me! poor maid,
> Born in a tempest when my mother died,

> This world to me is [like] a lasting storm,
> Whirring me from my friends. (IV.i.18-21)

The storm which suddenly interrupts Pericles' return to Tyre is, however, not only symbolically significant; it is also significant in the play's structure of recurrent occasion. It is like the earlier tempest which had left Pericles alone in Pentapolis inasmuch as it reminds Pericles again of mortality and of the necessity of accepting what "the powers above us" bestow. Both are also occasions of losses which threaten the lines of life. But as the correspondences between the two occasions emerge, carefully drawn differences also emerge to sustain the pattern of inverted parallels that links the latter half of the play with the first. Whereas the first tempest separated Pericles from his past by stripping him of all tokens of his ancestral inheritance, the present tempest separates him from the wife whose gentleness and beauty promise him a happy and bountiful future. Again his future depends precariously upon the elemental forces of nature and the benevolence of others. Following the first storm "the past," symbolically represented by his father's armor, was his source of hope. Now his source of hope and only connection with the future is the newborn child.

When Lychorida appears to inform him of Thaisa's death, she urges him to take comfort in the birth of the child and to be strong for the child's sake:

> Patience, good sir; do not assist the storm.
> Here's all that is left living of your queen,
> A little daughter. For the sake of it
> Be manly, and take comfort. (III.i.19-22)

Pericles wavers. His grief drives him to the edge of desperation, and for the second time in the play he questions the motives of the gods:

> O you gods!
> Why do you make us love your goodly gifts
> And snatch them straight away? We here below
> Recall not what we give, and therein may
> Use honour with you. (III.i.22-26)

Again Lychorida urges him to be patient and Pericles regains his composure, forgetting his own grief in the sympathy he feels for the child who has been so rudely welcomed to this world. He gains strength from the fact that in the child there is the promise that his lines of life will extend beyond him into the indefinite future. His acceptance of what the gods have bestowed is expressed in lines that are among the most moving in the entire play:

> Now, mild may be thy life!
> For a more blust'rous birth had never babe.
> Quiet and gentle thy conditions! for
> Thou art the rudeliest welcome to this world
> That ever was prince's child. Happy what follows!
> Thou hast as chiding a nativity
> As fire, air, water, earth, and heaven can make
> To herald thee from the womb. Even at the first
> Thy loss is more than can thy portage quit
> With all thou canst find here. Now, the good gods
> Throw their best eyes upon't!   (III.i.27-37)

More parallels emerge. Once again after a tempest Pericles is sustained by two acts of charity. The sea again restores in the very act of seeming to take away. Having demanded, according to ancient custom, the body of Thaisa, it washes her casket up at the feet of Cerimon, the one man whose skill in "secret art" and "physic" is sufficient to revive her.[22] The parallel is completed by the charitable Cerimon who restores Thaisa as the fishermen had restored Pericles. In each instance the benevolence of men and of the divinity that controls nature has sustained the lines of life that connect Pericles with past and future time.

In the later action the sea will again prove benevolent by bringing Pericles' ship to Mytilene and reunion with Marina. Humans, however, are not so reliable. The low-born fisherman proved worthy and "reverend Cerimon" testified to "the worth that learned charity aye wears" (V.iii.93-94); but the royal Cleon and Dionyza, who have professed their gratefulness to Pericles and sworn to care for Marina as they would for a child of their own, break their vow, succumbing to depraved love.

Within the general outlines of the pattern of time repeating itself, the play also continues to explore discrepancies between truth and seeming and to move toward the climactic moment in the play when love and trust are celebrated as the sustaining and redeeming forces in the universe.

When Pericles finds it necessary to leave Marina in the care of Cleon and Dionyza he has no reason to doubt them, nor does the play provide us with any reason to suspect them of being untrustworthy. Their oath seems to us as unnecessary as it does to Pericles.

> Fear not, my lord, but think
> Your Grace, that fed my country with your corn,
> For which the people's prayers still fall upon you,
> Must in your child be thought on. If neglection
> Should therein make me vile, the common body,
> By you reliev'd, would force me to my duty;
> But if to that my nature need a spur,
> The gods revenge it upon me and mine
> To the end of generation! (III.iii.17-25)

As his reply indicates, they are noble and good, and that fact makes such vows seem superfluous: "I believe you. / Your honour and your goodness teach me to't / Without your vows" (III.iii.25-27). Nor does he have any reason, years later, to doubt their story of Marina's death. When he eventually discovers that they have betrayed him, he will face his final test; and he will successfully meet it when he chooses to obey Diana rather than to seek revenge upon Cleon and Dionyza.

The theme of truth and seeming is also the center of dramatic focus in the brothel scene. When Lysimachus arrives at the brothel and encounters Marina for the first time, he assumes simply that her presence there is proof of her profession. She is judged initially on the basis of appearances just as, years earlier, her father had been judged by the courtiers and king of Pentapolis; and as her father had confirmed his royal identity through action, so she will prove her nobility and honor. Seeming and truth are also at odds in Lysimachus. He is noble by rank and birth, but his presence in the brothel, as Marina is quick to point out, suggests motives that are ignoble and mean. It is also evident from the way in which he is greeted by Boult and the Bawd that he is an old acquaintance and frequent purchaser of their wares. Whatever his protestations to Marina after he is convinced of her honor—"Had I brought hither a corrupted mind, / Thy speech had altered it" (IV.vi.111-12), and

> For me, be you thoughten
> That I came with no ill intent; for to me
> The very doors and windows savour vilely
>
> (IV.vi.115-17)

— it is clear that he has made a habit of lechery and that it is Marina who inspires him to mend his ways.[23]

Marina reforms Lysimachus by demanding that he prove his nobility in the way that she in fact verifies her maiden innocence. The debate in which Marina simultaneously confirms her honor and converts Lysimachus concerns the deceptiveness of appearances. Lysimachus' opening question makes clear that he interprets the Bawd's assurances of Marina's virginity as mere salesmanship:

Lysimachus: Now, pretty one, how long have you been at this trade?
Marina: What trade, sir?
Lysimachus: Why, I cannot name ['t] but I shall offend.
Marina: I cannot be offended with my trade. Please you to name it.
Lysimachus: How long have you been of this profession?
Marina: E'er since I can remember.
Lysimachus: Did you go to 't so young? Were you a gamester at five or at seven?
Marina: Earlier too, sir, if now I be one.

(IV.vi.72-82)

Marina's quiet insistence upon regarding her "profession" as virginal innocence effectively refutes what appearances suggest to Lysimachus, and he is brought around to acknowledging and admiring her nobility and virtue: "Thou are a piece of virtue, and I doubt not but thy training hath been noble" (IV.vi.118-19). His change of attitude commenced when in reply to his "Come, bring me to some private place, come, come" (IV.vi.97-98), she had demanded that he prove his noble birth:

> If you were born to honour, show it now;
> If put upon you, make the judgement good
> That thought you worthy of it.   (IV.vi.99-101)

Lysimachus' sudden conversion is only one more improbability in a play which is totally lacking in verisimilitude and psychological realism. But the fidelity of the scene is to another level of reality. As a "speaking picture" in an emblematic narrative its credibility rests upon the truth of the ideas embodied in its fiction. Marina verifies her noble birth by confirming her innocence and becomes an exemplar of redemptive love. She, in turn, inspires Lysimachus to prove that he is worthy of the noble legacy of which his public office is the visible sign. Purity and chastity have resolved discrepancies between truth and seeming and restored Lysimachus to the honor to which he was born.

The theme of truth and seeming receives its final statement in the moving scene in which Pericles is restored to the world of the senses and action and is finally reunited with Marina. For three months Pericles, whose obligations to the active world are implicit in the fact that he is a king, has withdrawn into himself, speaking to no one, taking sustenance, as Helicanus reports, "But to prorogue his grief" (V.i.26). The loss of Marina has left him without temporal hope. He has turned inward and withdrawn from the world of time. When he was shipwrecked in his youth, his father's armor had reminded him of the noble inheritance which ties him to the past and which he is obliged to keep alive through noble action and courtesy. When Thaisa apparently died, it was the infant Marina, his tie with the future, that gave him hope and the strength to endure. He was committed to protecting her and the legacy which she was to inherit from him in the same way he had earlier been committed to preserving what he had inherited from his father. Both were obligations which gave purpose and therefore direction to his life. But now, believing Marina has died, he has nothing to give meaning and shape to time. He has withdrawn from temporality and the world in the spirit of a

religious meditant. Years before, he had said, "We cannot but obey /
The powers above us" (III.iii.9-10). The complete passivity manifest in the silent king who drifts aimlessly on the seas, going wher-
ever wind and tide take him, is the ultimate obedience to which he
has been driven. He has surrendered himself utterly to "the powers
above us." Once again those powers prove beneficent: they carry
him to Mytilene. For a third time Pericles is the recipient of *caritas*.

Marina is brought to Pericles' ship on Lysimachus' recommendation as one who

> with her sweet harmony
> And other chosen attractions, would allure,
> And make a batt'ry through his deafen'd parts,
> Which now are midway stopped. (V.i.45-48)

Several critics have noticed the allusions to music and harmony in the
play. In addition to the general connotation of harmony and dishar-
mony those allusions evoke, they serve to reinforce certain of the
correspondences I have been discussing. For example, Pericles had
described Antiochus' daughter as a viol "untimely played."

> You are a fair viol, and your sense the strings;
> Who, finger'd to make man his lawful music,
> Would draw heaven down and all the gods to hearken.
> (I.i.81-83)

Now, Marina's "sweet harmony" will prove most timely. It will restore her father and "draw heaven down and cause the gods to heark-
en": Pericles will hear the harmony of the spheres and be visited by
Diana.

Marina's restoration of Pericles, consummated as it is by divine
illumination and extrasensory harmonies, is different in kind from
Cerimon's revival of Thaisa, to which it is linked by the play's pattern of correspondences. From Cerimon's first appearance, when he
tells a servant that his master will surely die, since "There's nothing
can be minist'red to nature / That can recover him" (III.ii.8-9), the
limits of his skill are stressed. His is a natural art. It is limited to a
knowledge of "the blest infusions / That dwells in vegetives, in

metals, stones," and to "the disturbances / That Nature works, and of her cures" (III.ii.35-38). He is, in short, a physician who has charitably dedicated himself to curing by natural means the sick and dying. He is able to revive Thaisa only because he has the skill to see what those who gave her to the sea could not, and to recommend the ministrations necessary to revive her. "They were too rough," he says, "that threw her in the sea" (III.ii.79-80). She is not dead, but "entranced" (III.ii.94). In her revival "Nature awakes" (III.ii.93).

Marina's patient is of course not entranced. His silence is willed. He has withdrawn from a world which has cruelly taken from him the people he has loved most. To "awaken" his nature Marina will have to minister to the inner man, to his soul, but first she will somehow have to awaken his senses. That will require all the art for which she is famed, but it will require something more, as well—something beyond the natural world and reason. Finally, it will require the patient's cooperation.

When Marina appears, her first effort to get Pericles to respond to song is unsuccessful. She appeals again to his sense of hearing, this time by speaking to him—"Hail, sir! my lord, lend ear" (V.i.83)— and is pushed away. She continues to speak, appealing this time to Pericles' sight by inviting him to look upon her:

> I am a maid,
> My lord, that ne'er before invited eyes,
> But have been gaz'd on like a comet.
>
> (V.i.85-87)

This appeal to sight also fails and she continues to speak to him, telling him of her own misfortunes and of her own noble ancestors who have been "rooted out by time."

> She speaks,
> My lord, that, may be, hath endur'd a grief
> Might equal yours, if both were justly weigh'd.
> Though wayward fortune did malign my state,
> My derivation was from ancestors
> Who stood equivalent with mighty kings;
> But time hath rooted out my parentage,

And to the world and awkward casualties
Bound me in servitude.   (V.i.87-95)

Her words seem to have no effect and she is about to give up, but
something prompts her to persist:

> I will desist;
> But there is something glows upon my cheek,
> And whispers in mine ear, "Go not till he speak,"
>
> (V.i.95-97)

and Pericles finally speaks. Marina has said enough to spur his memory and to perceive in her plight similarities to those he had earlier
suffered. He, too, has been a victim of wayward fortune and once
was cut off from a noble ancestry.

The cure has begun, and it has begun in the memory. It is the glim-
mer of a recognition that another person has suffered as he has suffered that prompts him to break his three-months' silence.

In the dialogue which follows, Pericles notices resemblances between Marina's sorrows and those which he had experienced in his
youth. The resemblances stir his curiosity and further stimulate his
memory.

> *Pericles:* My fortunes—parentage—good parentage—To equal mine!
> Was it not thus? What say you?
> *Marina:* I said, my lord, if you did know my parentage, You would not
> do me violence.
> *Pericles:* I do think so.   (V.i.98-101)

He next asks her to look at him, and when he looks into her face, another step has been taken. He remembers Thaisa: "You are like
something that—What country woman? / Here of these [shores]?"
(V.i.103-05). He is being drawn out of himself.

Through an act of memory he is led to consider another's sorrows, and in that extension of his consciousness his return to the
world outside himself begins. The senses of sight and hearing that
connect him to that world are awakened. As he looks into the face of
Marina her resemblance to Thaisa comes clearer, stirring his curiosity

and further stimulating his memory. Time seems to have reproduced in this girl the exact semblance of Thaisa.

> My dearest wife was like this maid, and such a one
> My daughter might have been. My queen's square brows;
> Her stature to an inch; as wand-like straight;
> As silver-voic'd; her eyes as jewel-like
> And cas'd as richly; in pace another Juno;
> Who starves the ears she feeds, and makes them hungry,
> The more she gives them speech.
>
> (V.i.108-14)

The repeated stress upon the senses of sight and hearing, throughout this and the preceding passages—even Marina's prompting from some invisible source sustains the stress in the something that "glows" upon her cheeks and "whispers" in her ear—and which concludes with Pericles' hearing the harmony of the spheres and seeing Diana, is surely no coincidence. Nor are the echoes merely coincidental in Pericles' speech comparing Marina with Thaisa or Cerimon's description of Thaisa as she begins to revive:

> behold,
> Her eyelids, cases to those heavenly jewels
> Which Pericles hath lost, begin to part
> Their fringes of bright gold. The diamonds
> Of a most praised water doth appear
> To make the world twice rich. Live, and make
> Us weep to hear your fate, fair creature,
> Rare as you seem to be. (III.ii.98-105)

Time, who is both the parent of men and their grave, seems now to be restoring for a second time what it has taken away.

The resemblance which has stirred Pericles' memory now in turn stimulates his senses. He wants to see and hear more, and his aroused curiosity leads him to ask questions that lead eventually to the discovery of who she is. But there is a climactic moment before that discovery, that moment at which Pericles wills to believe that the young woman who reminds him so strongly of Thaisa is indeed what she claims and what his own eyes and ears indicate her to be.

His pledge to believe is no mere rhetorical affirmation of her honesty. It is a pledge to trust in appearances despite past experience and the bitter knowledge that such trust makes one dangerously vulnerable. It will be this very act of trust—of choosing to believe in another's honesty, knowing that appearances may betray—that makes possible his climactic discovery of the girl's identity. Moments before, Marina had replied flatly to his query concerning her origins: "I was mortally brought forth, and am / No other than I appear" (V. i.105-06). Now when he questions her about her "history" she warns him that he will not believe her: "If I should tell my history, it would seem / Like lies disdain'd in the reporting" (V.i.119-20). Pericles replies:

> Prithee, speak.
> Falseness cannot come from thee; for thou look'st
> Modest as Justice, and thou seem'st a [palace]
> For the crown'd Truth to dwell in. *I will believe thee,*
> *And make [my] senses credit thy relation*
> *To points that seem impossible;* for thou look'st
> Like one I lov'd indeed.   (V.i.120-26)

It is the will to believe that is crucial to Pericles' recovery—the will to trust in the integrity of another human being.

The ensuing revelation strains his credulity. Marina seems at first to be an apparition "by some incensed god sent hither / To make the world to laugh at me" (V.i.144-45), and then merely a dream. But when Marina suggests " 'twere best I did give o'er," he reaffirms his vow: "I will believe you by the syllable." The confirmation of Marina's identity which follows produces in Pericles an ecstasy which finds appropriate expression in imagery of the sea:

> O Helicanus, strike me, honour'd sir;
> Give me a gash, put me to present pain,
> Lest this great sea of joys rushing upon me
> O'erbear the shores of my mortality
> And drown me with their sweetness.
>   (V.i.192-96)

Pericles, whom tempests at sea could not destroy, is rewarded for his constancy by an overwhelming sea of joy.

When he emerges from that sea of joy, he puts on fresh garments and a new life. Whereas only moments ago he had refused to see and hear, he is now able to hear and see in a dimension beyond the senses. The music he hears is a confirmation of the order and purpose in the universe and of the harmony beneath the surfaces of being and beyond the limits of unaided perception. The goddess he sees and hears after he has lapsed into sleep is Diana, goddess of chastity and the sea. Her influence in the lives of Marina and Thaisa is a necessary condition of his reunion, first with his daughter and finally with his wife and queen, and thus of the restoration of private and public time to its harmonious progression.

The scene in which Pericles and Marina are reunited is a moving celebration of the trust that in Shakespeare's view is essential if men are to live as members of the community of man—of the need to believe in the integrity of others even though one recognizes that such trust makes one vulnerable. Trust in other men is parallel to the trust or belief in a just and benevolent universe. Both transcend reason. Reason, art, or wit may sometimes enable one to penetrate dissembling appearances, as Pericles' discovery of the truth about Antiochus and his daughter indicates; but it is unable to foresee violations of trust—Dionyza's and Cleon's betrayal, for instance—or to fathom the purpose of sudden tempests, seeming change, and adversity. Reason, furthermore, may cure and accomplish much. Cerimon's "learned charity," an endowment "greater than nobleness and riches," revives Thaisa; but it is an art limited in its range to the natural world. On the other hand, it is faith that makes love renewing: Pericles' readiness to believe, first in Marina and then, despite his discovery of Cleon's and Dionyza's guilt and his desire for revenge, in Diana, makes possible his final reunion with Thaisa and her return as queen, wife, and mother to the world outside Diana's temple.

The alternative to faith and trust is the barren and isolating misanthropy of a Timon who exiles himself from humanity, cursing mankind as "fools of Fortune" and "time's flies" and finally committing suicide "to stop affliction." There is much in *Timon of Athens* in fact to suggest that its protagonist was conceived as the antithesis of the constant man, or that, having created Timon, Shakespeare proceeded to create in Pericles his opposite. Timon who, until he gives away his wealth, never experiences anything but prosperity is taken in by appearances, although the Poet, the Painter, and Apemantus have each endeavored to warn him.

Once Timon discovers the folly of his uncritical trust in appearances, he can see in man only depravity, total and irredeemable. He expresses his hatred of humanity through images that reflect his inverted view. The wall of Athens appears to him not as a protection of civilized man against the forces of barbarism, but as a wall in which to confine wolfish mankind. Even the earth and the sun's generative energy are included in his wrath.

The contrast with the generative powers of love celebrated in *Pericles* is striking. Timon's prayer to the sun is that it may use its generative power to scourge and torture man:

> O blessed breeding sun, draw from the earth
> Rotten humidity; below thy sister's orb
> Infect the air! Twinn'd brothers of one womb,
> Whose procreation, residence, and birth
> Scarce is dividant, touch them with several fortunes,
> The greater scorns the lesser; not nature,
> To whom all sores lay siege, can bear great fortune
> But by contempt of nature. (IV.iii.1-8)

Pericles found strength in the acceptance of his humanity and thus endured affliction patiently; Timon can endure only through his defiance of nature. He curses humanity:

> There's nothing level in our cursed natures
> But direct villainy. Therefore, be abhorr'd
> All feasts, societies, and throngs of men!
> His semblable, yea, himself, Timon disdains.
> Destruction fang mankind! (IV.iii.19-23)

Pericles celebrates the triumph of a constancy that is neither stoic forbearance nor, as one commentator has objected, mere passivity.

Pericles' constancy is a ready acceptance of what time bestows. It is a readiness to endure adversity when there is no alternative, or a readiness to act when the time is ripe. For time is occasion, as well as duration, and tries man with opportunities for choice which may decisively shape the course of future time. It derives its strength from the conviction that despite all appearances to the contrary the heavens are benevolent and just, punishing the guilty and rewarding the good, and from a human love, grounded in trust, that is an "ever-fixed mark / That looks on tempests and is never shaken." Its triumph in the cycles of individual lives is the renewal of "the lines of life."

The love which makes such constancy possible is the only source of reconciliation and of the generative renewal that assures the uninterrupted continuation of self and name. The alternative is the one witnessed in tragedy—in *Romeo and Juliet*, for instance, where reconciliation occurs through death and purgation and where, "as poor sacrifices to . . . ancient enmity" and horrible folly, the "lines of life" are cut.

In the later romances Shakespeare will be less overtly didactic; but he will continue to exploit the license of romance conventions to move beyond the boundaries of sense perception, and he will continue to present tales which ignore the criteria of verisimilitude and probability in order to imitate, in the Sidneian sense, ideal nature.

He will also return in the later romances to the themes he explores in *Pericles;* and his chief concern in each of those plays will continue to be the means by which man, having disrupted time, may restore it to its course of renewal. Thus each of the plays will disclose structures deriving from the dual aspects of time, as duration and occasion. Each play will also, despite shifts of focus and emphasis, be a "restorative" in which the renewing and sustaining power of a love grounded in trust is celebrated as the one and only source of gentleness and nobility.

Notes

[1] The complex problem of authorship that *Pericles* presents is beyond the concerns of this study. I am convinced that the play is Shakespeare's. The care with which the structure of the play is worked out is persuasive evidence that the replotting of Gower's narrative is the work of a single controlling intelligence; when the controlling ideas of the play and the ways in which they are dramatically explored are considered in the light of the concerns and techniques that are characteristic of *Cymbeline*, *The Winter's Tale*, and *The Tempest*, it seems incontrovertible to me that that controlling intelligence is Shakespeare's. I agree therefore with Donald Stauffer's conclusions that the play "is much more of a piece than is usually believed" and is probably "marred less by another hand than by a faulty and mismetred text," *Shakespeare's World of Images* (Bloomington, Ind., 1949, 1966), p. 345. The most elaborate, though not wholly convincing, theory in support of this view is developed by Philip Edwards in "An Approach to the Problem of *Pericles*," *Shakespeare Survey*, 5 (1952), III, 52.

[2] Acquaintance with the iconographical import of tempests has only recently led to at least a partial resolution of the interpretive problem posed by Giorgione's *La Tempesta*. The painting still presents problems; but it now seems certain that the rising storm in the background is emblematic of Fortuna and that the figures in the foreground, a soldier and a woman nursing a child, represent *Fortezza* and *Carità*. See Edgar Wind, *Giorgione's "Tempesta" with Comments on Giorgione's Poetic Allegories* (Oxford, 1969), pp. 1-4.

The fact that the painting remained so long a puzzle helps to explain the difficulties that *Pericles* has presented its readers. The painting and the play have a common theme and adopt symbolic referents from a common emblematic tradition which has only recently become known to us. Until one is familiar with that tradition, the play seems to be little more than a clumsy experiment in an outmoded form of dramatic narrative.

[3] The relationship defined by the play between Fortitude and *Caritas* perhaps provides a clue to the meaning of the broken column in Giorgione's painting. According to Wind (p. 18), the column is another emblem for Fortitude; that a broken column is used "is explained by the fact that Samson became a paragon of that virtue." But it is interesting to note that Pericles' fortitude is thrice extended to the breaking point, and that in each instance his strength is renewed by *Caritas*. Perhaps, then, the fact that the column in the painting is broken designates the physical limits of Fortitude. When Fortitude is broken, *Caritas* remains a source of inner, or spiritual, strength, offering hope of renewal.

[4] The most extensive study of Gower's role as chorus is that of Bertrand Evans in "The Poem of *Pericles*," *The Image of the Work* by B. H. Lehman and others (Berkeley and Los Angeles, 1955), and in *Shakespeare's Comedies* (London, Oxford, New York, 1960). His views of Gower's function in the play differ radically from my own. See, for instance, *Shakespeare's Comedies*, pp. 245-47. See also F. D. Hoeniger's Introduction to The New Arden *Pericles*, rev. ed. (Cambridge, Mass., 1966), p. lxxvii.

[5] Pericles' freedom, even when retreating in the face of necessity, has been generally ignored. Hoeniger's view that "Pericles is not in control of his fortunes" but only "endures them" (Introduction, The New Arden *Pericles*, lxxiii) is the prevailing view.

[6]G. Wilson Knight in *The Crown of Life,* 2nd ed. (London, 1948), pp. 41-42; and J. F. Danby, *Poets on Fortune's Hill* (London, 1952), pp. 88-89, remark Pericles' charity.

[7]The view of Pericles as a "passive hero" who endures adversity with a Job-like patience has numerous adherents. See Gerald A. Barker, "Themes and Variations in Shakespeare's *Pericles,*" *English Studies,* 44 (1936), 401-14; Donald Stauffer, *Shakespeare's World of Images;* F. D. Hoeniger, Introduction to The New Arden *Pericles;* J. M. S. Tompkins, "Why Pericles?" *Review of English Studies,* New Series, 3 (1952), 315-24.

The following quotations represent the commonly held and badly mistaken view of the play's structure. F. D. Hoeniger in "How Significant are Textual Parallels? A New Author for *Pericles,*" (*Shakespeare Quarterly,* 11 1960, 31-37), refers to the play as a "sprawling action of epic dimension" that is held together "only by the device of a chorus who acts as prologue and epilogue, and who several times supplies narrative links between scenes" (p. 36). Norman Rabkin dismisses the play as a work of "naive artifice" marred by "the pedestrian intrusions of Gower and ... a needlessly episodic plot ...," *Shakespeare and the Common Understanding* (New York, 1967), pp. 196-97. Bertrand Evans finds *Pericles* "the only play of Shakespeare's from which the entire first act could be removed without damage to the rest." *Shakespeare's Comedies,* p. 224.

[8]Equally distorting is the view of Pericles as a "wise and learned ... descendant of the wily Greek traveler" who relies on his wit and who knows when to retreat. See Thelma Greenfield, "A Re-Examination of the 'Patient' Pericles," *Shakespeare Studies,* 3 (1967), 51-61.

[9]Several critics have noticed the presence of various correspondences between the play's various actions. None, however, has examined them in any detail or considered the structural and thematic purposes to which they are put. See the Signet Classic *Pericles, Prince of Tyre,* ed. Ernest Schanzer (New York, 1965), Introduction, xxxv-xxxix, passim; the Laurel *Shakespeare,* ed. Francis Fergusson, with a Modern Commentary by R. N. B. Lewis (New York, 1966), pp. 18-31, esp. p. 21. Northrop Frye has seen something of the complex relationship of actions established through correspondences, although he has never, so far as I know, undertaken to analyze it. "The play opens with Pericles attempting to win the daughter of Antiochus, who lives in incest with her father and is consequently his wife as well. It closes with Pericles reunited to his own proper wife and daughter. These two contrasting episodes frame the whole play, and most of the intervening action is contained in two other repetitions of the same theme, which also contrast with each other. In one, Pericles wins the maiden Thaisa from her father; in the other, Marina, taken from the evil parental environment of Cleon and Dionyza to the still worse one of the pander and bawd, is approached by her lover in a brothel." *A Natural Perspective* (New York, 1965), p. 32.

[10]J. F. Danby touches in passing on the play's concern with truth and seeming: "The second part begins with the more inward loss of a wife, a loss, however, which brings the gain of a daughter. For Fortune always has a 'doutous' or double visage," *Poets on Fortune's Hill,* p. 95. See also G. W. Knight, *The Crown of Life,* pp. 47-48.

[11]The paradigm of "the just circle" appears in John Donne's "Obsequies to the Lord Harrington, brother to the Lady Lucy, Countesse of Bedford" and in "A Valediction: forbidding mourning." "Obsequies" provides, I think, an exact analogue:

O Soule, O circle, why so quickly bee
Thy ends, thy birth and death, clos'd up in thee?
Since one foot of thy compasse still was plac'd
In heav'n, the other might securely have pac'd
In the most large extent, through every path,
Which the whole world, or man the abridgement hath.

(ll. 105-10)

Throughout Pericles' wanderings, one foot of his soul's compass "still was placed in heaven." Thus, no matter how irregular those wanderings may seem, they reveal the circular pattern that constancy in the flux of time makes possible. In "A Valediction" the Beloved's "firmness"—

Thy firmness makes my circle just,
And makes me end, where I begunne—

is analogous to the "firmness" of the gods in whom Pericles trusts.

12F. E. Hoeniger correctly distinguishes between Lear's and Pericles' reaction to tempests. Lear first challenges the tempestuous elements "heroically" and then denounces them for collaborating with forces of ingratitude, whereas Pericles "expresses obedience and readiness to obey." Introduction to The New Arden *Pericles*, lxxxii-lxxxiii.

13Bertrand Evans, *Shakespeare's Comedies*, pp. 224-25.

14Jim Fahy, one of my students, has pointed out to me that *Caritas* is occasionally represented in medieval and Renaissance art as a human figure offering clothing to a naked person. For an example see Adolph Katzenellenbogen, *Allegories of the Virtues and Vices in Mediaeval Art* (New York, 1964), p. 76.

15Numerous analogues for Pericles' dry branch with its green tip as a symbol of renewal are to be found in Renaissance collections of emblems and *impresa* and in books of heraldry. See Gerhart B. Ladner, "Vegetation Symbolism and the Concept of the Renaissance," *Studies in Honor of Irwin S. Panofsky*, ed. Millard Meiss (New York, 1961), I, 303-22.

16See Thomas Elyot's discussion of "what very nobility is, and whereof it took first that denomination," *The Book Named The Governor*, ed. with an Introduction by S. E. Lehmberg (London, 1962), Everyman edition, pp. 103-06.

17*Shakespeare's Comedies*, p. 225.

18*Shakespeare's Comedies*, p. 225.

19Stauffer is right in finding thematic significance in Simonides' dissembling. Commenting on the speech in which Simonides reverses appearances and gives Thaisa to Pericles (II.v.81-84), he says: "Here in a brief four lines is the doctrine of obedience to a power assumed beneficent even when its ways appear bewildering or hostile, followed immediately by a blessing." *Shakespeare's World of Images*, p. 268.

20Samuel Daniel, *The Tragedie of Cleopatra*, ll. 554-58, in the *Complete Works of Samuel Daniel*, ed. Alexander Grosart (London, 1885), III, 52.

21Norman Rabkin notices similarities between the trials of Pericles and those of his daughter but makes nothing of them. *Shakespeare and the Common Understanding*, p. 211.

[22]Bertrand Evans finds in the "extraordinary billow" which casts Thaisa's casket up so near to Cerimon the first indication in the play that the sea is controlled by a beneficent power: "At its coming, the seas of Pericles, hitherto seemingly either uncontrolled or wickedly purposive, appear to manifest the force of a benevolence at work in mysterious ways." *Shakespeare's Comedies,* p. 232.

[23]Hardin Craig argues that "Lysimachus is not really a rake and frequenter of brothels but an observer who tests Marina's virtue." "*Pericles* and *The Painful Adventures,*" *Studies in Philology,* 45 (1948), 600-05.

III

Cymbeline: Legendary History and Arcadian Romance

IN *Cymbeline* Shakespeare returns to the general concerns of *Pericles* but with a shift of dramatic focus. The restorative pattern, which in *Pericles* takes the form of exemplars and exemplary episodes, is represented in a fiction which is intended, as J. P. Brockbank has observed, "to express certain truths about the processes that have shaped the history of Britain."[1] As the action gets under way, tragedy seems imminent. The body politic is diseased and has a fool for its head. Order and degree have been destroyed by a king who is unable to distinguish between authentic and apparent nobility. But tragedy is averted: the destructive action is miraculously transformed, and the body politic is restored to health. Virtuous action is again honored as the basis of true nobility, the ancient lines of Britain's kings are repaired, and an honorable reconciliation with Rome is won when surrender had seemed inevitable.

The demands made upon mimesis by such an action are intricate. If the play is going "to express certain truths about the processes that have shaped the history of Britain," an illusion of historicity must be established at the outset. At the same time, since the fiction of the play must demonstrate the process by which the fallen inhabitants and institutions of a real world are miraculously restored by love, mimesis must allow for the transition from representational to symbolic narrative.

The mimetic mode that Shakespeare devised to meet these requirements is unique to *Cymbeline*. For the initial destructive action he adopts the mode he had used in *Lear*; for the renewing action he returns to the emblematic mode that he had used so effectively in *Pericles*. The mode of *Lear*, while affording the means of establishing historical probability, is, nevertheless, sufficiently free to allow for the inclusion in *Cymbeline* of such improbable characters as the wicked Queen (an evil stepmother out of fairy tale lore) and the anachronistic Iachimo, and for such unlikely events as the wager and the means by which Iachimo gains entrance to Imogen's bedchamber. The mode of *Pericles*, by drawing attention to mimesis as artifice, calls attention to, and occasionally even isolates, the ideas it figures forth. Scenes, for instance, may introduce symbolic actions by serving as emblematic tableaux which isolate and announce the ideas that are central to that action; dreaming and awaking may introduce shifts in mimetic focus from one level of reality to another. Furthermore, the emblematic mode allows the greatest freedom in the visualization of abstractions and thus the fullest exploitation of the symbolic resources of dramatic illusion. Within such a mode the spiritual insight afforded by man's belief in the merciful heavens may be represented by a god descending from the heavens to speak with men, princes who have been raised in the wilderness may be exemplars of honor and courtesy, and a king's recovery of his lost heirs (together with his recognition of nobility where formerly he had been unable to recognize it) may represent the renascence of a nation.

There is nothing in the opening scene of the play to distinguish the world it introduces from the world of *Lear*. The setting is the court of an ancient British king. The concerns are public: a king's folly has bred a disorder which threatens to consume his heirs and the body politic. As the action progresses the impression that we are in the world of tragedy is strengthened. Cymbeline and Posthumus appear to be shaping a tragic future for themselves and for Britain.

But as the "tragic" action approaches its crisis, signs of the coming shift in mimetic modes begin to appear. The earliest indications of the change occur when the setting shifts from Cymbeline's court to the mountains of Wales. In a way that recalls Pericles and Marina, Belarius in his first appearance speaks metaphorically of his surroundings. For him, the cave in which he and his foster sons live, with its low door and ceiling, is an emblem of humility.

> A goodly day not to keep house with such
> Whose roof's as low as ours! [Stoop], boys; this gate
> Instructs you how t' adore the heavens and bows you
> To a morning's holy office. The gates of monarchs
> Are arch'd so high that giants may jet through
> And keep their impious turbans on without
> Good morrow to the sun. Hail, thou fair heaven!
> We house i' th' rock, yet use thee not so hardly
> As prouder livers do.
>
> (III.iii.1-9)

The hill, too, which he urges the boys to climb during the day's hunt, assumes emblematic significance. As a high place from which to look down upon the world—a "place which lessens and sets off" (III.iii.13)—it designates the circumspection that is a mark of prudence.[2] The impression that we are entering a new dramatic world is strengthened by the debate between Belarius and the boys which follows. Its subject, whether a contemplative life in the country or an active life in court is more desirable, is a familiar one in the world of pastoral. Thus it, too, calls attention to the setting as artifice.

As the pastoral action progresses it becomes increasingly clear that we have entered a new mimetic world in which universals are unabsorbed by particularity. It is the world of Arcadian romance, in which the miraculous may occur—and in which characters and actions, as well as caves and hills, may serve the purposes of emblematic narrative. Its inhabitants are pure exemplars. Belarius is Ideal Patriarch and Tutor;[3] Arviragus and Guiderius (as Belarius, himself, observes in IV.ii.169-81) are exemplars of Ideal Royalty—of Ideal Honor, Civility, and Valor. Involved, as they are, in actions which make no claim to historicity, their "reality" resides in the truths which they and their actions figure forth. The same thing is generally true of those characters who move into the emblematic world of Wales from the historical world of Cymbeline's court. Imogen becomes exemplar of a love which "alters not when it alteration finds" and Posthumus becomes the repentant sinner who through redemptive love regains his lost identity as his father's son, as husband to a princess, and as noble member of the body politic. Even Cloten, who, along with his mother, is primarily an exemplar in the opening action, acquires another symbolic dimension—as the "old" Posthumus who must die before the "new" Posthumus can be born.

Nowhere in Shakespeare is Sidney's theory of mimesis more strongly suggested. In creating an Arcadian Wales Shakespeare follows Sidney's Poet, who "disdayning to be tied to any subiection" of the sort the philosopher or the historian is obliged to endure,

> dooth growe in effect another nature, in making things either better then Nature bringeth forth, or, quite a newe, formes such as neuer were in Nature, as the *Heroes, Demigods, Cyclops, Chimeras, Furies,* and such like: so as hee goeth hand in hand with Nature, not inclosed within the narrow warrant of her guifts, but freely ranging onely within the Zodiack of his owne wit.
>
> (*Apology*, p. 156)

Wales is a "golden world" in which Shakespeare looks beyond even the laws of nature. From the moment we enter that world until the restorative action is completed and the play dissolves into pageantry,[4] the extravagant improbabilities of romance are a means of figuring forth a miraculous renewal in the time of Kymbeline of Britain's native line of kings and the no less miraculous preservation of an old agreement with classical Rome.

The failure to recognize in *Cymbeline* the inventive way in which Shakespeare met the mimetic problems inherent in the nature of his subject has obscured its meaning and led to repeated criticism of its construction and design. Dr. Johnson's charge of "unresisting imbecility" is based on grounds of verisimilitude, probability, and consistency:

> This play has many just sentiments, some natural dialogues, and some pleasing scenes, but they are obtained at the expense of much incongruity. To remark the folly of the fiction, the absurdity of the conduct, the confusion of the names and manners of different times, and the impossibility of the events in any system of life, were to waste criticism upon unresisting imbecility, upon faults too evident for detection, and too gross for aggravation.[5]

More recent criticism, while less harsh, generally agrees that the play is seriously flawed in conception and design. Granville-Barker finds it "a very lop-sided affair" and is especially troubled by the awkward way in which the stories of the marriage of Imogen and Posthumus and of Cymbeline's lost sons are joined.[6] Traversi is less harsh. For him the play is an experiment which, although flawed in its conception, nevertheless, made possible the brilliant symbolic achievements of *The Winter's Tale* and *The Tempest*. Evidence in the play of "diverse and even contradictory artistic purposes" suggests to Traversi "the work of an author feeling his way, with incomplete clarity of purpose, toward a fresh use of the dramatic conventions which lay to his hand."[7] Nosworthy, too, finds weaknesses in the play's conception and attributes them to its experimental nature: in "undertaking something hitherto unattempted," Shakespeare made some "easily detected errors," chief among which were his choice of the legend of Cymbeline for his plot and his failure to blend "tragedy and comedy in the right amounts."[8] Even G. Wilson Knight, whose general praise of *Cymbeline* is very high, finds the first two acts deficient in inspiration and imagination:

> The plot-construction and interweaving of themes and persons in *Cymbeline* are extremely interesting; so is its impressionistic subtlety. . . . We have, however, missed the imaginative density of *The Winter's Tale* . . . and not until we approach Belarius' cave do we find a comparable creative magic. We wait for it until the third act; but then the poet's genius functions with sovereign power.[9]

These critics have mistaken the transformation of the play's imitative mode and its corresponding shift in tone as evidence of inconsistencies in its conception and of flaws in dramatic unity. Only after the shift in modes is recognized as the means by which Shakespeare shifts dramatic focus from the "brazen world" of history to the ideal world of Arcadian romance is it possible to discover the ideas which order and give meaning to the action.[10]

The effect in *Cymbeline* of the shift from representational to emblematic narrative and the final transformation of illusion into ceremonial pageantry deserves the close attention of directors as well as of critics and scholars. Characters who introduce the emblematic world must establish and sustain the tone appropriate to that world. Other characters who in the opening scenes are representational—Imogen, Posthumus, and perhaps Iachimo—must become exemplars in the renewing action; and somehow their transformation must be made theatrically effective. Only then may the play in performance achieve coherence of tone and unity of effect. But the director will find a way out of these difficulties if he understands that the transformation of the play's mode of imitation is a way of representing the miraculous process by which a potentially tragic action in the life of a nation is transformed into an action worthy of national celebration. He will also find a way out of the difficulties that the final scene has always presented. Like the final scene of *The Winter's Tale* and the whole of *Pericles*, the scene should be acted as art which draws attention to the fact that it *is* art.[11] Its discoveries are gestures, as ritualistic in their celebration of love's restorative powers as the concluding ceremonial ballet of *As You Like It*.

One further mimetic aspect of the play remains to be considered before proceeding to an analysis of its destructive and renewing actions. *Cymbeline* is in some sense "historical." It represents as "true" the outlines of Geoffrey of Monmouth's account of "the Roman conquest and the tribute variously yielded and denied by the line of Cassibelane to Arviragus." It also represents the tribute settlement as "a momentous historical symbol."[12] The question therefore arises:

How are the historical truths, which are recreated and celebrated in the play, served by its fiction?

An answer to the question is to be found in Sidney's discussion of the advantages the poet enjoys over the historian. The historian is, in Sidney's view, limited to the "bare *Was*." "Manie times he must tell events whereof he can yeelde no cause; or, if hee doe, it must be poeticall" (*Apology*, pp. 168-69). The poet, on the other hand, deals with "universal considerations." He is concerned with setting things down as they should be; but if he is dealing with matters historical, with things as they actually happened, he is free to provide causes. He has, in short, the freedom to make intelligible in the light of universals what the historian is bound only to recount. *Cymbeline* is an excellent example of that freedom. Shakespeare accepts the "bare *Was*" of his historical source—the sequence of turbulent events during the reign of Kymbeline which concludes with the settlement of the tribute—and through a fiction offers an explanation of how the "bare *Was*" came to be. The fiction, too, is of course mimetic. It makes manifest the "universal considerations" in the light of which the historical particulars are interpreted. It figures forth the causes of disorder in the "tragic" action and of the resolution of disorder in the "renewing" action. The disruption of time and the violence which threatens to destroy Imogen and reduce Britain to Roman bondage originate in mistrust, malice, and perverse love. It will be trust and love, both human and divine, which eventually bring about reconciliation and the renewal of the lines of life for Sicilius Leonatus, the long-deceased father of Posthumus, as well as for the royal family of Britain.

The causal structure of the plot is conceived within the general terms of growth and decay and the dual aspects of time. *Tempus commodum* presents the play's principal characters with opportunities for decisive choice; *tempus longum* furnishes the basis for the pattern of recurrent occasion, which figures less obviously but no less importantly in this play than in *Pericles*. Twenty years before the action of the play commences Cymbeline disrupted generative time; he violates it again at the outset of the play, thus precipitating an action which parallels the result of his first error.[13] His violation is repeated by Posthumus when he succumbs to the clever Iachimo's "proof" of Imogen's infidelity.

The source of the destructive action in *Cymbeline* is not specifically identified as it is in *The Winter's Tale* and *The Tempest*. Initially, it appears to be Cymbeline's lack of trust in the proven loyalty of Belarius. Other indications point to Cymbeline's inability to discern between truth and appearances as the initial source. He is unable to fathom the Queen's deception or to distinguish the genuine nobility of Posthumus from the boorish strutting of Cloten when no one else at court has any difficulty in doing so.

Evidence in the play, in fact, strongly suggests that Cymbeline is the victim of an incurable folly and that he learns little in the course of the play. When, for instance, he is eventually made aware of the malice of his queen, he can only confess to his folly and say in his defense:

> Mine eyes
> Were not in fault, for she was beautiful;
> Mine ears, that [heard] her flattery; nor my heart,
> That thought her like her seeming. It had been vicious
> To have mistrusted her; yet— O my daughter!—
> That it was folly in me, thou mayst say,
> And prove it in thy feeling. Heaven mend all!
> (V.v.62-68)

These words ring hollow in the mouth of a king who chose to believe, in the face of compelling evidence to the contrary, that Belarius was a traitor and who refused to see nobility and worth in Posthumus when his own daughter and his entire court saw in him

> A sample to the youngest, to the more mature
> A glass that feated them, and to the graver
> A child that guided dotards.   (I.i.48-50)

It seems, then, that a weakness of mind accounts for Cymbeline's inability to trust in those who are deserving of trust and for the ease with which he falls victim to the calculated illusions devised by the Queen to further her son's interests.[14] It also explains why in the play's final scene he very nearly repeats his earlier errors by failing once again to recognize in Belarius and Posthumus a nobility that has been verified through virtuous action.

The consequences of Cymbeline's folly are both "public" and "private." His exiling of Belarius has led to the loss of his own male heirs and raises the question of royal succession. In refusing to recognize Posthumus as a worthy son-in-law, he further threatens his "lines of life." He denies Posthumus what according to "time's charter"[15] is rightfully his—his father's noble title, won in the wars against Rome and bestowed upon him by Tenantius—and he compounds that error by denying Posthumus what he has earned, for in the eyes of all (save Cymbeline, the Queen, and Cloten) Posthumus has earned his right to a noble name. Cymbeline has, furthermore, married an evil and vicious woman under whose influence he is persuaded to consider the brutish Cloten as heir to the crown and a desirable husband for Imogen. Finally, as the opening scene makes clear, he has forced men to pretend and feign. The First Gentleman introduces the subject in his opening lines:

> You do not meet a man but frowns. Our bloods
> No more obey the heavens than our courtiers
> Still seem as does the [King].　　　　　　　　(I.i.1-3)

All pretend to share Cymbeline's anger over Imogen's marriage. "All," the First Gentleman continues, "is outward sorrow" (ll. 8-9);

> 　　　　　　　　　　but not a courtier,
> Although they wear their faces to the bent
> Of the King's looks, hath a heart that is not
> Glad at the thing they scowl at.　　　　　　(I.i.12-15)

As a consequence of Cymbeline's folly, time threatens to destroy him, his heirs, and even the kingdom of Britain. His inability to fathom appearances, and hence his inability to trust in those who might offer him good counsel, have made him a slave to illusion and a fool of time. He is utterly under the influence of the Queen, whose sole motive is to advance her time-serving son. Thus the entire kingdom is in the service of folly; for Cymbeline in serving the Queen serves Cloten, and Cloten is a fool.

Such, then, is the fictional situation that Shakespeare invents to account for the public disorder during the reign of Kymbeline that he found recorded in Holinshed. Time has been violently disrupted and seems destined to run a tragic course. Imogen, the only remaining heir to Cymbeline's crown, is a prisoner of the Queen, who plots her death while Posthumus, denied his legacy, is ordered into exile. Cloten, with Cymbeline's approval, courts Imogen and seems destined to fall heir to the crown.

THE DESTRUCTIVE ACTION

When Posthumus is persuaded of Imogen's infidelity, he repeats the pattern begun by Cymbeline when he had believed the charges levelled against Belarius. He is transformed by sexual jealousy into an agent of destructive love and initiates a sequence of actions which reduce him, finally, to the level of the vicious and mindless Cloten.

His readiness to enter into the wager is itself evidence of the folly which makes him so ready to accept Iachimo's "proof" of Imogen's infidelity.[16] During his wanderings on the continent he has become infected with false notions of honor and courtly service to a lady. Once before, he has revealed how easily his passions are aroused. In France he has quarreled and come close to dueling with a courtier who challenged his claim that Imogen is the paragon of all French mistresses, and now in Italy he is similarly provoked by Iachimo's taunts. Confirming evidence of his folly is his readiness to wager the ring which Imogen has given him. When accepting it from Imogen, he had vowed never to take it off: "Remain, remain thou here/While sense can keep it on" (I.i.117-18). But under Iachimo's taunting, his passions are quickly aroused, and it is not long before he considers the ring as something that

> may be sold or given, or if there were wealth enough for the purchase,
> or merit for the gift; (I.iv.89-91)

and in spite of Philario's objections and his own initial reluctance he agrees to hazard the ring—breaking one covenant in the making of another and actually inviting Iachimo to test Imogen's constancy.

Whatever the folly of the wager itself, its outcome proves the vulnerability of Posthumus' trust. The evidence that Iachimo presents is insubstantial, and yet Posthumus accepts it with a readiness that appalls Philario. When Iachimo shows him the bracelet, Posthumus is shocked; and after considering only for an instant that Imogen may have "pluck'd it off/To send it me" (II.iv.104-05), he is ready to give the ring over to Iachimo and to assume, in a pique of adolescent cynicism, that all women are faithless and that beauty inevitably conceals corruption.[17]

> O, no, no, no! 'tis true. Here, take this too;
> It is a basilisk unto mine eye,
> Kills me to look on't. Let there be no honour
> Where there is beauty; truth, where semblance; love,
> Where there's another man. The vows of women
> Of no more bondage be to where they are made
> Than they are to their virtues, which is nothing.
> O, above measure false! (II.iv.106-13)

These lines indicate that he has already forgotten how ready he has been to wager the ring he had vowed never to take off and also (ironically) that he is being taken in by precisely what he is protesting, namely, "semblance."

Philario's responses throughout the scene underscore Posthumus' vulnerability to mere appearances.[18] When Posthumus first gives the ring to Iachimo, it is Philario who urges "patience," pointing out that Imogen may merely have lost the bracelet. He again urges patience when Posthumus accepts Iachimo's oath—"By Jupiter, I had it from her arm" (l. 121), as decisively confirming his wife's adultery:

> Sir, be patient.
> This is not strong enough to be believ'd
> Of one persuaded well of— (II.iv.130-32)

But Posthumus has been convinced. Like Othello and Leontes, he sees only what his passion allows him to see. The additional "proof"—the description of the mole "under" Imogen's breast, which Iachimo claims to have kissed—is quite unnecessary. It serves only to intensify his passion. By the time he rushes offstage he has been reduced to a raging fool, vowing in his madness to be avenged.

Posthumus is now afflicted with the same crippling inability to discern between truth and seeming that afflicts Cymbeline. The moral disintegration that follows is rapid. He rushes back onstage to deliver a soliloquy in which he completely undermines the claims he once had to a noble name. In lines that are reminiscent of Lear and Timon in their most cynical moments he concludes from Imogen's supposed infidelity the dishonesty of all women, even his mother's:

> Is there no way for men to be, but women
> Must be half-workers? We are all bastards;
> And that most venerable man which I
> Did call my father, was I know not where
> When I was stamp'd. Some coiner with his tools
> Made me a counterfeit; yet my mother seem'd
> The Dian of that time. So doth my wife
> The nonpareil of this. (II.v.1-8)

In denying his mother's honesty he denies his right to his father's noble name. As the soliloquy progresses the full significance of denying his patrimony becomes clear:

> Could I find out
> The woman's part in me! For there's no motion
> That tends to vice in man, but I affirm
> It is the woman's part: be it lying, note it,
> The woman's flattering, hers; deceiving, hers;
> Lust and rank thoughts, hers, hers; revenges, hers;
> Ambitions, covetings, change of prides, disdain,
> Nice longing, slanders, mutability,
> All faults that [may be nam'd], nay, that hell knows,
> Why, hers, in part or all; but rather, all.
> For even to vice
> They are not constant, but are changing still
> One vice but of a minute old, for one
> Not half so old as that. (II.v.19-32)

In rejecting his patrimony he denies the very notion of generative love as the means through which the lineal succession is assured.

Love is no more than lust, the means by which the legacy of sin and death are transmitted from generation to generation. The irony is unmistakable: in his madness Posthumus has renounced his patrimony and in effect proclaimed himself heir to all the depravities he has identified with woman; and by committing himself to a course of revenge he has lost all claim to the honors he had earned as a member of Cymbeline's household. His decision to defect to Rome completes the irony. His father had earned the title of "Sicilius Leonatus" in wars against the Romans—the very title which because of his mother's presumed dishonesty he now denies is legitimately his. He has renounced his private identity and dedicated himself to a course of action which will destroy his right to a noble title and rank within the body politic.

Posthumus has also unwittingly allied himself, in a moment of violent sexual jealousy, with the forces of depraved love, represented in the play by the Queen and Cloten, which threaten to destroy the royal line of Britain's kings. The alliance is underscored dramaturgically by the use of Cloten as foil.

At the outset of the play Posthumus and Cloten are as unlike as Thaisa and Dionyza, Marina and the Princess of Antioch, and Ferdinand and Caliban; but once Posthumus is sent into exile he comes increasingly to resemble Cloten. Cloten in his initial appearance (I.ii) is introduced as a gambler; in the opening scene of Act II we learn that he is a ready, if ineffectual, dueler; and in the third scene of the same act we see him react to Imogen's rejection of his crude attempts at courtship by planning a bizarre revenge to satisfy his sexual frustration. Unable to distinguish between appearances and reality, and therefore unable to comprehend why Imogen should prefer Posthumus to him, he dresses himself up in Posthumus' clothes and sets out on a course of rape and murder. Posthumus, during his wandering in Europe, exhibits similar inclinations and weaknesses; when he is overcome by jealousy and is no longer able to distinguish between truth and seeming, he, too, vows to be avenged.

Through a folly which has made him vulnerable to sexual jealousy, Posthumus has destroyed the very qualities of mind and spirit which once distinguished him from Cloten.[19] He, too, is now a vicious fool, to be distinguished from his counterpart only by his physical appearance. Eventually, even physical differences prove to be insignificant when the identities of the two fools are merged in the headless corpse discovered by Imogen.

Following Posthumus' fall, the destructive action rapidly moves toward crisis. The corrosive effects of the loss of trust threaten to consume Pisanio and Imogen. Initially, all hinges on Pisanio. Pressed on the one hand by Cloten to serve him and win a prince's esteem, and on the other by Posthumus to serve him faithfully, Pisanio holds Imogen's future and, as things eventually turn out, the future of Britain in his hands. In this critical time he emerges as exemplar of the love and trust from which the restorative action eventually emerges.

Pisanio faces two critical occasions: the first, when he receives the letter from Posthumus ordering him to kill Imogen; the second, when Imogen, discovering the contents of the letter, lapses into despair. In each instance, trust proves to be the only sure grounds for determining a course of action in a world in which the lack of trust and the inability to discern between truth and seeming have turned fair to foul and foul to fair. Because Pisanio's trust remains firm he continues to see clearly and truly and, therefore, never loses his hold on reality.

This vital epistemological role of faith (or trust) is brought out by Shakespeare's sharply drawn contrast between Pisanio's response to the charges Posthumus has levelled against Imogen and Posthumus' response to Iachimo's "proofs" of her infidelity. Posthumus' trust is immediately shaken and his passions quickly gain control of reason, corrupting his senses and destroying his ability to discriminate between appearance and reality. Pisanio, too, is deeply moved; but the firmness of his trust enables him not only to examine the contents of the letter in the clear light of reason, but to reconstruct with extraordinary accuracy what the audience knows to be the real situation:

> How? of adultery? Wherefore write you not
> What [monster's her accuser]? Leonatus!
> O master! what a strange infection

Is fall'n into thy ear! What false Italian,
As poisonous-tongu'd as handed, hath prevail'd
On thy too ready hearing? Disloyal? No!
She's punish'd for her truth, and undergoes,
More goddess-like than wife-like, such assaults
As would take in some virtue. O my master!
Thy mind to her is now as low as were
Thy fortunes. How? that I should murder her?
Upon the love and truth and vows which I
Have made to thy command? I, her? Her blood?
If it be so to do good service, never
Let me be counted serviceable. How look I
That I should seem to lack humanity
So much as this fact comes to? [*Reading.*] "Do't; the letter
That I have sent her, by her own command
Shall give thee opportunity." O damn'd paper,
Black as the ink that's on thee! Senseless bauble,
Art thou a fedary for this act, and look'st
So virgin-like without? Lo, here she comes.

Enter Imogen

I am ignorant in what I am commanded.

(III.ii.1-22)

Pisanio's trust leads him to question immediately the source of the charge. He surmises the truth and assumes, in a way of which Posthumus was utterly incapable, that the credentials of a newly-met Italian might at least be looked into before accepting his word about a woman with whom Posthumus has grown up. He realizes, too, what the preceding action has also confirmed for the audience—that Posthumus' mind "is now as low" as his fortunes once were. In short, whereas reason under the sway of passion leads Posthumus to mistake illusion for truth, reason grounded in trust leads Pisanio to reject illusion and to conjecture truth.

Trust proves again to be the only reliable basis for action when Imogen discovers that Posthumus has ordered Pisanio to murder her. Pisanio's unwavering trust in Posthumus' essential goodness proves to be the means by which he maintains his hold on truth and persuades Imogen to renew her faith, first in him and then in her husband.

Imogen's response to the letter parallels Posthumus' response to Iachimo's "proof" of her infidelity, but with one crucial difference— a difference which allows Pisanio eventually to break the pattern of mistrust and destruction that has been already thrice repeated in the "tragic" action of the play. She is shocked and deeply disillusioned, and she immediately concludes that Posthumus has been unfaithful to his marriage vows:

> Iachimo,
> Thou didst accuse him of incontinency;
> Thou then look'dst like a villain; now methinks
> Thy favour's good enough. Some jay of Italy,
> Whose mother was her painting, hath betray'd him!
>
> (III.iv.48-52)

Just as Posthumus had concluded from her supposed inconstancy that all women are irredeemably depraved, she seems about to conclude from his apparent inconstancy that all men are deceivers:

> O,
> Men's vows are women's traitors! All good seeming,
> By thy revolt, O husband, shall be thought
> Put on for villainy; not born where't grows,
> But worn a bait for ladies.   (III.iv.55-59)

However, as she continues it becomes clear that Posthumus' apparent infidelity has not destroyed her faith in the potential and actual goodness of men, but only her readiness to trust in proper-seeming men:

> True honest men, being heard like false Aeneas,
> Were in his time thought false, and Sinon's weeping
> Did scandal many a holy tear, took pity
> From most true wretchedness; so thou, Posthumus,
> Wilt lay the leaven on all proper men;
> Goodly and gallant shall be false and perjur'd
> From thy great fail.   (III.iv.60-66)

123

The difference is important. Posthumus' mistrust results in his rejection of what is real. To him, whatever seems in women to be good is only illusion—only seeming. Imogen doubts only the possibility of ever distinguishing between men who are true and honest from those who seem to be. Imogen, like Posthumus, succumbs to despair. She doubts Pisanio's honesty and asks him to do what the divine prohibition against self-slaughter makes her fearful of doing herself; but she never doubts the reality of the good or man's capacity to perform the good. Her spiritual recovery will require of her only that she regain her willingness to trust in the goodness of particular men; Posthumus' will require that he discover the essential nature of love and constancy.

In the moment of Imogen's despair mistrust runs its course. The destructive action, begun when Cymbeline mistrusted Belarius, has moved to the point where the innocent Imogen asks to be killed. But at this point Pisanio wins Imogen's confidence. By persuading her of his own honesty he removes "the leaven" which Posthumus' apparent dishonesty has cast "on all proper men" and finally convinces her of his own adamant conviction that Posthumus has not been dishonest, but, rather, a victim of "some villain" who is "singular in his art" (III.iv.124).

Here, then, is the turning point in the play, the moment in which the destructive action is circumvented and renewal commences. From the moment that Pisanio renews Imogen's faith and she decides to seek out Lucius the action moves steadily toward the restoration of trust and reconstruction of the social order which Cymbeline's folly, abetted by Posthumus', has brought to the edge of catastrophe. As that action proceeds, appearances will continue to deceive; but now they will serve the interests of renewal and reconciliation—a curious inversion of their consequences in the opening action.

THE RENEWING ACTION

Renewal begins in the wilderness. The pattern is a familiar one in Shakespeare's plays. In *As You Like It* good men, who have found no recourse to justice in a duchy governed by a tyrant, flee to the forest of Arden where they live patiently and civilly. In *The Win-*

ter's Tale rural Bohemia is a haven for Perdita where her natural nobility is nurtured by the simple but good shepherd. An island provides a similar haven for Prospero and Miranda in *The Tempest;* here, Prospero finds not only a second opportunity to govern but, finally, after years of contemplation have made him again worthy to govern, the opportunity to reform the society he had formerly failed to govern well. In *Cymbeline* Belarius, Guiderius, and Arviragus—joined briefly by Imogen and eventually by the repentant Posthumus—form the nucleus of a new and ideal community.[20] It is a patriarchy founded on the natural virtues of "humanity"—"those virtues In whom seemeth to be a mutual concord and love in the nature of man" (Elyot, *The Governor*, pp. 120-21).

Each of the scenes devoted to the depiction of the Ideal Community exploits the symbolic potentialities of Arcadian romance by presenting a "perfect picture" of "what should or should not be" (Sidney, *Apology*, p. 185). Each scene contributes, in short, to the portrayal of a "golden world" where, in contrast to the "brazen world" of Cymbeline's court, the appearances of things reveal rather than delude and where good and evil receive their due. For in that world ideas, virtues, and vices (for which the philosopher can provide only "a woordish description, which dooth neyther strike, pierce, nor possesse the sight of the soul") are visually set forth in "fayned examples" (Sidney, *Apology*, pp. 164, 169).

The first of these emblematic scenes is devoted to the knowledge of self which leads to humility and reverence—virtues without which the respect for order and degree is an impossibility. Belarius, like Duke Senior in *As You Like It*, has found the rough conditions of a life "exempt from public haunt" (*AYLI*, II.i.15) conducive to *nosce teipsum*. As the scene opens he draws a lesson in humility and reverence from the cave in which he and his foster sons live. The boys indicate by their responses that they have learned their lessons well. They know the meaning of humility and they are reverent in their respect for the heavens.

But they are less ready to accept the absolute dichotomy between rural and civic life that Belarius proceeds to develop in his next lesson:

> *Belarius:* Now for our mountain sport. Up to yond hill!
> Your legs are young; I'll tread these flats. Consider,
> When you above perceive me like a crow,
> That it is place which lessens and sets off;
> And you may then revolve what tales I have told you
> Of courts of princes, of the tricks in war;
> This service is not service, so being done,
> But being so allow'd. To apprehend thus
> Draws us a profit from all things we see;
> And often, to our comfort, shall we find
> The sharded beetle in a safer hold
> Than is the full-wing'd eagle. O, this life
> Is nobler than attending for a check,
> Richer than doing nothing for a [bribe],
> Prouder than rustling in unpaid-for silk.
> Such gains the cap of him that makes him fine,
> Yet keeps his book uncross'd. (III.iii.10-26)

However diligent Belarius has been in raising the boys he has kidnapped, instructing them in humility and reverence and training them in the noble art of the chase, he is, nevertheless, a spokesman at this point for an attitude toward the court and the active life which is contrary to the social ethic assumed in the play.[21] Nobility is obligated to sustain the social order; and the natural nobility of Arviragus and his brother expresses itself in their reluctant acceptance of what Belarius has found to be true.

> *Guiderius:* Out of your proof you speak; we,
>   poor unfledg'd,
> Have never wing'd from view o' th' nest,
>   nor know not
> What air's from home. Haply this life is best,
> If quiet life be best; sweeter to you
> That have a sharper known; well corresponding
> With your stiff age; but unto us it is
> A cell of ignorance, ... (III.iii.27-33)

When Arviragus has seconded his brother, the best Belarius can do is to appeal, on grounds that the youth of every generation seem destined to hear: "If you had only been through what I've been through."

> How you speak!
> Did you but know the city's usuries,
> And felt them knowingly; the art o' th' court,
> As hard to leave as keep: whose top to climb
> Is certain falling, or so slipp'ry that
> The fear's as bad as falling; the toil o' th' war,
> A pain that only seems to seek out danger
> I' th' name of fame and honour which dies i' th' search,
> And hath as oft a slanderous epitaph
> As record of fair act; . . . (III.iii.45-54)

It will be the boys who will eventually persuade Belarius to take up the active life he so long ago had rejected. He will fight alongside them against the Romans and by that action help to cure the British court of the very evils he has described so cynically in the lines quoted above. He will also cure himself, proving by that action that he has regained his faith in the social order.

The scene's emblematic content should now be apparent. Belarius' and the boys' views are complementary, rather than antithetical as the disillusioned old warrior argues. Taken together, they express in a primitive form the private virtues and public obligations on which community depends.

Those virtues and obligations will be delineated more fully in the action involving the family group and its encounters with Imogen and Cloten. In the scenes ensuing Imogen and Cloten are foils for the purpose of developing further the communal ideal that is represented in Belarius' patriarchal community. The development involves a good deal more than merely contrasting the way in which a needy outcast is received with benevolence and an arrogant fool is slain in self-defense. It begins with a consideration of knowledge of self as a fundamental requirement of personal and civic virtues and then proceeds to a delineation of those virtues upon which custom, order, and degree are founded.

The scene in which Imogen first encounters Belarius and his foster sons (III.vi.) is devoted to the love which, according to Thomas

Elyot, is the basis for "community" and "gentleness." Imogen's opening soliloquy indicates that from her own adversities she has come to know the meaning of *humanitas* ("I see a man's life is a tedious one") and thus to feel the need of the wretched for "foundations" (III.vi.6). Her love for Posthumus has provided her with the strength to endure; now, when she is at the point of complete exhaustion, she becomes love's recipient. She is welcomed by Belarius and the boys into their primitive communal life.

When she first encounters Belarius and his foster sons, she does not know what treatment to expect. The cave seems "some savage hold"; and when she is later discovered by the boys, her apology and appeals indicate that she anticipates anything but civil treatment. In representational drama the reassurances she receives and the readiness with which she accepts them would be too brief to be persuasive. But Shakespeare's concern here is not with things as they are but as they ought to be. He exploits the license of romance to present a "speaking picture" which "coupleth the generall notion" of community "with the particular example" of Belarius' patriarchy. The scene is "an image of that whereof the Philosopher bestoweth but a woordish description" (Sidney, *Apology*, p. 164). Elyot, the "Philosopher," writes:

> The nature and condition of man, wherein he is less than God Almighty, and excelling notwithstanding all other creatures in earth, is called humanity; which is a general name to those virtues in whom seemeth to be a mutual concord and love in the nature of man. And although there be many of the said virtues, yet be there three principal by whom humanity is chiefly compact: benevolence, beneficence, and Liberality, which maketh up the said principal virtue called benignity or gentleness. (*The Governor*, pp. 120-21)

Gentleness, Elyot continues, originates in benevolence ("charity," "love," or "amity") and expresses itself in a readiness to give unselfishly of one's efforts ("beneficence") or of one's goods ("liberality"). These are precisely the virtues figured forth in the scene. The readiness with which Imogen is taken in and given food and shelter is an example of "beneficence" and "liberality." Her acceptance as a "brother" by the boys is an example of "gentleness." The family group of which she has become a member is a community which is bound together by "the mutual concord and love" which is natural to man.

As night falls the scene concludes with lines that are symbolic and ceremonial. Belarius as patriarch directs all according to decorum:

> *Belarius:* Boys, we'll go dress our hunt. Fair youth,
>   come in.
> Discourse is heavy, fasting; when we have supp'd,
> We'll mannerly demand thee of thy story,
> So far as thou wilt speak it.
> *Guiderius:*   Pray, draw near.
> *Arviragus:* The night to th' owl and morn to th' lark
>   less welcome.
> *Imogen:* Thanks, sir.
> *Arviragus:* I pray, draw near.   (III.vi.90-96)

The *natural* and the *civil* are united in the little group as night draws down and its members share in the warmth and glow of "mutual concord and love."

The notion of community introduced in III.vi. is again taken up in the opening scene of the fourth act. The scene is devoted to Cloten, who confuses surface appearances with true nobility and whose depravity makes him a threat to the values represented at this point in the play by the cave community. From the beginning of the play he is committed by his folly to the peripheral, the transient, and the irrational. Now, as he enters the emblematic world of Wales, the metaphysical implications of his folly become explicit: as Fool,[22] he is Sapientia's foil, Time's Fool, and exemplar of all that is contrary to benevolence and the communal virtues.

Cloten's soliloquy is a parody of *nosce teipsum*. The Fool, failing to know himself, cannot know the meaning of "humanity"; he remains isolated in his own pride and blind to all but surfaces. Again Elyot provides an illuminating discussion of the ideas which are the subject of the scene:

a man knowing himself shall know that which is his own and pertaineth to himself. But what is more his own than his soul? Or what thing more appertaineth to him than his body? His soul is undoubtedly and freely his own. And none other person may by any mean possess it or claim it. His body so pertaineth unto him that none other without his consent may vindicate therein any property. Of what valour or price his soul is, the similitude whereunto it was made, the immortality and life everlasting, and the powers and of Qualities thereof, abundantly do declare. And of that same matter and substance that his soul is of, be all other souls that now are, and have been, and ever shall be, without singularity or pre-eminence of nature. In semblable estate is his body, and of no better clay (as I might frankly say) is a gentleman made than a carter, and of liberty of will as much is given of God to the poor herdsman as to the great and mighty emperor. Then in knowing the condition of his soul and body he knoweth himself, and consequently in the same thing he knoweth every other man.

If thou be a governor, or hast over other sovereignty, know thyself, that is to say, know that thou art verily a man compact of soul and body, and in that all other men be equal unto thee. . . . The dignity or authority wherein thou differest from other is (as it were) but a weighty or heavy cloak, freshly glittering in the eyes of them that be purblind, where unto thee it is painful, if thou wear him in his right fashion, and as it shall best become thee. And from thee it may be shortly taken of him that did put it on thee, if thou use it negligently, or that thou wear it not comely, and as it appertaineth. Therefore whiles thou wearest it, know Thyself, know that the name of a sovereign or ruler without actual governance is but a shadow, that governance standeth not by words only, but principally by act and example; that by example of governors men do rise or fall in virtue or vice. (*The Governor*, p. 165)

The figure of the fool, Cloten, studying his own image and soliloquizing on the nature of man, is itself a parody of the emblematic representation of Sapientia gazing in her mirror. His soliloquy is a study of self leading to wrath, pride, and stupidity reconfirmed. Elyot stresses that man "in knowing the condition of his soul and body . . . knoweth himself, and consequently in the same thing he knoweth every other man." Cloten knows only appearances and therefore cannot understand why Imogen prefers Posthumus. He sees only surface similarities between himself and Posthumus and takes them to be essential:

> the lines of my body are as well drawn as his; no less young, more strong, not beneath him in fortunes, beyond him in the advantage of the time, above him in birth, alike conversant in general services, and more remarkable in single oppositions; yet this imperceiverant thing loves him in my despite. What mortality is!
>
> (IV.i.9-16)

Failing to know himself, Cloten cannot know Posthumus, or any other human. Nor can he see that worth alone merits titles and rewards. To him success is merely a matter of chance and fortune.

The next scene, which returns to the communal group, is devoted to precisely those virtues which are contingent upon self-knowledge and which Cloten cannot comprehend. When the boys and Belarius set off for the hunt, the intimacy of the parting is again expressive of the "mutual concord and love" that is discoverable only through *nosce teipsum*. After Arviragus urges Imogen to remain in the cave —"Brother, stay here. Are we not brothers?" (IV.ii.2)—Imogen answers affirmatively by extending the concept of brotherhood to all men on the ground of their common mortality, and using Elyot's distinction between "common clay" and the "cloak of dignity."

> So man and man should be;
> But clay and clay differs in dignity,
> Whose dust is both alike. (IV.ii.4-6)

She also echoes Elyot when responding to Guiderius' offer to stay with her. She urges him to observe decorum: "Stick to your journal course. The breach of custom/Is breach of all" (IV.ii.10-11). The stability of the social order within the community of which she is now a member would not be served by a "breach of custom." The daily hunt is such a custom and it is Guiderius' duty to observe it.

The theme of *nosce teipsum* continues to echo in the language of the scene. When Cloten encounters Guiderius he again mistakes appearance for reality, assuming that Guiderius' rustic attire is evidence of baseness. "What slave art thou?" (IV.ii.72), he asks, and when Guiderius replies in a way he takes as impertinent, he accuses him of being a robber and a villain and demands that he surrender. Guiderius' response is made in the very terms that Cloten had used earlier to prove to himself that he was at least Posthumus' equal:

> To who? To thee? What art thou? Have not I
> An arm as big as thine? a heart as big?   (IV.ii.76-77)

Cloten next appeals unsuccessfully to his clothes as tokens of his nobility and, finally, with no more success, to the fact that he is a queen's son. Cloten's foolishness in confusing tokens of nobility for inner worth, his appeal to his mother's royalty, and, finally, his miserable defeat complete the portrayal of a "purblind" fool whose utter ignorance of self, and therefore of all other men and order and degree, identifies him as the antithesis of *sapientia*.[23]

Cloten's death and the double funeral complete the portrayal of Belarius' community. Cloten has threatened the life of one of its members and been killed. Nevertheless, even in his funeral the community he has threatened respects custom. As Belarius reminds the boys, who in their grief over the apparent death of Imogen have ignored Cloten's headless corpse, their slain enemy deserves funeral rites that befit his social rank:

> He was a queen's son, boys;
> And though he came our enemy, remember
> He was paid for that. Though mean and mighty, rotting
> Together, have one dust, yet reverence,
> That angel of the world, doth make distinction
> Of place 'tween high and low. Our foe was princely;
> And though you took his life, as being our foe,
> Yet bury him as a prince.   (IV.ii.244-51)

The funeral ceremony concludes one phase of the "pastoral" action. When Imogen awakens to discover the headless corpse of Cloten, she is again in the world of deceiving appearances. The transition from "golden" to "brazen" world makes brilliant use of the resources of emblematic mimesis. Imogen has a dual role—as daughter of Cymbeline and estranged wife of Posthumus, and as Fidele.

Imogen, herself, directs our attention to the symbolic significance of Fidele's awakening:

> Yes, sir, to Milford-Haven; which is the way?—
> I thank you.—By yond bush?—Pray, how far thither?
> 'Ods pittikins! can it be six mile yet?
> I have gone all night. Faith, I'll lie down and sleep.
> But, soft! no bedfellow!—O gods and goddesses!
> *These flowers are like the pleasures of the world;*
> *This bloody man, the care on't.* (IV.ii.291-97)

For a moment the stage has become a tableau in which Faith awakens from a death-seeming sleep to reflect upon the transient pleasures and mortal cares of the world. The tableau figures forth the "fore-conceit" which will be depicted in the final phase of the renewing action; for it is the awakening of faith—first in Imogen, then in Belarius, and finally in Posthumus—which leads ultimately to the recovery of lost heirs, to the renewal of Britain's ties with Rome, and to the restoration of order and degree in the body politic.

The tableau lasts only for a moment, and then Fidele again becomes Imogen, whose "awakening" marks her return to the "historical" world of deception and depravity. In returning to that world she remembers the cave community only as "a bolt of nothing, shot at nothing" (IV.ii.300). The irony here is intricate. We know that Imogen has not been dreaming—that she has indeed been "a cave-keeper/And cook to honest creatures" (IV.ii.298-99). We also know, as spectators who are aware that we are watching a play, that what she remembers and dismisses as merely an empty illusion "which the brain makes of fumes" is in truth a dramatic illusion created to represent the ideal virtues of humanity. The irony deepens as Imogen, after commenting on the frailty of man's eyes and judgment, proceeds to mistake as real what we know to be illusory:

> Our very eyes
> Are sometimes like our judgements, blind. Good faith,
> I tremble still with fear; but if there be
> Yet left in heaven as small a drop of pity

As a wren's eye, fear'd gods, a part of it!
The dream's here still, even when I wake. It is
Without me, as within me; not imagin'd, felt.
A headless man! The garments of Posthumus!
I know the shape of 's leg; this is his hand,
His foot Mercurial, his Martial thigh,
The brawns of Hercules; but his Jovial face—
Murder in heaven?—How!—'Tis gone.

(IV.ii.301-12)

Her mistaken identification of the corpse is a reminder to us that the virtuous and faithful, as well as fools like Cloten, can be misled by appearances. She repeats the very error Cloten had made when he compared himself with Posthumus and found no distinguishing physical differences.

The irony continues. Imogen's next conclusion indicates that her eyes are no blinder to the truth than her judgment; for the evidence from which she concludes that Pisanio, in the employ of Cloten, has murdered Posthumus and tried to murder her is utterly unsubstantial:

Pisanio?

'Tis he and Cloten. Malice and lucre in them
Have laid this woe here. O, 'tis pregnant, pregnant!
The drug he gave me, which he said was precious
And cordial to me, *have I not found it
Murd'rous to the senses?* That confirms it home.
This is Pisanio's deed, and Cloten's.　　　(IV.ii.323-29)

The final irony is in the fact that her errors in seeing and reasoning have led to the restoration of her faith in Posthumus. Even misleading appearances and errors in judgment may have fortunate consequences! The play at this point is moving toward the conclusion affirmed in each of the romances: the one source of constancy in a world of deceiving appearances is a love grounded in faith.

Shakespeare continues to exploit the resources of emblematic narrative in the final episode of IV.ii. When Lucius, his Captains, and the Soothsayer discover Imogen lying with her head on the bloody corpse of Cloten, the stage again becomes a tableau. Again a character in the tableau directs our attention to the symbolic significance of the action in which he is a participant. When the figure who appears to Lucius to be either dead or asleep has been aroused and given her name, Lucius comments on the appropriateness of her name. To him, she seems to be Faith personified:

> Thou dost approve thyself the very same;
> Thy name well fits thy faith; thy faith thy name.
>
> (IV.ii.380-81)

The emblematic prefiguration is clear: once again Faith has arisen from a deathlike sleep to face the adversity that is the common lot of fallen man. Imogen's own faith in Posthumus has been fully restored; and we shall presently see similar restorations of faith in Belarius and Posthumus.

Imogen's return to "the brazen world" also announces the public phase of the renewing action. In the historical world of Cymbeline and Augustus Caesar the conflict between Britain and Rome has come to a head, with all signs seeming to favor Rome. Lucius awaits a powerful army led by the "bold" Iachimo, and the Soothsayer finds in his vision an omen that seems favorable to the Romans. On the other hand, adversity closes in upon Cymbeline. The Queen, upset by Cloten's disappearance, is afflicted with "a madness, of which her life's in danger" (IV.iii.3). Cymbeline, his succession threatened, can only await the advance of the Roman legions. Pisanio, the one character whose faith and loyalty have not once wavered, now finds himself helpless. "Perplex'd in all," he can only trust in time and the benevolent heavens (IV.iii.41-46).

The final outcome will prove that Pisanio's trust is well founded. But it will not be merely time that finally reveals the truth, nor fortune that brings the ship of state into a safe harbor; and if the heavens do "work" in bringing order out of confusion, it is through human agencies—through Belarius, Arviragus, Guiderius, and Posthumus. Faced with occasions provided by time, they make the appropriate choices, basing them upon love and trust.

With the landing of the Romans, time presents Belarius with the opportunity to regain what he has lost. It is a recurring occasion. Twenty years earlier he had fought the Romans and for his efforts had been accused of treason and exiled. His immediate inclination on this new occasion is to retire, and when Guiderius objects, he reminds him of the torture and death they face for having killed Cloten. When the boys continue to argue with him, he is driven to what, in terms of the play's central thematic concern, is the crucial point at issue:

> the King
> Hath not deserv'd my service nor your loves,
> Who find in my exile the want of breeding,
> The certainty of this hard life; aye hopeless
> To have the courtesy your cradle promis'd,
> But to be still hot Summer's tanlings and
> The shrinking slaves of Winter.   (IV.iv.24-30)

The choice Belarius would make is based upon "desert" and certainty. His first argument is an expression of the logic which led him to repay Cymbeline for failing to trust him by kidnapping his sons. He has given Cymbeline what he deserves by repaying him in kind; and since Cymbeline has done nothing since to deserve Belarius' support, he finds no reason now to volunteer his service. This is the logic of natural justice. In the absence of love evil can only be avenged and service given only to those who merit it. Belarius' second argument is based upon his disillusion with the world of the court. He prefers the assurance of time's hard certainties, the revolutions of the seasons, to unreliable "courtesy."

But once again love proves renewing. The boys hear only the promptings of their noble blood; and when he realizes that they intend to engage the Romans with or without him, Belarius the Patriarch becomes a follower and agrees to go with them into their "country wars."

> No reason I, since of your lives you set
> So slight a valuation, should reserve
> My crack'd one to more care. Have with you, boys!
> If in your country wars you chance to die,

That is my bed too, lads, and there I'll lie.
Lead, lead! [*Aside.*] The time seems long; their
    blood thinks scorn
Till it fly out and show them princes born.

(IV.iv.48-54)

His love for the princes he has raised and his admiration for the patri-
otic and noble virtues he sees in them have awakened his faith in
"courtesy" and led him to resume, without concern for "desert," his
former role in the public world. He has made a choice which will
regain him the love, titles, and honors that once were his.

Posthumus eventually recovers what he has lost through a process
that is similar to the restoration of Belarius. But the conditions he
must satisfy are far more demanding. Belarius has only to recover his
faith in the integrity of the court. He has never denied man's capacity for honorable action, nor has he ever denied the notions of order
and degree. He has sought satisfaction through revenge, but not
through murder. Posthumus' mistrust, on the other hand, has been
total. He has denied the "mutual concord and love" of humanity itself. Before his return to the civil world he must return to the world
of man. Through *nosce teipsum* he must discover *humanitas*.

His return commences in V.i., when he confronts what he takes
to be the visible evidence of his own guilt. As he begins to reflect
upon the bloody "proof," we recognize that he has been given another opportunity to consider Imogen's "transgression," and on this
occasion in the light of his own. Iachimo's "proof" had provoked in
him a sexual jealousy so violent that he had charged all wives with
dishonesty and denounced all women as the vessels through which
original sin is transmitted from generation to generation. Now, on
this new occasion, the remorse he feels for his own guilt clears his
eyes. Discovering in his own guilt the legacy of sin to which all men
are heirs, he begins to "see feelingly" and to understand why justice
needs the tempering of mercy:

Yea, bloody cloth, I'll keep thee, for I wish'd
Thou shouldst be color'd thus. You married ones,
If each of you should take this course, how many

> Must murder wives much better than themselves
> For wrying but a little! (V.i.1-5)

By accepting the burden of his own guilt he affirms his humanity and begins to reclaim his nobility. As his former condemnation of all wives had led to the denial of his own legitimacy and, hence, of his right to his father's name, his forgiving of all wives, here, marks the beginning of his movement toward regaining his right to that name.

As Posthumus' soliloquy progresses, the question of justice (raised implicitly in his reflection on the folly of his seeking justice through revenge) emerges as the dominant concern. He regrets that Pisanio had not refused, in the name of justice, to carry out the command to kill Imogen, and then he briefly questions the justice of the gods:

> if you
> Should have ta'en vengeance on my faults, I never
> Had liv'd to put on this; so had you sav'd
> The noble Imogen to repent, and struck
> Me, wretch, more worth your vengeance. (V.i.7-11)

The acknowledgment of guilt in this protest is evidence of his new awareness. It is an awareness born of the knowledge of self: he shares the common guilt of "humanity" and in the strict terms of retributive justice is guilty of crimes, even before the crime of killing Imogen, that demand his death.

Posthumus, convinced of his own guilt, must now resolve the question he has raised—and in a way that is important to the next step he must undertake to reclaim his patrimony. Addressing the powers whose justice he has just questioned, he continues his meditation:

> But, alack,
> You snatch some hence for little faults; that's love,
> To have them fall no more: you some permit
> To second ills with ills, each elder worse,
> And make them dread it, to the doers' thrift.
> But Imogen is your own; do your best wills,
> And make me blest to obey! (V.i.11-17)

Seeing himself as among those whom the gods permit "to second ills with ills," each succeeding ("elder") ill worse than its successor, so as to allow the ill-doer to grow increasingly horrified by what he has done, he resolves to interrupt the sequence now, rather than to continue it by fighting against Britain. He stands ready to obey the will of the gods and to satisfy what their law demands. His most recent evil, the killing of Imogen, has accomplished its purpose, "the doers' thrift." The law and his own "thrift" demand his death, and he will seek it as a Briton fighting the Romans:

> I am brought hither
> Among th' Italian gentry, and to fight
> Against my lady's kingdom. 'Tis enough
> That, Britain, I have kill'd thy mistress; peace!
> I'll give no wound to thee. Therefore, good heavens,
> Hear patiently my purpose: I'll disrobe me
> Of these Italian weeds and suit myself
> As does a Briton peasant; so I'll fight
> Against the part I come with; so I'll die
> For thee, O Imogen, even for whom my life
> Is every breath a death; and thus, unknown,
> Pitied nor hated, to the face of peril
> Myself I'll dedicate.   (V.i.17-29)

In seeking death by fighting against the Romans, he will die for having killed Imogen and thus satisfy the justice of the gods.

The means Posthumus chooses to satisfy the gods are as important as the end—both to his spiritual regeneration and to his eventual reconciliation with Imogen, Cymbeline, and the civil state of Britain—for they are also the means by which he confirms his legacy as a Briton and as his father's son. His regeneration began when he acknowledged his "humanity." By accepting death as the just punishment for sin and by forgiving Imogen and all wives their transgressions, he has acknowledged the dual legacy of justice and love to which all men fall heir. Now, by donning the humble attire of a "Briton peasant" to face death "unknown" and "to shame the guise o' th' world" (V.i.32) by making "men know/More valour in me than my habits show" (V.i.29-30), he reaffirms the patrimony which in his jealous rage he had renounced. He is now ready—as atoning man, as British subject, and as Posthumus Leonatus—to prove through action his nobility of purpose.

In the scenes devoted to the miraculous military action in which Posthumus joins Belarius, Arviragus, and Guiderius to turn a rout into a victory, authentic nobility succeeds in shaming "the guise o' th' world." Iachimo, having been defeated by an opponent whom he assumes to be a mere "carl,/A very drudge of Nature's" (V.ii.4-5), is made aware of the extent of his own dishonor and of the hollowness of his own knighthood and honors. Belarius and the three youths, holding their ground against an enemy force of three thousand and inspiring the fleeing gentry to return to the fight, have also shown up the hollowness of the knighthood and titled nobility of Cymbeline's realm by displaying a "nobleness, which could have turn'd/A distaff to a lance, gilded pale looks" (V.iii.33-34). They have visibly confirmed their nobility in valorous action.[24] Dressed in their humble country attire, they have proved what Pericles in his rusty armor proved in Pentapolis and what Perdita, in the floral scene of *The Winter's Tale*, proves: virtuous action is the only proof of true nobility.

But Posthumus has still more to learn about truth and seeming. He has failed to find death on the battlefield where it seemed most likely to be found and been disappointed. He has also been surprised:

> I, in mine own woe charm'd,
> Could not find Death where I did hear him groan,
> Nor feel him where he struck. Being an ugly monster,
> 'Tis strange he hides him in fresh cups, soft beds,
> Sweet words; or hath moe ministers than we
> That draw his knives i' th' war.   (V.iii.68-73)

So long as he conceives of death as a punishment, it will necessarily seem to him a thing to be feared. Punishment must be painful or else it is no punishment; moreover, it must, in his view, fit the crime, and the crime he believes he has committed is fearful in the extreme. Eventually his vision will be clarified. He will see death differently. But for the present he sees death only as a punishment, a way of satisfying divine justice. It is this desire to pay for what he believes he has done, not despair, that leads him to change clothes again and to be taken prisoner as a Roman and held for treason.

This action, too, contributes to clarification. Posthumus has been a defector to the Roman cause, and the Roman dress he assumes is a public admission of his disloyalty. Once again he corrects a variance between truth and seeming. It is also true, as several commentators have observed, that the action initiates an exercise in repentance.[25] In surrendering himself to the Britons, Posthumus confirms his readiness to answer to both divine and civil justice, to answer with his life for the crime he has committed against both his country and the gods. The fact that he is finally reprieved is the consequence of mercy granted by both authorities—a mercy freely given, but which his own efforts to remake himself prepare him to receive.

Posthumus' soliloquy following the Gaoler's exit (V.iv.3) is crucial to these matters. It commences with an acceptance of "bondage" as a way to "liberty" inasmuch as it points to death. The liberty Posthumus seeks is a release from a tormented conscience. The point, however, is subtler than it first seems, for in his reflections Posthumus has ascended from the notion of physical captivity and release to a spiritual notion. Death now seems to him a "penitent instrument" which will release him from the debt he has incurred by his crimes of murder and treason. To die is to satisfy both the civil and divine law and thus to be free from the debt incurred.

From this point on in the soliloquy Posthumus concentrates upon the divine law and its satisfaction. The civil law demands his death, and his surrender is sufficient proof of his willingness to satisfy it. Divine law seems to him not so easily satisfied. Now, for the first time since the beginning of his remorse, he considers the gods in terms other than as exactors of justice.

> Is't enough I am sorry?
> So children temporal fathers do appease;
> Gods are more full of mercy. (V.iv.11-13)

As he had earlier discovered the justice of the gods in allowing him to live, murder Imogen, and still go seemingly unpunished, now, through the strength of his own powers of self-examination and reflection, he discovers their mercy. They will be merciful if they will accept his life as satisfactory payment for the life of Imogen, even though his life is not equal in worth to hers:

> I know you are more clement than vile men,
> Who of their broken debtors take a third,
> A sixth, a tenth, letting them thrive again
> On their abatement. That's not my desire.
> For Imogen's dear life take mine; and though
> 'Tis not so dear, yet 'tis a life; you coin'd it.
> 'Tween man and man they weigh not every stamp;
> Though light, take pieces for the figure's sake;
> You rather mine, being yours; and so, great powers,
> If you will take this audit, take this life,
> And cancel these cold bonds. (V.iv.18-28)

When Posthumus had agreed to Iachimo's wager, he had talked of love as if it could be measured quantitatively. He now realizes that love's "worth's unknown, although his height be taken"—that no value can be placed upon it because it is of a spiritual rather than material order.

The proof that Posthumus has satisfied the justice of the gods, that they have cancelled "these cold bonds," is the vision that follows. He is now given, in a way that has been anticipated in *Pericles*, the most profound ability to see and therefore to understand.

Proof of his newly gained awareness is his confident attitude toward his own death. It is no longer an "ugly monster" to him, but the way to freedom—not from the fetters he wears or from the prison where he awaits his execution, but from the bonds of divine law. In the light of his newly awakened faith in the gods' mercy he is able to see in a way which utterly mystifies the Gaoler. When he announces "I am merrier to die than thou art to live" (V.iv.176), the Gaoler curtly reminds him of what one who awaits execution ought to consider: people awaiting execution know not which way they go after death. Posthumus' reply, "Yes indeed do I, fellow" (V.iv.183), occasions a sardonic rejoinder from the Gaoler. His lines clearly identify for the audience the source of that new power of vision which has given Posthumus such assurance:

> Your Death has eyes in's head then; I have not seen him so pictur'd.
> You must either be directed by some that take upon them to know, or
> to take upon yourself that which I am sure you do not know, or jump
> the after-inquiry on your own peril; and how you shall speed in your
> journey's end, I think you'll never return to tell one.
>
> (V.iv.184-91)

Of the three possibilities listed by the Gaoler the audience is easily able to dismiss the third, for it has seen in earlier scenes that Posthumus is certainly not indifferent to "the after-inquiry." The second seems, momentarily, a possibility, but only until we realize that we have only moments earlier seen Posthumus "directed" in these matters by someone who takes it upon himself to know, namely, Jupiter. Posthumus' reply, which again picks up the sight metaphor, befuddles and exasperates the Gaoler, though by now it should prove no problem to us.

> *Posthumus:* I tell thee, fellow, there are none want eyes to direct them
> the way I am going, but such as wink, and will not use them.
> *Gaoler:* What an infinite mock is this, that a man should have the best
> use of eyes to see the way of blindness! I am sure hanging's the way
> of winking. (V.iv.192-97)

Such talk is nonsense to the Gaoler because he can only think of sight in the ordinary sense. Posthumus, on the other hand, has discovered through the renewal of faith a kind of sight that is available to all men if they will choose to exercise it. Transcending the limits of phenomenal nature, it is a way of seeing that achieves final clarification for Posthumus, resolving for him the difference between what death and cosmic justice seem and in fact are. It is a way of seeing made possible only by an initial affirmation of belief in the mercy of the gods.

Returning to Posthumus' dream, we realize, then, that the vision it presents is not only Jupiter's way of confirming Posthumus' belief that the gods are merciful as well as just, but also the dramatist's means of portraying the kind of vision that Posthumus has been given by the gods as a reward for his trust in their benevolence. It is a mode of dramatic illusion, permitted by the conventions of romance, which allows the dramatist to portray what he conceives to be a reality beyond the phenomenal world. As such, the vision is a means—and in this it is similar to Pericles' dream and to the music of the spheres which he hears—of illuminating the audience as well as Posthumus. In its presentation of Jupiter descending from the heavens to answer the questions raised by the Shades of Posthumus' parents and brothers it answers the central questions raised by the play's action about justice and mercy and truth and seeming.

No less real than the assurance that Jupiter gives Posthumus are the assurances that he gives the spirits of Posthumus' deceased family. Sicilius Leonatus, thanks to Posthumus' atonement, may rest in peace, confident that his name will live on in a son who has proved worthy of it and that it will pass on to the heir which the predicted reunion with Imogen promises. The two dead brothers may also rest peacefully, knowing that their brother's heroism will be acknowledged. As for Posthumus, the appearance of his family constitutes a spiritual reunion with parents and brothers he has never known. It is a reunion that all but completes the process of renewal begun by Posthumus after receiving the bloody "proof" of Imogen's death. Having initially been denied his patrimony by Cymbeline and then having denied it himself in both word and action, he has now, as the spirits of his brothers point out, reclaimed it by serving Cymbeline exactly as his father and brothers had once served Cymbeline's father, Tenantius. He has recovered a vital part of his long-lost past by using the occasion of his own guilt and the Roman war in such a way as to regain for himself and his father a future that promises harmony and fruitfulness. All that remains to complete the restorative action in the life of the family of Sicilius Leonatus is Cymbeline's final reunion with Imogen and Cymbeline's acknowledging the noble title of Sicilius Leonatus that he had formerly denied Posthumus.

The parallel remarked by Posthumus' brothers between the occasion many years ago when they and their father fought for Tenantius against the Romans and the present occasion on which Posthumus has fought for Britain and Cymbeline is only the first of several to emerge in the final phase of the action. Belarius again proves his honor against the Romans. Exiled on that earlier occasion for treason, he is now granted, along with the two boys whose identities are yet to be revealed, a dignity becoming his estate (V.v.21-22); and then, after he has revealed himself to the king and confessed publicly to the treasonous act of having kidnapped the king's sons, he is forgiven. Cymbeline, too, finds time repeating itself. Once again he is faced with the opportunity to recognize and properly acknowledge the nobility of those whose loyalty he had either refused to see or had openly denounced. Before he discovers the true identity of Belarius and Posthumus he publicly acknowledges their merit. He promises rewards to anyone who locates the "poor soldier that so richly fought" and "whose rags sham'd gilded arms" (V.v.3-4). He confers knighthood upon Belarius and his two boys, promising to fit them "with dignities becoming your estates" (V.v.22).

It seems, however, that Cymbeline is about to repeat the very mistake he had made those many years ago. He remembers only that Belarius is a banished traitor; and when the old warrior whom he has just rewarded for heroism reveals that he is Belarius, Cymbeline orders him to be seized, evidently with the intent to execute him. At this point the audience recognizes another recurrent moment. Posthumus in his guilt had hoped the gods would mercifully release him from the bond incurred by his guilt, and found his hope fulfilled. Now Belarius speaks in legalistic terms of the bond that Cymbeline has incurred:

> First pay me for the nursing of thy sons;
> And let it be confiscate all so soon
> As I've receiv'd it.   (V.v.322-24)

His crime is treason. He has kidnapped the king's heirs, and, like Posthumus earlier, he accepts death as the means of fulfilling the debt demanded by law. Now Cymbeline proves himself capable of mercy, not only by forgiving Belarius for his act of treason but by embracing him a few moments later as a brother (V.v.399). Acknowledgment of proven worth and forgiveness has broken the final strand in the pattern of destruction and retribution that Cymbeline began so long ago. Impressed by Posthumus' forgiving of the contrite Iachimo, Cymbeline now announces that "Pardon's the word to all" (V.v.422).

It is love and trust, then, which sustain Pisanio, Posthumus, and Imogen in the darkest moments in the play, when the discrepancies between truth and seeming are so pervasive that their resolution seems impossible. It is also love and trust that initiate the processes of clarification, restoration, and renewal that culminate finally in the realization of "mutual concord and love" in the families of Leonatus and Cymbeline and in those larger families, the community of Cymbeline's court and the British and Roman nations. In the newly gained civil and familial concord, the ideals manifest in the family and communal life of Belarius' primitive patriarchy (which Imogen had remembered only as a dream) are fully realized. Order and degree have been re-established in the "brazen world" of Britain by children who have confirmed their right to their noble patrimonies through noble action and by fathers who, having once failed, have redeemed their civil and familial rights—Cymbeline by forgiving, Belarius by rejoining and defending the social order he had rejected in his time of disillusionment.

A final word about the extent of divinity's involvement in *Cymbeline* is in order. The concluding scene of the play affirms and reaffirms the role that the heavens have had in bringing about the harmonious conclusion of events. The Soothsayer, who from his first appearance in the play has had difficulties in reading natural phenomena, concludes that the peace restored between Rome and Britain has been the work of the heavens: "The fingers of the powers above do tune/The harmony of this peace" (V.v.466-67). He has reinterpreted the omen of the Roman eagle which "wing'd/From the spongy south to this part of the west" and "There vanish'd in the sunbeams" (IV.ii.348-50) as a sign that the reunion of Britain has been divinely ordained. Cymbeline accepts the Soothsayer's reading, announcing in the opening lines of his exit speech sacrifices to the gods and a ratification of the newly won peace in the temple of Jupiter.

But the audience from its vantage point has seen more than the

Soothsayer and Cymbeline have been permitted to see and knows the extent to which Britain's destiny has been shaped by men. We have seen the gods intervene, but primarily through human agents— through men who like Posthumus and Belarius have atoned fully for their crimes against heaven and country and thus transformed themselves into agents of renewal. We know, therefore, that the destination of the Roman eagle's flight has been determined by men. It was unleashed and directed toward Britain by Cymbeline's refusal to continue to pay tribute to Rome; and, as the Soothsayer had initially suggested, it seemed to promise a Roman victory. But that victory was circumvented by Belarius and the three boys, who in asserting their nobility won the favor of the god who rides on the back of the eagle and who is the dispenser of justice.

The audience also knows that the eagle seen by the Soothsayer, whose knowledge of the future is based solely upon natural phenomena, is not to be identified only with Rome. Having seen Posthumus identified with the eagle on several occasions in the play, we realize in retrospect that the eagle seen by the Soothsayer may also have designated the vengeful Posthumus' return to England with the invading Romans. We realize, therefore, that retributive justice in the form of the Roman invasion, and in the person of Posthumus, has been circumvented by atoning man and a merciful and forgiving Jupiter. We know, in short, that the heavens have intervened at a decisive moment in the history of Britain, but only after human agents have taken the initiative.

NOTES

[1]"History and Histrionics in *Cymbeline*," *Shakespeare Survey*, 11 (Cambridge, 1969), 42-49.

[2]Thomas Elyot observes that the circumspect "may, as it were on a mountain or place of espial, behold on every side far off, measuring and esteeming everything, and either pursue it, if it be commendable, or abandon it or eschew it, if it be noyful." Circumspection, he continues, "is not only expedient but also needful to every estate and degree of men, that do continue in the life called active." *The Book Named The Governor*, ed. with an Introduction by S. E. Lehmberg (London, 1962), Everyman edition.

[3]J. M. Nosworthy recognizes the symbolic role of Belarius, describing him as a character who "impresses us as a piece of virtue, but not as a man of character. . . . His speeches consist, almost exclusively, of abstract moral generalizations which impress us only by their ineptitude, and clearly serve no useful ethical purpose. They enable him, however, to remain a puppet, and to retreat, at practically every turn, from such realities as threaten his symbolic anonymity." The New Arden *Cymbeline* (London, 1955), Introduction, liv.

[4]Harley Granville-Barker comments on the play's pageantlike conclusion: "There need be no stage directions . . . to show us Cymbeline and Lucius, Posthumus, Iomgen and her brothers, Belarius, Iachimo and the rest setting out in elaborate procession; the play dissolving into pageantry." *Prefaces to Shakespeare*, I (Princeton, N.J., 1946), 496.

[5]Quoted by Nosworthy (New Arden *Cymbeline*, Introduction, xli) from *General Observations on the Plays of Shakespeare* (1756).

[6]*Prefaces to Shakespeare*, I, 461-62.

[7]Derek A. Traversi, *Shakespeare: The Last Phase* (New York, 1953), p. 43.

[8]New Arden *Cymbeline*, Introduction, l-li.

[9]*The Crown of Life* (London, 1948), p. 157.

[10]One critic, Mr. Norman Rabkin, after failing to discover any ideas in the play, reaches the vacuous conclusion that Shakespeare wrote *Cymbeline* merely to demonstrate his power over his plot materials: "The world of tragedy can be redeemed in *Cymbeline* as it could not in earlier Shakespearean tragedy, the play seems to say, simply because the playwright can deny its tragic inevitability by his power over the plot." *Shakespeare and the Common Understanding* (New York, 1967), p. 211.

[11]Granville-Barker's discussion of the dramatic purpose of this deliberate display of art in *Cymbeline* misses the point by suggesting that it is Shakespeare's means of reminding his audience that he does not expect them to take his play seriously. Shakespeare "has an unlikely story to tell, and in its unlikelihood lies not only its charm but largely its very being; reduce it to reason, you would wreck it altogether. Now in the theater there are two ways of dealing with the inexplicable. If the audience are to take it seriously, leave it unexplained. They will be anxious—pathetically anxious—to believe you . . . The other play is to show one's hand, saying in effect: 'Ladies and gentlemen, this is an exhibition of tricks, and what I want you to enjoy among other

things is the skill with which I hope to perform them.' This art, which deliberately displays its art, is very suited to a tragi-comedy, to the telling of a serious story that must yet not be taken too seriously, lest its comedy be swamped by its tragedy and a happy ending become too incongruous." *Prefaces*, I, 466-67.

[12]Brockbank, "History and Histrionics in *Cymbeline*," p. 44.

[13]Bernard Harris recognizes the importance of the past as history in the late plays and, specifically, in *Cymbeline*: the "problem of the shaping or misshaping destiny of the past is natural to those themes of the late plays which treat of loss and restoration, disjunction and pattern. But in *Cymbeline*, more than perhaps in any of Shakespeare's plays, the problems of structure and utterance are complicated by the necessary attention to the past as history." " 'What's Past is Prologue': *Cymbeline* and *Henry VIII*," *Later Shakespeare* Stratford-upon-Avon Studies, 8 (London, 1966), 203.

[14]Bertrand Evans assumes that Cymbeline's blindness is due to the Queen and that "all follows from her deception." *Shakespeare's Comedies*, p. 250.

[15]The phrase is from *Richard II*, II.i. York is speaking to Richard just after learning that Bolingbroke's "royalties and rights" are to be seized:

> Take Hereford's rights away, and take from Time
> His charters and his customary rights;
> Let not to-morrow then ensue to-day;
> Be not thyself; for how art thou a king
> But by fair sequence and succession? (ll. 195-99)

[16]Several commentators have emphasized the folly of Posthumus' wager. Robert G. Hunter accurately notes that in Shakespeare's view "true love would feel no necessity for a test," and that the ease with which Posthumus succumbs to Iachimo's villainy is indicative of his "naivete and lack of confidence." *Shakespeare and the Comedy of Forgiveness* (New York, 1965), p. 152. Homer D. Swander rejects the view that Posthumus' acceptance of the wager is to be seen as simply a convention of romance. Shakespeare, according to Swander, in portraying Posthumus exposes beneath his "apparently perfect gestures, an essential meanness in the man himself and in the conventional virtue that he embodies." "*Cymbeline* and the Blameless Hero," *English Literary History*, 30 (1964), 259-70.

[17]Robert G. Hunter's observation that Posthumus' soliloquy "regales us with the clichés of Pauline anti-feminism" (*Shakespeare and the Comedy of Forgiveness*, p. 153), completely misses the mark.

[18]The corruption of reason and perception which results from the loss of trust is systematically traced in the first three acts of *The Winter's Tale*. Donald Stauffer is one of the few commentators who have recognized in the late plays the importance given to trust. Shakespeare's "ultimate simplicity is that all mistrust is vicious. How easily, then, may slander and false appearance play upon the trustful! The ideal is reciprocal trust and virtue." *Shakespeare's World of Images*, p. 283.

[19]For discussion of Cloten as a reflection of the fallen Posthumus, see Homer D. Swander, "*Cymbeline*: Religious Idea and Dramatic Design," *Pacific West Coast Studies in Shakespeare*, pp. 251-52; and Robert G. Hunter, *Shakespeare and the Comedy of Forgiveness*, pp. 157-58.

[20]G. Wilson Knight refers to Belarius' "community," noting that it "has its own rough aristocracy" which is "to be daily reasserted and rewon." *The Crown of Life*, p. 129.

[21]Derek Traversi, failing to recognize *humanitas* as the controlling idea of the communal scenes in Wales, offers a distorted interpretation of the actions they contain. He sees Belarius' rejection of the world of court as justified (*Shakespeare: The Last Phase*, p. 67) and finds that the King's lost sons bring with them in their return to court "the virtues of barbaric honesty which are henceforth to be integrated into the order of true courtliness." "The Last Plays of Shakespeare," in *The Age of Shakespeare*, ed. Boris Ford (Baltimore, 1955), p. 263.

[22]William Barry Thorne accurately identifies Cloten as a fool: "The Second Lord actually describes Cloten as the professional 'fool', with his cockscomb and bladder." "*Cymbeline:* 'Lopp'd Branches' and the Concept of Regeneration," *Shakespeare Quarterly*, 20 (1969), 143-59.

[23]Cloten's beheading may symbolically announce the public phase of the play's renewing action. The idea of *reform* is represented in numerous Renaissance emblems and *imprese* by the "cutting away" of dead or rampant growth. See, for instance, Gerhardt Ladner's discussion ("Vegetation Symbolism and the Concept of Renaissance," *Studies in Honor of Irwin Panofsky*, I, 303-22, 303) of Cesare Ripa's suggestion of how "to represent pictorially the idea of 'reform'" by a pruning knife or shears: "...just as a pruning knife or shears cut away superfluous branches which sap the strength of trees and prevent them from bearing fruit, so reform removes abuses and transgressions: the virtue of lawful observance, which though lost by evildoers never perishes in itself, is thus reformed and through it good government." Cloten is a "superfluous branch" which has sapped the vitality of the royal tree of Britain's kings. Before the renewal of the royal tree can begin, Cloten must be "cut away."

[24]The battle as described by Posthumus is also unmistakably emblematic. Belarius, along with Arviragus and Guiderius, emerges as an exemplar. He is the representative of the courageous warrior of common but ancient British stock who in moments of national crisis joins with royalty in his country's defense (V.iii.15-18). The boys are models of the ideal virtues of royalty; their faces are models from which copies ("with faces fit for *masks,* or rather fairer/Than those for preservation cas'd, or shame," V.iii.19-22) ought to be made, and when, in fact, those models are eventually copied, the tide of battle is turned:

> some, turn'd coward
> But by example—O, a sin in war,
> Damn'd in the first beginners!—gan to look
> The way that they did, [i.e. Belarius and the two boys],
>   and to grin like lions
> Upon the pikes o' th' hunters. Then began ...
> A rout, confusion thick.   (V.iii.35-41)

[25]Hunter (*Shakespeare and the Comedy of Forgiveness*, pp. 163-72) and Swander ("*Cymbeline:* Religious Idea and Dramatic Design," pp. 159-63) provide full and on the whole sound analyses of Posthumus' attempt to fulfill the demands of divine justice.

IV

The Winter's Tale: An Old Tale with "Matter to Rehearse"

THE WINTER'S TALE returns to the general concerns of *Cymbeline*—the dependence of seeing upon belief, the confirmation of nobility through action, natural love and concord as the only basis of community—but with an economy and clarity of structure that make it dramatically more successful than its predecessor. The folly and mistrust of Cymbeline and Posthumus, from which the destructive action in *Cymbeline* proceeds, are concentrated in Leontes, who, as untrusting husband and purblind ruler, is the sole initiator of the action which very nearly consumes the royal family of Sicilia. No clever Iachimo deceives him; no vicious but beautiful woman misleads him. He deceives himself; and in the depiction of the moral disintegration that follows his loss of faith in Hermione we see fully explored what in *Cymbeline* is postulated as a given, or is only cursorily depicted.

In *Cymbeline* the king is presented to us as unable either to discern between the true and the apparently true, or to trust in those who have earned his trust; and while Posthumus' acceptance of Iachimo's proof is developed in some measure, the immediate consequences of his loss of faith in Imogen are confined mainly to the contents of a single soliloquy. But in *The Winter's Tale* the consequences of Leontes' loss of trust take up the greater part of three acts, in which we watch a gracious king and husband very nearly bring himself and his family to ruin. Once the suddenness of Leontes' jealousy is gotten over, the progression is as clear and as compelling as that of Macbeth's moral disintegration.

The renewing action of the second half of the play, while disclosing a number of similarities with the renewing action of *Cymbeline*, gains in effectiveness from the clarity of its plotting. The progression of the opening action is reversed. Whereas the loss of trust and love turned destructive by "affection" in the opening action beget near calamity, love grounded in trust restores almost all that has been lost. Old enmities are reconciled and the marriage of children promises renewal of the "lines of life" that seemed to have been cut in the opening action. It is one of the most brilliantly sustained pieces of writing to be found anywhere in Shakespeare.

The play's mode of imitation is a refinement of the mode Shakespeare had used in *Pericles* and in the latter half of *Cymbeline*.[1] Its characters have something of the substantiality of *Cymbeline*'s, and yet there is a remoteness about them that suggests the characters of the earlier play. They have a psychological and physical dimension that *Pericles*' Ideal Exemplars lack. They are fallible and they live in a world that is more particularized than *Pericles*' emblematic world of tempests, strange seas, and remote shores. At the same time, perhaps because the countries in which they live are somewhere between the real world and that of Arcadian fiction in a kind of no-man's-land which is nevertheless everyman's land, they lack the substantiality of *Cymbeline*'s Britons, Romans, and Italians.

The effect I am describing is also due to the remote and unspecified time in which they live.[2] The characters in *Cymbeline* also obviously live in a remote time, but time in *Cymbeline* has a measure of specificity that is lacking in *The Winter's Tale* and *Pericles*. *Cymbeline*'s Romans and Britons evoke in us shadowy recollections of a specific pre-Christian era—recollections of a time preserved largely only by legend and myth and yet sufficiently confirmed by genuine history and artifact to gain our belief. They have local habitations and sometimes even historical names. The characters in *The Winter's Tale*, on the other hand, lack even the kind of temporal identity that legendary history provides. They exist in a fiction which, like Gower's old "song," deliberately avoids particularizations of place and time, and exploits the license of romance to focus upon a reality beyond the level of physical and psychological verisimilitude. It is "an old tale" which has "matter to rehearse, though credit be asleep and not an ear open" (V.ii.66-68).

In such a tale it is pointless to expect the kind of psychological probability that is so much admired in *Othello* or *Macbeth*. We may object to the genre of romance and argue the superiority of realistic mimesis, of Shakespearean tragedy or Jonsonian comedy, for instance; but to be troubled by Leontes' jealousy because its suddenness and lack of motivation detract from or violate the illusion of realism is no more to the point than objecting (on the grounds that such things just do not happen in the real world) to the scene in which Hermione is brought back into the play as a "statue." In each instance, our concern ought to be the "matter" rehearsed in events that make no claim to verisimilitude.

Shakespeare's indifference to the ways in which he might easily have made Leontes' jealousy probable is in itself a clear indication that his concerns lay elsewhere. Greene's account is leisurely and full.[3] Bellaria (Hermione's counterpart in *The Triumph of Time*), who is "willing to show how unfeignedly she loves her husband by his friend's [Egistus'] entertainment," comes gradually to spend more and more time with him. Eventually they become intimate friends:

> This honest familiarity increased daily more and more betwixt them; for Bellaria, noting in Egistus a princely and bountiful mind, adorned with sundry and excellent qualities, and Egistus, finding in her a virtuous and courteous disposition, there grew such a secret uniting of their affections, that the one could not well be without the company of the other: insomuch, that when Pandosto was busied with such

urgent affairs that he could not be present with his friend Egistus, Bellaria would walk with him into the garden, where they two in private and pleasant devices would pass away the time to both their contents.

(p. 5)

Only gradually does Pandosto grow suspicious. Remarking the mutual affection that Bellaria and Egistus show to each other and the amount of time they spend together, he grows melancholy, and the humor drives him "into sundry and doubtful thoughts."

> First, he called to mind the beauty of his wife, Bellaria, the comeliness and bravery of his friend Egistus, thinking that love was above all laws and, therefore, to be stayed with no law; that it was hard to put fire and flax together without burning; that their open pleasures might breed his secret displeasures. He considered with himself that Egistus was a man and must needs love, that his wife was a woman, and therefore, subject unto love, and that where fancy forced, friendship was of no force. (pp. 5-6)

Gradually his suspicions increase until finally they become convictions and jealousy is born. It would have been a simple thing for Shakespeare to condense the evidence provided by Greene and introduce it early in the play through an expository aside or soliloquy. Or he might just as easily have represented Leontes, as J. Dover Wilson believes he did, as already jealous before the opening of the play.[4]

Either of the above alternatives would have eliminated the problem that has so troubled the critics. But Shakespeare's concerns here are not with realistic illusion. In his depiction of Leontes' sudden affliction he is concerned—as he will be throughout the remainder of the play and again in *The Tempest*—to "rehearse" the ways in which the past may affect the present and shape the future.

Leontes' jealousy originates in an act of memory. The critical section of the scene commences when Hermione, having persuaded Polixenes to agree to extend his visit, proceeds to ask him of the childhood days he spent with Leontes. It concludes with Leontes, too, being led to remember his youthful days—in such a way that he is struck by a violent passion which destroys in an instant a love that has flourished through the years.

In his responses to Hermione's questioning Polixenes summons up out of his memory a pastoral picture of timeless and innocent boyhood days eventually interrupted by awakened passions. The intimacy of his boyhood friendship with Leontes was a shared innocence.[5] They were unaware of time—

> Two lads that thought there was no more behind
> But such a day to-morrow as to-day,
> And to be boy eternal—   (I.ii.63-65)

and as yet uncorrupted by, or even conscious of, sin:

> We were as twinn'd lambs that did frisk i' th' sun,
> And bleat the one at th' other. What we chang'd
> Was innocence for innocence; we knew not
> The doctrine of ill-doing, [no], nor dream'd
> That any did.   (I.ii.67-71)

Together, they discovered the paradoxical legacy of man's fall—the "stronger blood" of the passions which are the mark of The Fall but which may lead, nevertheless, to the ennobling of "our weak spirits":

> Had we pursu'd that life,
> And our weak spirits ne'er been higher rear'd
> With stronger blood, we should have answer'd Heaven
> Boldly, "Not guilty"; the imposition clear'd
> Hereditary ours.   (I.ii.71-75)

Polixenes in his account has introduced one of the two ways, crucial in the play, in which the past affects the present and shapes the future. The loss of innocence and the discovery of time is an experience which, in terms of the myth of The Fall, the young of every generation are bound to repeat. The circumstances may vary, but the discovery of sin and the punishment it has occasioned is the discovery of a legacy which is always vitally contained in the present and always momently to be reckoned with. The "imposition" which is "hereditary ours" is the shaping influence of the past contained in the present and the ominous presence of death in the future.[6]

The past, then, in the form in which Polixenes' reminiscings have introduced it, has determined for all time conditions which man can only accept. He is subject to strong and unruly passions; and he is mortal. Both the micro- and the macrocosm are subject to sudden and violent tempests, and over both worlds Time the Destroyer casts his shadow. Nevertheless, man is free to temper his unruly passions and to determine how he will face the fact of his mortality. In the orthodox Christian view the way in which he exercises that freedom is obviously crucial, since it determines the soul's future in eternity. It is no less critical in *The Winter's Tale*, in which the concerns are not (at least openly) eternal but temporal, since the choices made by its principal characters vitally affect the "lines of life" and the succession of rulers.

As Polixenes proceeds in his recollections, we learn of the particular circumstances in which he and Leontes discovered hereditary guilt:

> O my most sacred lady,
> Temptations have since then been born to 's; for
> In those unfledg'd days was my wife a girl,
> Your precious self had then not cross'd the eyes
> Of my young play-fellow. (I.ii.76-80)

Their discovery was in the "stronger blood" of sexual desire, aroused by the women they eventually marry—in the awakening of a passion which may lead either to love, marriage, and the begetting of heirs, or to jealousy, madness, sin, and death.

Manifest, then, in the awakening of desire that Polixenes describes are the antithetically opposed forces of generative and destructive love which are the source of conflict in *Pericles* and *Cymbeline*. The proof that Polixenes and Leontes have transformed passion into love—the proof of how they have met the trial of the awakening of "stronger blood"—is the history of their love from the moment of its awakening down to the present moment in dramatic time. By meeting the initial trial of hereditary guilt, the element of necessity (or tempestuousness) in the continuum of time, they have kept private and public time on a course of renewal. Each has married, begotten an heir, and governed his kingdom in tranquillity; each now enjoys an idyllic present.

But trust and love are vulnerable from moment to moment because of the presence of hereditary guilt in the personal present. They are always subject to sudden eruptions of violent feelings which by clouding the mind and distorting perception may lead an Othello to accept a handkerchief or a Posthumus to accept a bracelet as ocular proof of infidelity. Such fits of passion are unpredictable. There was no way of predicting Posthumus' sudden loss of trust in Imogen; nor could Pericles have known that Dionyza and Cleon would eventually betray him. Now, the serene present in Sicilia is about to be suddenly and violently disrupted by another awakening of "stronger blood."

That disruption proves to be an instance of the second way in which the past is depicted in this play as a vital influence upon the present. The past also exists in the personal present as memory. The past as memory is obviously essential to all deliberation and choice, since the knowledge called upon in moments of choice is a part of what is retained in the memory. The past is equally and unavoidably essential to perception and, potentially, a source of feeling. The quality of perception is determined by what from past experience we bring to bear on sense data in the moment of perceiving. Feelings, too, necessarily bear the mark of the past, since how we have been trained to think and to see determines from moment to moment how we feel. On the other hand, by an act of specific remembering, of focusing and reflecting upon a given event or sequence of events, feelings may be awakened or re-experienced which can deeply affect perception and deliberation and hence the future. The results of such feelings may be beneficial. In the meditative exercises examined by Louis Martz, for instance, and in the verse which appears to have been influenced by them, the controlled use of memory aims at motivating states of fear, love, and sorrow that in the Christian view are essential to salvation.[7]

Shakespeare's interest in the influence of memory upon feeling, perception, and action is evident throughout the poems and plays.

One thinks of *Hamlet*, immediately, and of such sonnets as "When to the sessions of sweet, silent thought," "Thy gift, thy tables, are within my brain," and of the numerous sonnets among the marriage group in which the poem as memorial is conceived as a way of preserving the young man from relentless encroachments of time. More directly pertinent to the matter at hand is the role of memory in Pericles' return to the world of the senses. Only after Marina has awakened memories which stir the feelings of compassion that take him outside of himself does Pericles begin to see and to hear.

But the memory may also awaken feelings which distort perception and destroy the subject's contact with the real world just as effectively as they restore Pericles' contact with it. And this is precisely what happens to Leontes.

Leontes' conviction that his wife and friend have betrayed him originates in an act of remembering. Pleased to learn that his old friend has agreed to extend his visit, Leontes compliments Hermione on her persuasiveness: "Hermione, my dearest, thou never spok'st/ To better purpose" (I.ii.88-89). She responds by playfully challenging her husband's extravagant compliment and getting him to make a qualification, "Never, but once" (I.ii.89). She then pursues the issue in the spirit of polite banter and in language that contains erotic overtones similar to those present in her last remarks to Polixenes:

> What! have I twice said well? When was 't before?
> I prithee tell me; cram 's with praise, and make 's
> As fat as tame things
> . . . .
> you may ride 's
> With one soft kiss a thousand furlongs ere
> With spur we heat an acre. (I.ii.89-96)

She then asks him directly:

> But to th' goal:
> My last good deed was to entreat his stay;
> What was my first? It has an elder sister,
> Or I mistake you. O, would her name were Grace!
> But once before I spoke to th' purpose; when?
>
> (I.ii.96-100)

The question forces Leontes to reflect on that one time, years earlier, which had been exceptional—that moment when Hermione had finally agreed to accept his love:

> Why, that was when
> Three crabbed months had sour'd themselves to death,
> Ere I could make thee open thy white hand
> And clap thyself my love; then didst thou utter,
> "I am yours for ever." (I.ii.101-05)

Now she gives her hand to Polixenes, just as on that occasion years earlier she had given her hand to him:

> Why, lo you now, I have spoke to th' purpose twice:
> The one for ever earn'd a royal husband;
> Th' other for some while a friend. (I.ii.106-08)

The identification of present and past for Leontes is complete. In recalling that earlier occasion he re-experiences the feelings that Hermione's pledge "after three crabb'd months" to return his love had awakened in him; and now in a moment of delirium, when the "stronger blood" of passion has been reawakened and he is overcome by *tremor cordis*, he attributes his own feelings to Polixenes and believes that he sees actual proof of his wife's infidelity. As he will later disclose to Antigonus (II.i.152-55), he "sees feelingly"; and since the feelings that color and shape his vision are erotic, he sees eroticism in the actions of Polixenes and Hermione.

Shakespeare's purpose in replotting Leontes' jealousy should now be apparent. Sexual passions are a mark of The Fall, a legacy of the past with which all men must contend in the personal present. In an unguarded moment they may surface, suddenly and seemingly without reason, to destroy relationships that have lasted through the years. In such a moment they may infect even the memory and, as a consequence, distort perception and destroy trust and love.

In addition to being of the deepest conceptual importance throughout the play, the relationship between past and present time also furnishes the controlling principles of progression and unity for its action. The contrasting parallels between the past and present occasions of the awakening of "stronger blood" introduce the same pattern of cyclical recurrence that shapes *Pericles* and *Cymbeline*. On the initial occasion of the awakening of desire Leontes successfully met the trial of hereditary guilt. By transforming erotic passion into love he became an agent of the creative, sustaining, and renewing forces of Nature. On the second occasion of its awakening he joins Antiochus, Cleon, Dionyza, Cymbeline, and Posthumus as an agent of the destructive forces that are also manifest in mutability. On its first awakening "stronger blood" had been sanctified and consummated in marriage and had begotten heirs, but on its second awakening it threatens to destroy all that it had originally begotten, and more.

The pattern of recurrence that is evident in these two occasions of innocence destroyed by "stronger blood" will be even more strikingly apparent in the play's renewing action.[8] The reversal of the destructive action proceeding from Leontes' madness will prove to be once again contingent upon how the young meet the urgent demands of awakened desire and upon how men of winter exercise memory. Under the guidance of Paulina, Leontes will remember his guilt and thus keep alive the sorrow which enables him to see compassionately. He will also remember the prophecy of the oracle and thus resist arguments that he should remarry in the interest of Sicilia's future. The children will confront the fact of hereditary guilt in the awakening of their feelings for each other and will have to prove the quality of their affection by meeting the several tests to which time will put them. Finally, the reversal and the play's "circle" of action will be completed when Leontes is brought face to face, as it were, with the past in what he takes to be the statue of Hermione. In that moment by an act of believing he "renews" his own life and the life of the queen whom sixteen years earlier he had refused to believe and had consequently condemned to death.

The replotting of Leontes' jealousy, then, is only the initial step undertaken by Shakespeare in transforming Greene's simple tale of "The Triumph of Time" into a moving celebration of how errant man, born into sin and condemned to die, may finally triumph over time by using Time Past (memory) and Time Present (*occasio*) to recover what has been lost, to sustain himself in the tempestuous present, and to preserve what is preservable of the self in the future.[9]

THE DESTRUCTIVE ACTION

Leontes' violent and suddenly awakened passion quickly spreads from his infected memory to the rest of his faculties.[10] When his heart begins to dance and he feels his trust in wife and friend begin to waver, he begins to doubt his own senses. What he sees may be innocent; but then again it may not:

> This entertainment
> May a free face put on, derive a liberty
> From heartiness, from bounty, fertile bosom,
> And well become the agent; 't may, I grant;
> But to be paddling palms and pinching fingers, . . .
>
> (I.ii.111-15)

The associational progression in the speeches that follow depicts the further corruption of all the faculties by the passions that have been aroused by memory. As Leontes turns his attention to Mamillius—"Art thou my boy?"—it is evident that his memory has been corrupted further; for in questioning Mamillius' legitimacy he questions Hermione's honesty, perhaps even during those "three crabbed months" when he had courted her. In the language of the then current psychology, fancy is freed from the control of reason; it moves freely, following passion's dictates, contaminating Leontes' memory, and thus distorting his apprehension of the present:[11]

> Why, that's my bawcock. What, hast smutch'd thy nose?
> They say it is a copy out of mine. Come, captain;
> We must be neat; not neat, but cleanly, captain,
> And yet the steer, the heifer, and the calf
> Are all call'd neat.—Still virginalling
> Upon his palm!—How now, you wanton calf!
> Art thou my calf? (I.ii.120-27)

After the faculty of sight presents a simple sense perception to the understanding, fancy intervenes, leading reason to reflect upon a fact of memory—"They say it is a copy out of mine." Under the continued domination of fancy, Leontes is drawn to reflect upon a meaning of "neat" that he had not intended and thus to the question of Mamillius' legitimacy, "Art thou my calf?" Fancy next leads him to distort the fact of Mamillius' strong physical resemblance to his father. In his jealousy Leontes is unable to see it, for Mamillius lacks the shaggy head and horns of a cuckold.

> Thou want'st a rough pash and the shoots that I have,
> To be full like me; yet they say we are
> Almost as like as eggs; women say so,
> That will say anything. But were they false
> As o'er-dy'd blacks, as wind, as waters, false
> As dice are to be wish'd by one that fixes
> No bourn 'twixt his and mine, yet were it true
> To say this boy were like me. Come, sir page,
> Look on me with your welkin eye. Sweet villain!
> Most dear'st! my collop! Can thy dam?—may 't be?—
>
> (I.ii.128-37)

Once memory and sight have been infected, reason, too, is clouded and enlisted in the cause of affection. In the lines cited above, Leontes struggles to combat his feelings with reason, and in the lines following he reminds himself that affection makes "possible things not so held" and communicates merely "with dreams"; but reason surrenders and Leontes loses the ability to read appearances accurately. In the service of affection reason panders to affection's dictates with the following grotesque rationalization:

> Affection! thy intention stabs the centre.
> Thou dost make possible things not so held,
> Communicat'st with dreams;—how can this be?—
> With what's unreal thou co-active art,
> And fellow'st nothing. Then 'tis very credent
> Thou mayst co-join with something; and thou dost,
> And that beyond commission, and I find it,
> And that to the infection of my brains
> And hardening of my brows. (I.ii.138-46)

Affection's conquest of Leontes is virtually complete. The events that follow disclose the total enslavement of his faculties. He imagines that the entire court is whispering about Polixenes' decision to extend his visit. He turns on Camillo, his personal adviser, charging him with deception and complicity; and when Camillo attempts to defend himself and the queen, he is viciously attacked as a liar, who is either "a mindless slave" or "a hovering temporizer" (I.ii.301-02).

Up to the end of I.ii., affection's influence has been confined to the personal and the private. Its initial conquest has been of Leontes' memory, imagination, reason, and sight. The immediate result has been to interpret the actions and words of others as proof of his conviction that wife, friend, and personal adviser have betrayed him. The second act traces the spread of affection's corruptive influence into the public sphere. Whereas in I.ii. Leontes spoke as a betrayed husband he now speaks as king, spreading the corruption of his jealousy throughout the court and abusing the power of his public office. Hearing that Camillo has helped Polixenes escape, he convinces himself that they are part of a plot against his life and crown, and that Hermione is a traitor as well as an adulteress. He refuses to address Hermione as queen

> Lest barbarism, making me the precedent,
> Should a like language use to all degrees,
> And mannerly distinguishment leave out
> Betwixt the prince and beggar. (II.i.84-87)

and orders her imprisoned for her supposed crime against the crown. When his counsellors endeavor to intercede on her behalf and remind him of his royal responsibilities to justice, he is unable to hear them. It is they who, according to Leontes, are unable to perceive what is perfectly obvious:

> Cease; no more.
> You smell this business with a sense as cold
> As is a dead man's nose; but I do see't and feel't,
> As you feel doing thus; and see withal
> The instruments that feel. (II.i.150-54)

The irony is unmistakable: the lines describe precisely Leontes' own corrupted senses in a way which the audience is ready to understand. His vision is controlled wholly by what he feels. Hamlet, too, sees feelingly. Perceived through his sorrow and disillusion, the world seems to him rank and disordered. But whereas Hamlet never completely loses touch with the world beyond his consciousness, Leontes is wholly caught up in the illusory. His final position in the scene is one of self-righteous and blind self-assurance:

> Why, what need we
> Commune with you of this, but rather follow
> Our forceful instigation? Our prerogative
> Calls not your counsels, but our natural goodness
> Imparts this; which if you, or stupefied
> Or seeming so in skill, cannot or will not
> Relish a truth like us, inform yourselves
> We need no more of your advice.

(II.i.161-68)

The disease that in its first stage overcame Leontes, corrupting all of his faculties, has now spread to the body politic. The diseased head has transmitted its infection, refusing even to listen to the pleas of counsellors and corrupting even its court and its laws. Leontes has become a tyrant who in his enormous folly has surrendered himself and his kingdom to a blinding passion and thereby exposed both to the violent forces of destructive time.

The final stage of personal and public corruption occurs in the court scene (III.ii). The absolute confidence with which Leontes awaits the oracle, which will prove what a disinterested champion of justice he is, is chilling. Like the Julius Caesar whom Shakespeare portrays on the morning of the assassination, Leontes represents here, in the moments before the shocking revelation of Hermione's innocence, a "wisdom consum'd in confidence," deaf to counsel and blind to the truth.[12] He is a man made tragically vulnerable by an unshakable confidence in his own moral rectitude which isolates him from the real world and makes him an unseeing prisoner of his own illusions. Not even the word from Delphos can get through to him, and it is only the swift and violent retribution following upon his rejection of the oracle that frees him from the prison of his own illusions.

His denial of the oracle completes the disintegration of his trust. His initial refusal to believe in the honesty of Hermione and Polixenes has spread to include Camillo, his public advisors, and Paulina. He has questioned even the legitimacy of Mamillius and denied the legitimacy of his newly born daughter. Now, standing alone in his blindness and believing only in his own honesty, he denies the words of divinity.

Among Shakespeare's victims of jealousy and mistrust, Leontes is unique. Othello and Posthumus are worked on from without. Iago and Iachimo are both masters of pornography who cleverly lead their victims to a state of feeling in which they accept the flimsiest kind of evidence as proof of infidelity. But Leontes' affliction is self-generated. Its origins are in hereditary guilt. Held in check during the years of a happy and fruitful marriage, it is awakened by an act of memory and suddenly emerges again in the form of violent passion to destroy innocence, corrupt perception, and disrupt time.

It is possible now to see more fully than before what Shakespeare is concerned to rehearse in the opening action of this old tale. In its rehearsal of archetypal experience it returns again to a concern of the earlier romances, the pattern of recurrence in the cycle of human life. Since the sins of fathers are visited upon sons and daughters, the loss of innocence and the discovery of time are bound to be repeated by the children of every generation. As Leontes and Polixenes discovered hereditary guilt in the passions aroused by the women they eventually married, so will Florizel when he meets Perdita. How he meets the test of time and the urgencies of "the red blood that reigns in the winter's pale" will be decisive in determining which way time will proceed. But the awakening of "stronger blood" is repeated not only by the youth of successive generations; it is also repeatable, as Leontes' sudden loss of trust indicates, in the cycle of a single life. The legacy of The Fall is always a threat to present and future harmony. One moment of weakness and all that generative love has accomplished can be undone. The moment of weakness from which the nearly-tragic action of the first three acts proceeds is Leontes' moment of "tremor cordis," when his trust in Hermione commences to waver and his grasp of what is real to weaken.

The exploration of the precarious interdependence of belief and perception which ensues brings us to the second major concern rehearsed in the opening action, the general question of illusion and reality. Leontes at a relatively early point in the opening action remarks to an attending Lord how fortunate he has been to discover the truth and then proceeds to draw an analogy between himself and one who, having innocently drunk of a cup, is later told that the cup contained a venomous spider.

> How blest am I
> In my just censure, in my true opinion!
> Alack, for lesser knowledge! How accurs'd
> In being so blest! There may be in the cup
> A spider steep'd, and one may drink, depart,
> And yet partake no venom, for his knowledge
> Is not infected; but if one present
> Th' abhorr'd ingredient to his eye, make known
> How he hath drunk, he cracks his gorge, his sides,
> With violent hefts. I have drunk, and seen the spider.
>
> (II.i.36-45)

A poisonous distrust has infected his knowledge and produced imaginings that are as real to him as the spider in the cup to which he alludes. His belief that he has drunk "and seen the spider" distorts his vision, causing him to imagine as real in others what is actually real within him.

The primacy of faith, or belief, is insisted on in each of the earlier romances, but in neither so emphatically as here. What Leontes believes determines his interpretation of what he sees and how he reasons. As his mistrust spreads, his contact with the real weakens proportionately, until, believing only in himself, he denies the heavens and stands wholly isolated in his own illusions.

Leontes' eyes are opened and he is brought to his knees by retribution swiftly exacted. Mamillius is dead, and so, reportedly, is Hermione. His guilt bears down upon him. He has brutally treated an innocent wife and friend. He has denied the legitimacy of his own daughter and has caused her to be cast away. He has wrongly accused Camillo, abused justice, and openly defied the heavens. He has interrupted the natural process of renewal through the begetting of children, and he has deprived his kingdom of a successor.

But even in this darkest of moments for Leontes, when he despairs in the face of his horrible guilt, the generative powers of love begin the process of renewal. Love's agents in this instance are principally human: Paulina, overcoming her momentary passion for revenge, asks forgiveness; Leontes assumes the burden of remembering, which years later will finally contribute to the restoration of what his jealousy so nearly destroyed; and on the storm-ridden coast of Bohemia a shepherd, searching for lost sheep, discovers the infant Perdita and takes her to his cottage. The guilt-ridden king has no alternative but to fix his mind on the past, hoping only that he may satisfy Apollo's justice by remembering his fault and thus experiencing "shame perpetual." The shepherd, meeting in the tempest "with things newborn," takes up the infant and charitably serves "great creating Nature" by raising it as his own.

We see, then, two distinct ways in which the heavens demand that time be used. The heavens sustain creation through an act of love. The shepherd participates in that sustaining act by caring for Perdita. Through his natural benevolence he serves the future. The heavens also exact retribution from those who through the perversion of love have interrupted the natural process of generation. The guilty king must accept the wages of his own sin and seek to satisfy the rigorous law by which he is judged guilty. He must use the present to atone for the past. Proof of his obedience to the law will be the rigor with which he exercises his memory. He must keep alive his sorrow, and he must remember the prophetic warning of the oracle—the "King shall live without an heir, if that which is lost be not found" (III.ii.136-37). Memory, in fact, will play a vitally important role in determining the way in which the prophecy is fulfilled. Leontes has lost more than an heir. He has lost his capacity to trust. Recovery of Perdita will depend upon his recovery of his readiness to trust. The means of recovery will prove to be "grace and remembrance."

THE RENEWING ACTION

When the play's action resumes after sixteen years of "growth untried," an important contrast in the representation of appearances begins to emerge: whereas in the opening action appearances and reality were in perfect accord, in the renewing action there is a pervasive ambiguity in appearances that provides men of winter and the audience with cause for doubt.[13] By realistic standards, the contrast is obviously "artificial." We know the world of appearances remains from generation to generation substantially what it has always been. But Shakespeare is pursuing another reality, a psychological and epistemological one. The results are some of the most impressive to be found in this magnificent play.

Leontes' mistrust very nearly destroys within Sicilia the values which communal man has embodied in his institutions and upon which he has grounded his civilization: love, marriage, friendship, family, the law, justice. Whether or not we accept the myth of The Fall, we recognize the truth of the opening action. We find persuasive Shakespeare's version of the truth that the feelings and assumptions we bring to bear in our act of perceiving "reality" determine our interpretation of what we see. His mode of representing that truth has been, in the Sidneian sense, "poetic" rather than "mimetic." He has endeavored to go beyond the limiting provincialities of time and place in order to represent truths which are universal; and the contrast developed in the two distinct actions of the play between simple and ambiguous appearances is simply another example of the technique of contrasting parallels which Shakespeare has used so extensively in the earlier romances. In the renewing action of *The Winter's Tale* it is the means of completing the exploration of the relationship between believing and seeing that is begun in the opening action. Granted that the loss of trust leads to the destruction of the relationships on which the survival of private and communal man depends: what are the means by which a man may restore or recover what he has destroyed? Men of winter, seasoned in the duplicity and depravity of the world, have good cause to be disillusioned and suspicious and must prove that they are able to trust and to love. Confronted by ambiguous appearances, overt deception, and their own fallibility, they must prove their belief in man's capacity for good by forgiving the lapses of others.

Trust and forgiveness, then, are what the renewing action demands of the men of winter as they confront a world of ambiguity and open deception. Conscious of their own errant ways and always vulnerable to hereditary guilt, they perceive the present in the light of the past; and the shape of the future depends upon the choices they make.

The future depends also upon the children—a fact that commentary on the play has not adequately taken into account. Florizel and Perdita must resolve the ambiguity surrounding their affections. They inherit from their fathers a dual legacy, a noble name and hereditary guilt. The quality of their affections must be confirmed by time: the way in which they use present time will determine which inheritance from the past will shape the future.

With these generalizations in mind we may proceed to examine the renewing action.

The crucial scene, in which the love of Florizel and Flora is confirmed as generative and which draws together the two halves of the play, is the festival scene. Within the play's structure of recurring occasion it repeats in the lives of Florizel and Perdita that interval of time when Polixenes and Leontes met the women they eventually married and thus discovered "stronger blood" and hereditary guilt. It is a return, as well, to the concerns that have dominated the nearly tragic story of Leontes' affections—truth and seeming, honesty and trust, and the renewing or destructive potentialities of "stronger blood."

Those who have written about the scene have misread it. They have assumed that Perdita's and Florizel's love is naively genuine and honorable, perhaps because they have been predisposed by the pastoral setting to take for granted the innocence and purity of rural Bohemia's inhabitants, or because they have assumed, along with G. Wilson Knight and E. M. W. Tillyard, that the sheepshearing festival is simply a ritualistic celebration of the renewing power of "great creating Nature" presided over by a Perdita who is symbolic of the goddess and her creative powers.[14] Neither view comes close to the truth.

The festival is indeed a celebration of natural renewal, but Perdita is no goddess. In fact, her refusal even to pretend that she is is a matter of the greatest importance. Nor is rural Bohemia a place of pastoral innocence. It is as much a part of the fallen world as the locale in which Leontes and Polixenes as boys lived innocently and ignorant of time. It is inhabited by rustics who have not been corrupted by the specific affectations and follies of court; nevertheless it shares tempestuous as well as calm weather with the rest of the world, and its inhabitants, temporary or permanent, must reckon with time and fallen human nature. Subject to tempests and the maraudings of savage beasts, it is also a place where between the ages of "ten and three-and-twenty" there is nothing but "getting wenches with child, wronging the ancientry, stealing, [and] fighting" (III.iii.59-63).

It is Autolycus who, at the outset of the renewing action, initially alerts us to the presence in rural Bohemia of folly, deception, lawlessness, and unrestrained passion. He will continue throughout the festival scene to remind us of man's vulnerability and fallen nature and to keep us aware of the ambiguities that are present. His opening song serves not only, as Bethell has noticed, "to bring the ideal world of romance into unmistakable relation with contemporary life, even in its least savory aspects," but also to bring pastoral Bohemia into unmistakable relation with the courtly world of Sicilia and the activities in that world that have been depicted in the play's first three acts.[15] The opening stanzas, a celebration of "doxies" and "aunts," are a reminder that the "red blood" that "reigns in the winter's pale" and is a source of renewal may also be only the quickening of erotic affection. Succeeding stanzas identify him as an outlaw. Once a part of the social order as a servingman to Prince Florizel, he is now "out of service," and, like Falstaff, one of the "moon's men":

> The pale moon shines by night;
> And when I wander here and there,
> I then do most go right.
>
> (IV.iii.16-18)

Subsequent events bear out the fact that Autolycus makes a virtue of inconstancy, practicing expedience as deftly as he changes disguises. In the amusing episode which Knight identifies as a parody of the parable of the Good Samaritan,[16] he easily dupes the Clown by pretending he has been robbed and beaten and by picking the Clown's pocket at the very moment his victim is helping him to his feet. He is an extemporizing opportunist who accommodates himself to the circumstances of the moment and who proves eventually to be time's and fortune's fool. A celebrant of unrestrained sensuality who lives outside the law and uses his wits to deceive, he is a reminder to the audience of the presence in pastoral Bohemia of sensuality unredeemed and of wit devoted to deception and selfish ends.

To recognize that rural Bohemia is not the never-never land of pastoral innocence is to realize that Perdita and Florizel are as vulnerable to "stronger blood" as the rest of Bohemia's inhabitants. Perdita, as Polixenes initially fears, may be angling for a prince; Florizel may be seeking only a tumble in the hay. The quality of love remains unknown even to lovers until it is revealed by the trials of time and adversity. The sheepshearing festival, rather than being a simple folk celebration of nature's bountiful fertility, is the occasion of the trials which test and confirm the authenticity of Perdita's and Florizel's love. It offers two kinds of trial: the temptations presented by festival time when folly has the license of custom and the celebrants under a lord of misrule "let the world slip";[17] and the impediments and threats of tempestuous time which threaten to destroy love by forcing the lovers to abandon their ship to the winds of fortune. During festival time, which reigns in the scene until the stormy Polixenes discloses his identity, Perdita will prove to Camillo and perhaps even to the suspicious Polixenes that her love is not self-seeking. Florizel's affections, on the other hand, remain ambiguous, and in fact the strongest test of Perdita's, during the reign of festival time. They will not be definitively tested until festival time has given way to tempestuous time and he faces first the alternatives presented him by his angry father and then the alternatives of entrusting his ship to chance or to the sagacious pilot Camillo.

The scene's opening episode, in which Florizel repeatedly urges

Perdita to forget the obstacles the everyday world presents their love and to enjoy her role as Flora, begins the testing of Perdita and at the same time raises doubts about her lover's motives. Is his love honorable as he believes and repeatedly affirms? Or is it an instance of the sensuality which Autolycus had celebrated in his song? Time, the Tryer and Revealer, will eventually tell. Florizel's opening speech indicates his readiness to let the world slip and accept Perdita in the role in which the holiday has apparently cast her:

> These your unusual weeds to each part of you
> [Do] give a life; no shepherdess, but Flora,
> Peering in April's front. This your sheep-shearing
> Is as a meeting of the petty gods,
> And you the queen on't.   (IV.iv.1-5)

Perdita, on the other hand, is reluctant in spite of the license that has been always accorded by holiday custom. She is disturbed by her violation of decorum in donning "unusual weeds" and appearing "most goddess-like pranked up," and is equally concerned about Florizel:

>   Even now I tremble
> To think your father, by some accident,
> Should pass this way as you did. O, the Fates!
> How would he look to see his work, so noble,
> Vilely bound up? What would he say? Or how
> Should I, in these my borrowed flaunts, behold
> The sternness of his presence?   (IV.iv.18-24)

She resists her lover's persuasions; even in the face of his repeated request that she enter and enjoy the world of illusion she insists upon remembering who she is—"a simple lowly maid" whose love faces insurmountable obstacles in the real world. She may wear the robes of Flora, but she refuses to assume the goddess's identity. Her refusal is initial proof of the innocence and integrity of her love.

Florizel's own readiness to forget the everyday world and his urging of Perdita to "Apprehend/Nothing but jollity" (IV.iv.24-25), raise doubt about the innocence of his intentions. The doubt is strengthened by the analogies he draws between himself and the several gods who, "Humbling their deities to love, have taken / The shapes of beasts upon them" (IV.iv.26-27). It is true that having listed those deities he avows that his own "humbling" transformation is for reasons that are chaste:

> Their transformations
> Were never for a piece of beauty rarer,
> Nor in a way so chaste, since my desires
> Run not before mine honour, nor my lusts
> Burn hotter than my faith. (IV.iv.31-35)

Nevertheless, the suggestion that he would seize upon holiday folly in the interest of "stronger blood" has been made. He has admitted that his desires "run" and that his lusts "burn," and subsequent allusions throughout the scene keep the suggestion alive. At the very least, his readiness to forget the real world and his repeated coaxing of Perdita to do likewise detract from the vow of constancy that he presently makes. Present mirth seems of greater concern to him than the problems that Perdita refuses to dismiss.

In returning to those problems Perdita shifts her concern—from Polixenes' response as a father to Florizel's courtship, to his response as king:

> O, but, sir,
> Your resolution cannot hold when 'tis
> Oppos'd, as it must be, by th' power of the King.
> One of these two must be necessities,
> Which then will speak that you must change this purpose,
> Or I my life. (IV.iv.35-40)

The "necessities" to which she alludes have not been made explicit, but they are clear. Florizel has resolved to love her chastely, honorably, and faithfully; but his resolution will be unalterably opposed by the king. Therefore Florizel will have to give up his resolution, by giving up his love or by pursuing it unchastely; or else Perdita will have somehow to "change" her life. Again Florizel's response detracts from the reassurances he offers. He continues to be more concerned with festive time than with real time:

> Thou dearest Perdita,
> With these forc'd thoughts, I prithee, darken not
> The mirth o' th' feast. Or I'll be thine, my fair,
> Or not my father's; for I cannot be
> Mine own, nor anything to any, if
> I be not thine. To this I am most constant,
> Though destiny say no. Be merry, gentle!
> Strangle such thoughts as these with anything
> That you behold the while. Your guests are coming.
> Lift up your countenance, as it were the day
> Of celebration of that nuptial which
> We two have sworn shall come.   (IV.iv.40-51)

The day is not their marriage day and no amount of pretending will make it so. The point to be made is not that Florizel is deliberately attempting to seduce Perdita, or that his vows are not seriously offered. It is, rather, that not even lovers can speak with certainty about their feelings. Since amorous passion in Shakespeare's view is inseparable from love, love can only be distinguished from physical longing by the way in which it meets impediments. It can only be confirmed, therefore, retrospectively—by observing the constancy with which it has endured time and adversity. Its future, as Leontes' and Posthumus' sudden loss of trust reminds us, is precarious and unpredictable. Florizel has made vows which he sincerely intends to keep, but Perdita has confirmed her love through action. Her refusal to surrender to holiday folly confirms that she is not, as Polixenes fears, an angler for his son's affections. At the same time it saves Florizel from the consequences into which his ardor might have led them both, had it received the kind of encouragement he has been seeking.

The events following, in which Perdita finally does participate in the festival by assuming her filial duties as hostess and "mistress of the feast" and welcoming her guests, prove further the quality of her affections. The role she assumes—the point is crucial to an understanding of what next occurs—is neither the one pressed on her by Florizel nor precisely the one urged by the Shepherd. Florizel had appealed to the licensed folly of the festival and urged her to be Flora. The Shepherd appeals to familial duty and social custom:

Fie, daughter! when my old wife liv'd, upon
This day she was both pantler, butler, cook,
Both dame and servant; welcom'd all, serv'd all;
Would sing her song and dance her turn; now here,
At upper end o' th' table, now i' th' middle;
On his shoulder, and his; her face o' fire
With labour; and the thing she took to quench it,
She would to each one sip. You are retir'd,
As if you were a feasted one and not
The hostess of the meeting. Pray you, bid
These unknown friends to 's welcome, for it is
A way to make us better friends, more known.
Come, quench your blushes, and present yourself
That which you are, mistress o' th' feast. Come on,
And bid us welcome to your sheep-shearing,
As your good flock shall prosper.   (IV.iv.55-70)

She accepts her duties as mistress in her father's house and, still
wearing the "borrowed flaunts" of Flora, proceeds to greet the
guests; but the manner of her greeting is entirely her own—a confirmation of her innocence and noble birth. Nothing she does even so
much as hints of the wholesome but country manners of the Shepherd's wife; and while she proceeds with the flower ceremony as
Flora, she remains ironically aware of the incongruous role that she
has assumed. She, a maiden whose love may never bear fruit, is cast
in the role of Flora, a goddess of fertility, and must celebrate the
renewing and creative powers of nature. Her awareness of these
incongruities prevents folly from winning the day.

Under Perdita's direction a folk ritual customarly associated with
sensual license is transformed into a graceful and witty lamentation
of a love condemned by circumstances of birth to barren virginity
and sorrow. Autolycus, who at the close of the flower ceremony will
enter to burlesque the action just completed,[18] has greeted spring
with a song praising the "red blood" that "reigns in the winter's
pale." Now Perdita greets Camillo and Polixenes in the early winter
or late autumn of their lives with rosemary and rue, herbs associated
with remembrance and grace. Rather than promising renewal with

the advent of spring, they preserve and sustain through winter only the lingering scent, the memory, of summer's fullness. Such nostalgic offerings are not in keeping with a festival celebrating the arrival of spring and the renewal of life, but they are all that a maiden whose own love cannot be consummated may offer. When Polixenes responds in lines that reflect surprise at being greeted so unconventionally by Flora, she acknowledges that gillyflowers and carnations would be more suitable:

> Sir, the year growing ancient,
> Not yet on summer's death, nor on the birth
> Of trembling winter, the fairest flowers o' th' season
> Are our carnations and streak'd [gillyflowers].
>
> (IV.iv.79-82)

They would represent symbolically the renewal of life within the seasonal cycle and, by implication, renewal within the cycle of the lives of her aging guests. Flourishing before "summer's death" and the "trembling" winter's birth, they would sustain the continuum of organic process and promise to men in their late autumn continuation of the "lines of life." The notion alluded to here occurs in the marriage sonnets. A father who is on the threshold of "trembling winter" finds comfort in his fair issue, in whom he will continue to live after death. But carnations and gillyflowers are "by some called Nature's bastards," and appropriately so in Perdita's view:

> Of that kind
> Our rustic garden 's barren; and I care not
> To get slips of them.   (IV.iv.83-85)

Her disapproval seems prudish, or at best naïve, until we remember that she continues to speak metaphorically as Perdita and not as Flora. From the beginning of the scene she has refused to "strangle" such thoughts as may "darken" the "mirth of the feast"; and now, still reflecting on the problems she faces as a low-born rustic who is in love with a prince, she adopts the same metaphor that Shakespeare had used in Sonnet 16

Now stand you on the top of happy hours,
And many maiden gardens, yet unset,
With virtuous wish would bear your living flowers,
Much liker than your painted counterfeit

(ll.5-8)

to affirm that she will not bear illegitimate children into the world.

Once we perceive the kind of garden and planting to which she is actually alluding, the difficulties presented by the next stage of her debate with Polixenes, which have proved so troublesome to the commentators, disappear. Seizing upon Perdita's refusal to plant carnations and gillyflowers as an opportunity to test her determination not to breed bastards, Polixenes provides her with what seems to be a perfectly rational justification for her having children by Florizel.

> *Polixenes:*   Wherefore, gentle maiden,
> Do you neglect them?
> *Perdita:*   For I have heard it said
> There is an art which in their piedness shares
> With great creating Nature.
> *Polixenes:*   Say there be;
> Yet Nature is made better by no mean
> But Nature makes that mean; so, over that art
> Which you say adds to Nature, is an art
> That Nature makes. You see, sweet maid, we marry
> A gentler scion to the wildest stock,
> And make conceive a bark of baser kind
> By bud of nobler race. This is an art
> Which does mend Nature, change it rather, but
> The art itself is Nature.
> *Perdita:*   So it is.
> *Polixenes:* Then make [your] garden rich in gillyflowers,
> And do not call them bastards.
> *Perdita:*   I'll not put
> The dibble in earth to set one slip of them;
> No more than were I painted I would wish
> This youth should say 'twere well, and only therefore
> Desire to breed by me.   (IV.iv.85-103)

She accepts the argument that nature provides the art by which nature is mended and changed, but she rejects Polixenes' final suggestion because she is thinking of her own "maiden garden." What may be natural in the breeding of flowers is unnatural in the breeding of men. A gardener may nurture nature, changing the appearance of a flower by marrying "a gentler scion to the wildest stock"; but maidens' gardens are subject to higher laws, and the art which alters the appearance of a flower by actually changing its nature can only change human appearances. It cannot alter human nature, and therefore, though natural when used to alter a flower's appearance, it is unnatural when used to change human appearance.

As the scene progresses Perdita continues to exploit the role of Flora to comment ironically on her own predicament. "The marigold, that goes to bed wi' th' sun / And with him rises weeping" (IV.iv.105-06) with which she greets her middle-aged guests probably alludes to the sorrows attendant upon the physical satisfaction of unsanctioned love. Polixenes' son has earlier identified himself with the sun. Her reply to Camillo's admiring response,

> I should leave grazing, were I of your flock,
> And live only by gazing.   (IV.iv.109-10)

is also expressive of ironic self-awareness. Camillo's response is an endorsement of Perdita. He has accompanied Polixenes to the festival to find out something about the rustic maiden who seems to have lured Florizel away from court. He has just heard her reject an argument which she might have used to justify her eloping with Florizel if her interest in the prince were self-seeking. Camillo is impressed and says so; but Perdita is no more interested in neo-Platonic adulation, of the sort advanced by Bembo in *The Courtier* in defense of the superiority of aging lovers, than she is in the grossly sensual love with which Flora had become associated in sixteenth-century England. Barren in its other-worldliness, Platonic love offers Camillo no means of enduring his approaching season of winter:

> Out, alas!
> You'd be so lean, that blasts of January
> Would blow you through and through.
>
> (IV.iv.110-12)

Up to this point in the ceremony Perdita has observed an order and decorum. She has greeted the oldest of her father's guests first, honoring the "ancientry," and then she has proceeded to welcome those of middle age. She has provided both groups with the most appropriate herbs and flowers that she has to offer. Now when she turns to Florizel and the other youthful guests, she is unable to complete the flower ritual: she lacks any flowers that might be even roughly appropriate to their spring:

> Now, my fair'st friend,
> I would I had some flowers o' th' spring that might
> Become your time of day; and yours, and yours,
> That wear upon your virgin branches yet
> Your maidenheads growing.   (IV.iv.112-16)

Flowers designating innocence remain her concern here; and as the passage progresses it becomes a personal lamentation of unfulfilled womanhood:

> O Proserpina,
> For the flowers now, that frighted thou let'st fall
> From Dis's waggon! daffodils,
> That come before the swallow dares, and take
> The winds of March with beauty; violets dim,
> But sweeter than the lids of Juno's eyes
> Or Cytherea's breath; pale primroses,
> That die unmarried, ere they can behold
> Bright Phoebus in his strength—a malady
> Most incident to maids; bold oxlips and
> The crown imperial; lilies of all kinds,
> The flower-de-luce being one!   (IV.iv.116-27)

Her emphasis is upon the fragility and beauty of life, upon flowers that do not outlast the spring and which are therefore no more indicative to her of hope than rosemary and rue. The reference to the primroses "That die unmarried, ere they can behold/Bright Phoebus in his strength" almost certainly alludes to the speech in which Florizel had likened himself to "Golden Apollo." Thus Perdita is lamenting that she shall die unwed before she beholds Florizel in his full strength as king.

When Perdita turns finally to Florizel, she concludes the ceremony with a complaint that indicates how completely the ritual of renewal has, from her point of view, broken down:

> O, these I lack,
> To make you garlands of, and my sweet friend,
> To strew him o'er and o'er! (IV.iv.127-29)

For men of winter she had at least been able to provide herbs that preserved the memory of life. Her garden contains no flowers suitable to men of autumn, but after pausing to explain their absence, she had gone on to greet her middle-aged guests. But now she is unable to proceed further. The lack of spring flowers makes it impossible for her even to lament the barren virginity the future holds for her. Her springtime appears to her to be as barren and unpromising as her garden. Time as renewer and restorer seems frustrated, and Perdita concludes the ritual with a reference to death. She lacks even the flowers suitable for a garland "to strew . . . o'er and o'er" her "sweet friend."

What follows is climactic. Florizel picks up the reference by asking, "What, like a corse?" (IV.iv.129), and Perdita replies, introducing the only alternative to barren virginity and death:

> No, like a bank for love to lie and play on;
> Not like a corse; or if, not to be buried,
> But quick and in mine arms. (IV.iv.130-32)

Since Autolycus' entrance in IV.ii., the promiscuous impulses of the red blood that quickens in the spring have been present in rural Bohemia. It has been Florizel who, by proclaiming so insistently the purity of his motives and by his coaxing of Perdita to enjoy festival time, has kept the audience aware of them. Now for the first and only time in the scene she seems to be on the verge of forgetting herself—of allowing herself the license of misrule that Flora is allowed by festive custom. For an instant she forgets that she is "mistress of the feast" and becomes Flora, ready to lie on a flower-strewn bank with her lover. But her awareness of self returns and she observes:

> Methinks I play as I have seen them do
> In Whitsun pastorals. Sure this robe of mine
> Does change my disposition. (IV.iv.133-35)

At this moment when Perdita completes her ritualistic celebration of the seasonal cycle and confronts the only alternatives that future time appears to allow, either barren virginity or promiscuous love— at this break in time—Florizel responds with an expression of adoration that is "formulated," as Eubank has noticed, "as a desire to arrest time, to achieve permanence outside the flux of time."[19] Although the quality of his admiration seems to correspond generally with that earlier expressed by Camillo, the response it elicits from Perdita alerts us to an intention that was not present in Camillo's praise:

> O Doricles,
> Your praises are too large. But that your youth,
> And the true blood which peeps [so] fairly through't,
> Do plainly give you out an unstain'd shepherd,
> With wisdom I might fear, my Doricles,
> You woo'd me the false way. (IV.iv.146-51)

Her suspicion that Florizel's praises may be persuasions to seduction suggests that she has recovered her composure, but the grounds on which she dismisses that possibility indicates that her recovery may not be complete. She may remember that she is not Flora, but she assumes all too easily that appearances are sufficient proof of Florizel's integrity, that things are indeed what they seem.

Perdita's own innocence and purity make her peculiarly vulnerable to the appearance of innocence and purity. There is no mistaking the irony of the evidence from which she concludes that her lover's wooing is honest. It depends upon ambiguities that are central to the scene and in fact to the entire play: "youth/And the true blood which peeps so fairly through't" are not proof of innocence. The "blood" which appears in Florizel's face may indeed be the "true blood" of nobility, but it may also be the "red blood" of sensuality celebrated by Autolycus in his song, tainted, as Polixenes and Leontes discovered when they fell in love, by hereditary guilt. The quality of Florizel's love will not be settled by his own proclamations of honorable intentions, nor by his seeming to be an unstained shepherd. It remains to be tested by the impediments it faces in real time.

The question raised concerning the "true blood" that Perdita accepts so easily as proof of her lover's innocence is kept alive by the Shepherd's remarks to Polixenes as they stand together watching the dance of the shepherds and shepherdesses. The possibility that Florizel, despite his vow, is under the sway of the "stronger blood" of affection is manifest in the metaphor the Shepherd innocently chooses as a means of describing Florizel's devotion to Perdita. His opening lines echo Perdita's lines about "true blood." He, too, believes Florizel and finds proof of his claim of "worthy feeding" in his appearance:

> They call him Doricles; and boasts himself
> To have a worthy feeding; but I have it
> Upon his own report, and I believe it.
> He looks like sooth. (IV.iv.168-71)

He also believes Florizel's claim that he loves Perdita:

> for never gaz'd the moon
> Upon the water as he'll stand and read,
> As 'twere, my daughter's eyes; . . . (IV.iv.172-74)

The comparison seems innocent enough; but the moon is often associated with inconstancy and lawlessness—Falstaff and Autolycus are both moon's men and Juliet urges Romeo to "swear not by the moon"—and those connotations of inconstancy cannot be avoided here. The allusion occurs in a context which has consistently pointed up the possibility that Florizel's ardor is neither what he himself may believe it to be nor what it appears to be to others. The allusion makes its own contribution to that possibility.

The Shepherd continues to be Shakespeare's unwitting instrument of irony when he replies to Polixenes' "She dances featly," with

> So she does anything, though I report it,
> That should be silent. If young Doricles
> Do light upon her, she shall bring him that
> Which he not dreams of. (IV.iv.177-80)

His intended meaning is obvious enough: if Doricles chooses her to be his wife, he will be astonished by her grace and accomplishments. He is also surely thinking of the chest and the proof of gentle birth which he has kept a secret for sixteen years; but the context suggests another meaning of which the audience, from the advantage of its perspective, cannot but be aware: if Doricles *lights* on her, he will find her a partner in love who will bring him pleasures he "not dreams of."

Besides keeping alive in the minds of the audience a truth about appearances that is central to the entire play, the Shepherd's unintentionally ambiguous remarks to Polixenes beautifully prepare for events to come. They serve to feed Polixenes' suspicion about the antics of his son and the low-born maiden he is courting in the same way that Hermione's innocent remarks years earlier had made Leontes vulnerable to affection. They also prepare for the entrance Autolycus will presently make. Innocence and integrity have dominated the festival up to that point in the action when Perdita accepts "youth" and "true blood" as proof that Florizel is "an unstain'd shepherd." Now at the moment when sensuality and deception may have gained the advantage, the entrance of Autolycus, master of deception and exploiter of unsanctioned sensuality, is announced.

His role as Perdita's foil is unmistakable.[20] Perdita had greeted her guests with herbs and flowers that were suited to their ages and appropriate to the ceremony as she chooses to direct it. Autolycus, an outlaw disguised as a peddler, has "songs for man or woman, of all sizes"; in fact, "no milliner can so fit his customers with gloves" (IV.iv.191-93). His wares include obscene songs and trinkets as enticements to seduction. Whereas Perdita had refused to allow Flora's robes to change her disposition and made a point of refusing to deceive, Autolycus exploits his disguise to line his own purse by selling his wares and by cutting the purses of others. The songs and trinkets he offers for sale are aids to seduction, either as means of buying pleasures or as ways of making physical appearances more enticing. In the latter respect they are similar in kind and effect to the painting of the face earlier rejected by Perdita. Autolycus' art is, in short, devoted to the exploitation of folly, personal and festive. It is devoted to the artful manipulation of appearances to deceive the mind and appeal to lust. It is only appropriate, therefore, that if Perdita's flower giving should end with a dance of real shepherds and shepherdesses, then Autolycus' reign of misrule should conclude with a rough and lively dance by twelve rustics made up as satyrs.

The parallel between the Perdita and Autolycus episodes is completed by the brief dialogue between Polixenes and his son that takes place during the dance of the satyrs. Its content contrasts sharply with the dialogue between Polixenes and the Shepherd that had taken place during the dance of shepherds and shepherdesses. The burden of the earlier dialogue had been the Shepherd's conviction that Florizel's devotion to Perdita is honorable. He has trusted appearances and, along with Perdita, accepted Florizel at his word; innocence had dominated his mind as it had seemed to dominate the stage in the dance they watch. Now, however, it is sensuality that seems to dominate, both on the stage in the dance of the satyrs and in Polixenes' mind. He wonders why Doricles has not "ransack'd the pedlar's silken treasury" (IV.iv.359-60); Florizel's reply, a confident affirmation hinting at princely gifts he has already promised her, seems to confirm his belief that things are "too far gone" (IV. iv.354):

> O, hear me breathe my life
> Before this ancient sir, [who], it should seem,
> Hath sometime lov'd! I take thy hand, this hand,
> As soft as dove's down and as white as it,
> Or Ethiopian's tooth, or the fann'd snow that's bolted
> By the northern blasts twice o'er.   (IV.iv.370-75)

In the completion of the parallel between the Perdita and Autolycus episodes the depiction of nature as represented by rural Bohemia is completed. It is dominated by contraries—lawlessness and order, folly and reason, honesty and deception, "true blood" and "stronger blood," love and eroticism, trust and suspicion. Its inhabitants are not in any sense unique. Furthermore, in Bohemia as in the rest of the world, innocence and purity can be finally verified only by action. Perdita's honesty has been borne out by her actions as hostess of the festival; but about Florizel's love there is still a tinge of doubt. The constancy of his vow to marry Perdita will be confirmed by the way he meets the adversity that time will presently bring when Polixenes throws off his disguise and brings an end to festive time.

With the completion of the parallel between the Perdita and Autolycus episodes another correspondence begins to emerge. A temporal pattern is repeating itself: the violent affections of a father and a king again disrupt a serene and happy time. Leontes' affection was provoked when he was asked to remember the time of his own youthful love. Now Florizel begs Polixenes to remember how he felt when he was young and in love—

> O, hear me breathe my life
> Before this ancient sir, [who], it should seem,
> Hath sometime lov'd!— (IV.iv.370-72)

and then he takes Perdita's hand, just as Polixenes had taken Hermione's the moment before Leontes had been overcome by jealousy. Polixenes appears to be persuaded by his son's proclamation of love and perhaps even ready to give his approval. As he proceeds to ask Florizel about his father, it seems that all Florizel need do to receive his father's approval is to agree to confide in him. What finally enrages Polixenes is Florizel's refusal even to explain why he will not take his father into his confidence. It is an admission of his intent to deceive and of his lack of trust.

Whether the destructive pattern acted out sixteen years earlier in Sicilia will now be repeated in Bohemia depends upon whether folly or trust and reason prevail during the tempestuous time of Polixenes' rage and Florizel's desperation. This brings us to the second test that the lovers face on the day of sheepshearing.

Perdita has presided over festive time. By controlling and using it, rather than surrendering to it, she has confirmed the integrity of her love and proved her noble birth. She has also prevented affection from seeking the sensual excesses to which Florizel's ardor, left unchecked, might have carried it. During her rule over time, innocence and noble blood have prevailed. Now, when the stormy rage of Polixenes has put an abrupt end to festive time, and the lovers face the realities which Florizel had been so anxious to ignore, the future rests with Florizel. He must prove in the face of tempestuous time not only that he is constant in his love for Perdita, but also that he is able to trust a man of winter and listen to reason.

As I have pointed out in the opening chapter of this study, Florizel's choice is emblematically depicted. He may surrender his future to Fortuna by allowing his desperate feelings to direct his course on a tempest-tossed sea; or he may entrust it to the sagacious Camillo, who now steps forward to assume the same role he had undertaken sixteen years earlier. Unable on that earlier occasion to deal effectively with Leontes' madness, Camillo had gone to Polixenes, asking him to trust in him:

> If therefore you dare trust my honesty,
> That lies enclosed in this trunk which you
> Shall bear along impawn'd, away to-night!
>
> (I.ii.434-36)

Polixenes chose fortunately to believe Camillo's story and placed his future in his hands:

> I do believe thee;
> I saw his heart in 's face. Give me thy hand.
> Be pilot to me, . . . (I.ii.446-48)

Now Camillo again faces the problem of dealing with passion's folly, the fury of a father and the despair of a young lover. Leaving Polixenes' anger to spend itself, he turns his attention to the lovers.

His situation is similar to Friar Laurence's when Romeo, facing exile for his slaying of Tybalt, threatens suicide. Florizel's reaction to his father's anger is nearly as desperate. It may, like Romeo's, be proof of his devotion, but its reckless indifference to the consequences it invites can lead only to catastrophe. That it threatens destruction rather than generation is clear from the language in which it is expressed:

> Let Nature crush the sides o' th' earth together
> And mar the seeds within! Lift up thy looks.
> From my succession wipe me, father; I
> Am heir to my affection. (IV.iv.488-91)

To surrender to affection is, in the language of the navigational emblem, to surrender to Fortune and the winds of chance. Somehow, Camillo must get Florizel to entrust the helm to him; and when all else fails and Florizel announces that he will "let myself and Fortune/Tug for the time to come" (IV.iv.506-07), the old counsellor is forced to extreme measures. Friar Laurence, with a potential suicide on his hands, offers Romeo the hope of reunion with Juliet in the strategem of the sleeping potion. Camillo, too, is driven by a lover's desperation to chart a course of deception and duplicity. Since Florizel refuses to wait for his father to calm down, and since he is determined to marry Perdita, Camillo suggests that the lovers marry while he endeavors to persuade Polixenes to accept his new daughter.

Following Florizel's tacit acceptance of his proposal, Camillo must persuade him to accept the course he has charted. The course he proposes offers Florizel a means of reconciliation with his father and fulfillment, therefore, of his love without forfeiting his duties as son and heir-apparent. Although it is risky—its success depends upon the readiness of men of winter to remember, to repent, and to forgive—it is

> A course more promising
> Than a wild dedication of yourselves
> To unpath'd waters, undream'd shores, most certain
> To miseries enough; . . . (IV.iv.575-78)

Florizel's acceptance of Camillo's plan proves not only that he is willing to listen to reason, but also that he is now ready to trust in the benevolence of men of winter. His testing is now complete. From this point on in the action he is a passive agent. His future is entirely in the hands of those in whom he has placed his trust.

Although trust and reason win an important victory over folly when Camillo succeeds in gaining Florizel's trust, folly remains active in Bohemia in the wrathful Polixenes and the conniving Autolycus—and in fact will win a temporary victory over the Shepherd and his son in the scene's final episode. But trust and reason enjoy the advantage in the main action. Folly's first defeat came at the hands of Perdita when she insisted upon presiding over the flower ceremony as mistress in her father's house rather than as Flora. Now when innocence is no longer able to hold off folly and both Polixenes and Florizel have succumbed to passion, reason in the person of Camillo comes forward.

Camillo's victory is driven home by the dramatic metaphor he uses to describe the role he has assumed. Responding to Florizel's expression of concern over the fact that he is not suitably attired to appear in Sicilia "like Bohemia's son," Camillo says:

> It shall be so my care
> To have you royally appointed as if
> The scene you play were mine. (IV.iv.601-03)

From this point on both Florizel and Perdita play roles in the action designed by Camillo. He dresses Autolycus in Florizel's garments, Florizel (temporarily) in Autolycus', and persuades Perdita to disguise herself. Even Autolycus in his new garments, quite against his own will and unbeknownst to Camillo, will play a role that contributes to the success of Camillo's plan.

Camillo's play metaphor and the way in which Perdita picks it up —"I see the play so lies/That I must bear a part" (IV.iv.668-69)— point up another dimension of the victory over passion that Camillo's success represents. The scene began with Florizel's "high self . . . obscured with a swain's wearing" and Perdita in "borrow'd robes." Her refusal to forget her identity as a lowly maid proved that she is not selfishly angling for a prince. Now, only because she sees that she has no alternative but to "bear a part" in Camillo's design, she agrees to the ruse of disguise. Disguise, formerly sanctioned by folly and used by Autolycus to deceive for selfish and evil ends, now becomes a means directed by reason to unselfish and honorable ends.

The final episode of the pastoral scene, which begins with Autolycus' entrance while Camillo, Florizel, and Perdita move off to the side and talk among themselves, has been dismissed as a clumsy and "rather heavy piece of machinery" devoted to the purpose "of getting everyone to Sicilia."[21] But grounds for such criticism disappear when Autolycus' continuing role as foil is recognized. He had earlier furnished a contrast for Perdita's innocence by extolling the pleasures of sensuality, and raised a doubt about the quality of Florizel's feelings by his presence in the scene. He now performs a similar function with respect to Camillo. He congratulates himself on his recent success, mocking the values which are at the center of the play: "Ha, ha! what a fool Honesty is! and Trust, his sworn brother, a very simple gentleman!" (IV.iv.605-06). He has exploited rustic folly by selling all of his trumpery, and the enthusiasm with which the peasantry has sought to buy his trinkets has, in turn, allowed him to cut most of their festival purses. Now he finds that time again provides him with an opportunity to serve his own ends.

After exchanging garments with Florizel, he encounters the Clown and the Shepherd worrying over what Polixenes' wrath holds in store for them. The situation parallels exactly the one in which Camillo finds himself after the enraged Polixenes threatens to disinherit Florizel and the young prince determines to surrender himself to affection and chance. On the occasion of Florizel's desperation Camillo had seen a double opportunity:

> He's irremoveable,
> Resolv'd for flight. Now were I happy, if
> His going I could frame to serve my turn,
> Save him from danger, do him love and honour,
> Purchase the sight again of dear Sicilia
> And that unhappy king, my master, whom
> I so much thirst to see.   (IV.iv.517-23)

Autolycus, too, finds that he has been given a double opportunity which, like Camillo's, allows him to serve both himself and his "master":

> If I had a mind to be honest, I see Fortune would not suffer me; she drops booties in my mouth. I am courted now with a double occasion, gold and a means to do the Prince my master good; which who knows how that may turn back to my advancement? (IV.iv.861-66)

The significance of the parallel is clear. Camillo, motivated by a desire to help the young lovers as well as by his own desire to return to Sicilia, has set about to gain Florizel's trust by reminding him of his own years of honest service to Polixenes. Having won Florizel's trust, he put his skill to work to dissuade the Prince and Perdita from putting to sea without a pilot. He has used time well. Autolycus, on the other hand, has gained the trust of the rustics by appealing to appearance. He wears the clothes of a gentleman. He has exploited the folly of the natural fool, the Clown, and he has deceived the simple Shepherd. An extemporizer and opportunist from the beginning, he has seized occasion as self-serving opportunity. His motives are selfish; Camillo's are benevolent.

But there is more to Autolycus' role. In seeking to use time to his own advantage he unwittingly becomes an instrument of renewing time. Commenting on his good fortune in being forced to change clothes with Florizel, he commits himself to the very forces from which Camillo has just saved the lovers:

> I see this is the time that the unjust man doth thrive. What an exchange had this been without boot! What a boot is here with this exchange! Sure the gods do this year connive at us, and we may do anything extempore. The Prince himself is about a piece of iniquity, stealing away from his father with his clog at his heels. If I thought it were a piece of honesty to acquaint the King withal, I would not do 't. I hold it the more knavery to conceal it; and therein am I constant to my profession. (IV.iv.687-97)

From this point on in the action his own folly makes him Time's Fool; and since Time has been transformed by Camillo, Florizel, and Perdita from Destroyer to Renewer, Autolycus' knavery serves the ends of renewal.

The good fortune Autolycus enjoys in the resolution of the play also underscores the power of regenerative process. When men cooperate with time by using rationally the opportunities it presents, time's renewing energies cannot be thwarted. Now the guilty are caught up in the restorative process just as the innocent had been caught up sixteen years earlier in the destructive. Deception and self-interest now inadvertently produce good, and as a result Autolycus' opportunism carries him to a place within the social order. He had originally served the Prince and worn three-pile; now after living by his wits as an outlaw, he is given the opportunity to wear the clothes of a gentleman, to serve the Prince, and, finally, to join the human community both as gentleman and as kinsman.

The success of Camillo's plan, however, depends upon a good deal more than Autolycus' efforts as Time's Fool. Final reconciliation will be achieved only after men of winter, and especially Leontes, prove their readiness to trust and forgive. The testing of Leontes gets underway immediately in the opening scene of the final act. That scene, by raising the issue of Sicilia's lack of an heir apparent, goes directly to one of the play's principal concerns, the preservation of "the lines of life." The issue facing Leontes is whether or not to marry in order to provide himself and Sicilia with an heir.

The issue is presented in terms of what ought to be remembered and what forgotten. Cleomenes urges Leontes to appreciate the fact that his "saint-like" penitence has been more than sufficient to assure his redemption and that he should now

> At the last
> Do as the heavens have done, forget your evil;
> With them forgive yourself. (V.i.4-6)

Having satisfied the heavens, he should now turn his attention to the serious problem his lack of a successor will pose for future time, and thus use the opportunity afforded by present time to marry and beget a child. In terms of remembering, Leontes expresses his reluctance to accept Cleomenes' advice:

> Whilst I remember
> Her and her virtues, I cannot forget
> My blemishes in them, and so still think of
> The wrong I did myself; which was so much

That heirless it hath made my kingdom, and
Destroy'd the sweet'st companion that e'er man
Bred his hopes out of.   (V.i.6-12)

Paulina opposes Cleomenes' argument by urging Leontes to remember Hermione with a particularity that calls to mind the instructions in the Ignatian exercises on how to meditate on the crucified Christ. Her purpose, too, is similar: by remembering Hermione and the cruel suffering he caused her, Leontes continues to experience the contrite sorrow that Cleomenes moments earlier described as "saint-like."

Cleomenes, whose concern is the urgent present and the perilous future, politely advises Paulina that she might "have done the time more benefit" by speaking of "a thousand things" other than Hermione and thus distracting Leontes (V.i.21-22). He is seconded by Dion. "What were more holy," he asks, "Than to rejoice the former queen is well?" (V.i.29-30). Not to consider the dangers attendant upon "fail of issue" is to "pity not the state nor the remembrance/ Of his most sovereign name" (V.i.25-26). Leontes must marry:

What holier than, for royalty's repair,
For present comfort and for future good,
To bless the bed of majesty again
With a sweet fellow to't?   (V.i.31-34)

Marriage is the desirable means of serving "*present* comfort" and "*future* good." Paulina, Dion continues, by urging Leontes to remember Hermione and opposing a new marriage does a disservice to both the state and the king.

Paulina's refutation draws together the acts of remembering Hermione and of obeying the oracle. The latter follows as a consequence of the former. To forget Hermione and marry is to oppose the will of the gods. To remember is to obey and, as Paulina points out, to *trust* that the heavens will provide the crown with an heir.

There is none worthy,
Respecting her that's gone. Besides, the gods
Will have fulfill'd their secret purposes;
For has not the divine Apollo said,

Is't not the tenor of his oracle
That King Leontes shall not have an heir
Till his lost child be found? which that it shall.
Is all as monstrous to our human reason
As my Antigonus to break his grave
And come again to me, who, on my life,
Did perish with the infant. 'Tis your counsel
My lord should to the heavens be contrary,
Oppose against their wills. [*To Leontes*,] Care not for issue;
The crown will find an heir. (V.i.34-37)

In accepting Paulina's argument Leontes meets successfully the test that his well-meaning counsellors have unwittingly presented him. The future seems to require that he marry and beget heirs, but now through the proper exercising of memory he chooses to obey the oracle, entrusting the future to Apollo.

The right use of memory in this scene gains an important dimension when considered in the total context of the action up to this point in the play. As we have seen, memory rightly and wrongly used has been a concern from the beginning of the action. It is one means by which the past may vitally affect the present. Hermione inadvertently provided the tinder for the jealousy which consumed Leontes when she playfully asked him to remember an earlier time when she had spoken to a good purpose. On that occasion memory proved graceless and the source of a mistrust that led eventually to Leontes' flat dismissal of the oracle's proof of Hermione's honesty. When the shock of Mamillius' death brings Leontes to his senses, the subject of memory is again raised. Paulina, in her grief and momentary desire for revenge, urges him to remember so that he may despair:

But, O thou tyrant!
Do not repent these things, for they are heavier
Than all thy woes can stir; therefore betake thee
To nothing but despair. (III.ii.208-11)

Moments later, she urges that he forget—advice no less erroneous than her revengeful recommendation that he remember in order to despair:

> What's gone and what's past help
> Should be past grief. Do not receive affliction
> At my petition; I beseech you, rather
> Let me be punish'd, that have minded you
> Of what you should forget ...
> . . . .
> I'll speak of her no more, nor of your children;
> I'll not remember you of my own lord,
> Who is lost too. (III.ii.223-32)

But Leontes neither forgets nor despairs; his way of remembering proves to be most "saint-like."

The use of memory continues in the fourth act to be crucial to the shaping of future time. In the second scene Polixenes' memory presents an obstacle to reconciliation. Camillo requests that he be given the opportunity to return to Sicilia. Polixenes' response reveals that he has never forgiven Leontes:

> Of that
> fatal country, Sicilia, prithee speak no more; whose very naming pun-
> ishes me with the remembrance of that penitent, as thou call'st him,
> and reconciled king, my brother; whose loss of his most precious
> queen and children are even now to be afresh lamented.
> (IV.ii.21-29)

Reconciliation will depend not upon Polixenes' forgetting past injustices suffered at the hands of Leontes, but upon remembering that he, too, along with all men, is in need of grace and forgiveness.

It is evident, then, that Perdita's greeting of Polixenes and Camillo in the next scene with rue and rosemary for "grace and remembrance" is more appropriate than she can possibly realize. Although at the time she offers them they seem at best pale substitutes for flowers that might symbolize the renewal of life, in the overall context of the play they designate the means by which forgiveness and reconciliation are finally realized. Grace and remembrance restore what "graceless" memory sixteen years earlier very nearly destroyed.[22]

Memory misused presents obstacles to the restorative action of the final two acts by contributing to the wrath which leads Polixenes to threaten Florizel with disinheritance and the Shepherd and Perdita with torture and death. The incident in which this occurs—when Florizel appeals to Polixenes to remember how he felt when he was young and in love—is surely intended as a parallel to the opening episode in which Leontes' recollection of the past provokes jealousy. Men of every generation, the play appears to say, are made vulnerable by the common imperfections of humanity and stand in need of grace and the kind of remembrance that leads to forgiveness.

Given the carefully developed context in which memory as the use of Time Past has been repeatedly identified with the use of Time Present as *occasio* to shape Time Future, Leontes' proper use of memory at the outset of the regenerative action appears to be a deliberately conceived parallel to his abuse of memory at the outset of the nearly tragic action of the first three acts. Whereas his erring memory led him to deny Hermione and his daughter, to deny the honesty of his friends and counselors of state, and eventually the heavens themselves, his right use of memory reverses the process. In remembering Hermione and his own guilt and in rejecting the appeal to "benefit" future time in Sicilia by marrying, he demonstrates his recovered trust in the gods. These acts of grace and remembrance initiate the process which will recover all possible of what was destroyed sixteen years earlier.

The very next episode in V.i. confronts Leontes with another opportunity to exercise proper trust and memory. The occasion he is afforded sustains the pattern of recurrences by presenting him with a situation analogous to the one in which he had fallen a victim to *tremor cordis*. The occasion occurs shortly after Paulina has gotten him to swear never to marry,

>   Unless another,
>   As like Hermione as is her picture,
>   Affront his eye;   (V.i.73-75)

who will not be

>   so young
>   As was your former; but . . . shall be such
>   As, walk'd your first queen's ghost, it should take joy
>   To see her in your arms.   (V.i.78-81)

A servant then enters, announcing the arrival of Florizel and a princess. Before their interview with Leontes is over, each has been identified with a parent and the occasion of the interview with the occasion of Leontes' jealousy in I.ii.

Leontes in greeting Florizel remarks his resemblance to his father:

> Your mother was most true to wedlock, Prince,
> For she did print your royal father off,
> Conceiving you. Were I but twenty-one,
> Your father's image is so hit in you,
> His very air, that I should call you brother,
> As I did him, and speak of something wildly
> By us perform'd before. (V.i.124-30)

The effect that Florizel's likeness to his father has upon Leontes' memory contributes to the process, begun with Paulina's insistence on his remembering Hermione, of reconstructing the past with extraordinary fidelity. In the lines immediately preceding, Paulina had contributed to that reconstruction by identifying Florizel with Mamillius:

>   Had our prince,
> Jewel of children, seen this hour, he had pair'd
> Well with this lord. There was not full a month
> Between their births. (V.i.115-18)

Leontes recognizes Florizel's resemblance to his father, whereas on that earlier occasion he was unable to see his own likeness in Mamillius. Perdita, too, awakens memories:

> And your fair princess,—goddess!—O, alas!
> I lost a couple, that 'twixt heaven and earth
> Might thus have stood begetting wonder as
> You, gracious couple, do; . . . (V.i.131-34)

The reconstruction of the past and the parallel between past and present occasions is briefly interrupted by Florizel's fallacious explanation of why he has come to Sicilia and by Leontes' discovery of the real reasons that have driven him to Sicilia. Florizel abjectly and openly confesses the truth to Leontes and then in a final appeal asks

Perdita to "look up" so that Leontes may understand why he feels so deeply about her.

> Though Fortune, visible an enemy,
> Should chase us with my father, pow'r no jot
> Hath she to change our loves. Beseech you, sir,
> Remember since you ow'd no more to time
> Than I do now. With thought of such affections,
> Step forth mine advocate. At your request
> My father will grant precious things as trifles.
>
> (V.i.216-22)

Leontes' response indicates that he does indeed remember. His affections are deeply moved, but by Perdita's beauty rather than by Florizel's plea. From the moment Florizel has asked her to "look up" Leontes has been gazing upon her in a way that is discomforting to Paulina. When he has responded to Florizel's "At your request/My father will grant precious things as trifles" with "Would he do so,/I'd beg your precious mistress,/Which he counts but a trifle" (V.i. 223-24), Paulina warns him:

> Your eye hath too much youth in't. Not a month
> 'Fore your queen died, she was more worth such gazes
> Than what you look on now.   (V.i.225-27)

The implication is clear. Sensuality flickers in Leontes' eye, and the parallel between the two occasions is all but completed. On that earlier occasion he had been asked to remember his youth, the stirring of "stronger blood," and Hermione's consent after "three crabbed months" to marry him. Now again, when gazing upon Perdita, he remembers Hermione and the feelings she had awakened in him: "I thought of her,/Even in these looks I made" (V.i.227-28). Experiencing something of how Florizel feels, and in spite of his recent discovery of Florizel's deception, he chooses to trust Florizel's avowal that his love is honorable:

> I will to your father.
> Your honour not o'erthrown by your desires,
> I am friend to them and you; . . .   (V.i.229-31)

Time in its revolutions has given Leontes the opportunity to redeem himself for his failure to trust wife and friend on that terrible
occasion in the past. Facing Florizel and Perdita just as he had faced
Polixenes and Hermione years earlier, and being strongly reminded
of that earlier occasion by Paulina's remarks as well as by the lovers'
resemblance to their parents, he is once again urged to remember
his own youth. That initial act of remembering had produced violent
suspicion and distrust. Now from grace and remembrance comes a
readiness to trust even in the face of appearances which suggest dishonesty and deception.

The testing of Leontes is now complete. By remembering and
obeying the oracle to the letter he has confirmed his renewed faith
in the gods. By accepting Florizel at his word he has proved his
readiness to believe in the honesty of youthful love. In each instance
his "saint-like sorrow" has graced remembrance. Now, the truth of
the oracle is about to be confirmed—and in a way which could not
have been foreseen. What seemed initially to be tautological in the
prophecy, "the King shall live without an heir, if that which is lost be
not found," will prove to have been conditional. Having found his
lost faith, he will presently discover his lost heir.

Only one final affirmation of faith will be required of Leontes,
and it will be ceremonial and exemplary rather than critical. He initiated the play's destructive action by losing his faith in Hermione.
That loss of faith led to his mistaking appearance for reality and to
the apparent death of his wife and queen. He will complete the play's
restorative action by an affirmation of faith which not only "resur-
rects" her from apparent death, but which also completes his return
to reality from a solipsistic world of illusion.

The play's final scenes (V.ii., V.iii.), which we are now ready to
consider, are among the most puzzling and least understood in all of
Shakespeare. Both have been severely criticized for their crude, outmoded, and creaking dramaturgy.[23] The exposition in V.ii. through
which Leontes' discovery of Perdita is reported has been widely
criticized and variously defended.[24] The "staginess" of the final
scene has been applauded, puzzled over, and wildly explained.[25] The

question of why Shakespeare deliberately leads the audience to assume that Hermione has been long dead has been raised many times but, so far as I have been able to discover, never successfully answered.

I am convinced that the approach to the play that I have presented in this study leads not only to the resolution of the major difficulties that the critics have always encountered in these scenes, but also to the discovery of some of the most persuasive evidence to be found anywhere in the romances of the soundness of my approach to the play, and to the romances generally. I shall proceed with the consideration of the scenes by demonstrating the thematic contribution made by the Autolycus-Shepherd-Clown episode to the restorative pattern. I shall next consider a final series of correspondences that is completed in the moment of Hermione's return to the world of flesh and feeling—correspondences which in completing the renewing action also complete the recursive structure of the play. I shall then conclude the chapter by demonstrating that the opening expository section of V.ii. and the greater part of the final scene present a fully developed statement of the dramatic theory informing the play itself and of what the play requires, finally, of its audience.

The Autolycus-Shepherd-Clown episode

The dramaturgical purposes of the episode are obvious enough. It tidies up loose ends by disclosing the futures of characters who have played peripheral but necessary roles in the restorative action, and it prepares the audience for the high seriousness of the final scene by providing a brief and amusing interval of "comic relief." What is not so obvious is that it also serves as an exemplum of the trust upon which community depends.

When Autolycus enters, he is still unwittingly playing the role of Time's Fool. Only his appearance has changed. He wears the clothes of a courtier, but to the same purpose he had worn those of a peddler. His presence in Bohemia served to remind the audience that beneath the seeming innocence of pastoral shepherds and shepherdesses there may also be present the unredeemed depravity of hereditary guilt. In his courtier's clothes he serves as a reminder that beneath the appearances of gentility and civility the same depravity is to be reckoned with.

After the reunion of Leontes and Perdita has been reported and the three Gentlemen have left the stage, Autolycus reflects on what for him is a frustrating state of events. The only thing preventing him from receiving preferment is his former life. "Now," he reflects, "had I not the dash of my former life in me, would preferment drop on my head" (V.ii.122-23). Fortune, it seems, has turned against him. If it had not been for the storm at sea, he would have had the credit for disclosing the contents of the fardel. But when "every wink of an eye" sees "some new grace . . . born" (V.ii.119-20), even the unregenerate Autolycus is rewarded. Again Time presents him with an opportunity—in the play's pattern of recurrent occasions—analogous to the one afforded him in the final episode of the pastoral scene. The Shepherd and Clown appear, those two gulls "I have done good to against my will, and already appearing in the blossoms of their fortune" (V.ii.134-36). They have been taken into the communities of family and society, and they now proceed, on the condition that he will "amend" his life, to offer Autolycus the same opportunity that has been given them.

That the Shepherd and his simple-minded son have worn the title and clothes of gentlemen for four hours of course no more makes them gentlemen in fact than the shepherd robes worn by Florizel in his role of Doricles guarantee the honor and innocence of his intentions. Action is the proof of integrity. On the other hand, the two rustics now enjoy a position in the social order which they may fulfill honorably or abuse. Verification will depend on their actions, just as their actions during the preceding sixteen years have verified the simple humanity which the royal family recognizes in embracing them as brother and son.

From what the audience knows of the Shepherd and his son, it will be the Shepherd and not the son who will live up to the new status they now enjoy. The boy as early as IV.ii. has mistaken courtly affectation and folly as evidence of gentlemanly behavior; and as a natural fool there is little chance that he can even begin to distinguish between gentleness and its surface tokens. His opening address to Autolycus is sufficient evidence that he is unable to make the distinction:

> You deni'd to fight with me this other day, because I was no gentle-man born. See you these clothes? Say you see them not and think me still no gentleman born. You were best say these robes are not gentle-men born. Give me the lie, do, and try whether I am not now a gen-tleman born. (V.ii.139-45)

There is also an element of parody in the situation that is the-matically important. One recalls that Leontes' readiness to speak on Florizel's behalf was the expression of trust based upon love. We dis-cover here that fools may also trust, and thus make themselves vul-nerable once again to deception, simply because they are fools; for now Autolycus "humbly" begs the Clown to speak on his behalf to the prince. Time has again provided Autolycus with an opportunity. There is no hint of how he will use it. He may, indeed, be capable of amending his life in the sense the Clown has intended when he asks "Thou wilt amend thy life?" Autolycus' word, as the audience knows, is worth nothing. He has duped the Clown and his father before, and the chances are good that he will again. The Clown's father, who from the moment he appears in the scene has expressed a healthy caution, is nevertheless concerned to be gentle, urging his son to pardon Autolycus' faults and to speak on his behalf with Prince Florizel: "Prithee, son, do; for we must be gentle, now we are gentlemen."

Gentleness demands a readiness to trust, a readiness to risk the chance that one's trust in another human being makes him vulner-able. Autolycus may be lying and seeking to take advantage of the Shepherd and his son; but gentleness proves itself by risking vulner-ability for the sake of even the Autolycuses in the world. That is the serious point which lies beneath the surface comedy of the scene's concluding dialogue:

Clown: Thou wilt amend thy life?
Autolycus: Ay, an it like your good worship.
Clown: Give me thy hand: I will swear to the Prince thou art as honest a true fellow as any is in Bohemia.

Shepherd: You may say it, but not swear it.
Clown: Not swear it, now I am a gentleman? Let boors and franklins say it, I'll swear it.
Shepherd: How if it be false, son?
Clown: If it be ne'er so false, a true gentleman may swear it in the behalf of his friend; and I'll swear to the Prince thou art a tall fellow of thy hands and that thou wilt not be drunk; but I know thou art no tall fellow of thy hands and that thou wilt be drunk; but I'll swear it, and I would thou wouldst be a tall fellow of thy hands.
Autolycus: I will prove so, sir, to my power. (V.ii.166-83)

The Shepherd's silence is as meaningful as his last remark. He has said all he can say about true gentlemen, and despite his doubts, he tacitly approves of trust.

Autolycus' final remark, "I will prove so, sir, to my power," is of course ambiguous. The intent of his vow to amend his life is a matter which only future time will reveal. What is not ambiguous is the fact that the Shepherd and his son, in giving him the opportunity to rejoin the social order all but complete another cycle in the play. Only Autolycus' own efforts are needed to complete in spirit what has in letter been completed. To give him that opportunity is to risk being deceived; but without trust or faith in man's capacity to do the good, community itself is impossible.

Memory, passion, fancy, and the awakening of belief

The destructive action of *The Winter's Tale* began when a violent passion, awakened by an act of memory, led Leontes to charge Hermione with infidelity and to lose himself in an illusory world of his own creation. Now, sixteen years later, another strong passion, awakened and nourished by remembering, awakens his faith and completes his return to reality from a world of illusion. The correspondences between the past and present occasions are striking.

The psychological progression is exactly the same on both occasions. Gazing upon what he takes to be Hermione's statue, Leontes recalls the girl he had once courted and reflects again upon the harms he has done her. The sorrow resulting *pierces* his soul, just as sixteen years before "affection" awakened by memory had *stabbed* "the center." Her "statue" makes her appear "As she liv'd now" (V. iii.32); and as he gazes on it, he recalls the "majesty" and "warm life" of the girl he courted so long ago:

> As now she might have done,
> So much to my good comfort as it is
> Now piercing to my soul. O, thus she stood,
> Even with such life of majesty, warm life,
> As now it coldly stands, when first I woo'd her!
> I am asham'd; does not the stone rebuke me
> For being more stone than it? O royal piece
> There's magic in thy majesty, which has
> My evils conjur'd to remembrance, and
> From thy admiring daughter took the spirits,
> Standing like stone with thee.   (V.iii.32-42)

During the next few moments while Leontes silently meditates upon the "statue," his sorrow is the subject of the dialogue. Camillo assures him that he has grieved long enough, and Polixenes urges Paulina to close the curtain. When Leontes finally speaks, it is to direct Paulina not to draw the curtain. His continuing study of the statue is neither nostalgic indulgence nor despair. It is an exercising of the memory which keeps alive contrite sorrow.

Now a second correspondence emerges: once again intense feelings inspired by an act of remembering stir the fancy. Lest we miss the point Shakespeare has Paulina underscore it:

> No longer shall you gaze on't, *lest your fancy*
> *May think anon it moves.*   (V.iii.60-61)

Paulina's "warning" directs our attention to an imporant transition in Leontes' meditation. He is drawn out of his intense sorrow by the lifelike appearance of the "statue." He "imagines" that the "statue" is alive:

> See, my lord,
> Would you not deem it breath'd, and that those veins
> Did verily bear blood?   (V.iii.63-65)

and again:

> The fixture of her eye has motion in't,
> As we are mock'd with art. (V.iii.67-68)

Fancy stirred by affection sixteen years earlier created an illusion which eventually replaced the real. Now, under the guidance of contrite sorrow, fancy creates an illusion which will shortly prove itself real and the "statue" merely an illusion.

The final steps in the process of recovery are the engaging of reason and then the affirmation of belief. Paulina again draws our attention to the important particulars:

> I'll draw the curtain
> My lord is almost so far transported that
> He'll think anon it lives. (V.iii.68-70)

Reason, under the domination of fancy, is utterly distracted. Once again Leontes experiences a madness which dislocates the senses. He "sees feelingly":

> O sweet Paulina,
> Make me to think so twenty years together!
> No settled senses of the world can match
> The pleasure of that madness. (V.iii.70-73)

Once again he is ready to believe in what his senses, under the influence of a powerfully distracting passion, present to him as true. "Transported" beyond the "settled sense of the world" into what he takes to be illusion, faith awakens and he believes in the reality of the illusion. As Hermione descends to rejoin him, all that is required is that he take her hand as he had done years earlier when "after three crabbed months" she had agreed to marry him. The restorative action is complete, and the last of the ambiguities that have complicated perception during the final two acts is resolved.

In the moment of final clarification and reunion the audience is reminded for a final time in this extraordinary play of correspondences and recurrent occasions of the cyclical movement of time and of the options it allows man. Unable to separate himself from the past and always precariously vulnerable to the claims of hereditary guilt, he is nevertheless able to affirm through action another legacy —the legacy of a love which is sustaining, restoring, and renewing. It is a legacy which allows him to move into the winter season of the life cycle, confident that his lines of life will be sustained and his name renewed.

Illusion, wonder, and belief: the play as "speaking picture"

The Gentlemen who enter the play in V.ii. to serve as agents of exposition are also the means by which Shakespeare focuses audience attention upon the play itself as a "speaking picture." They, too, have witnessed strange and wonderful events—events which when recounted resemble the improbable fictions of "an old tale"; and in recounting them they raise and reflect upon questions that the play itself raises—questions concerning belief and wonder, illusion and reality, sight and hearing. They are also the means by which Shakespeare brilliantly prepares us for the climactic revelation scene and the final statement it makes about the fiction of *The Winter's Tale* and the act of belief that it requires of its audience.

Through the reports and commentary of the Gentlemen Shakespeare delimits the senses of sight and hearing in order to affirm the superiority of the "speaking picture" of drama, as a mode of depicting the extraordinary events that comprise the fiction of the play, over painting and the purely verbal arts. As the exposition progresses it carefully prepares us for the final "proof" of the mimetic superiority of the art of drama that occurs in the final scene when, suddenly, we find ourselves in the very position in which the Third Gentleman found himself when he witnessed the discovery of Perdita. That preparation is accomplished through a sequence of metaphors which makes us increasingly aware of the appropriateness of the comments about wonder, credibility, belief, and the limitations of painting and the verbal arts to the "old tale" that is being acted out on the stage before us.

The First Gentleman's "broken delivery" of Camillo's and Leontes' response to the opening of the fardel and the Shepherd's account of how he found it identifies the limitations of the purely visual.

Camillo and Leontes in the moment of their discovery become the very *picture* of wonder:

> . . . the changes I perceived in the King and Camillo were very notes of admiration. They seem'd almost, with staring on one another, to tear the cases of their eyes. There was speech in their dumbness, language in their very gesture; they look'd as they had heard of a world ransom'd, or one destroyed. A notable passion of wonder appeared in them;
> (V.ii.11-18)

But the picture is incomplete; as emblem it leaves something unexplained:

> . . . the wisest beholder, that knew no more but seeing, could not say if th' importance were joy or sorrow; but in the extremity of the one, it must needs be.
> (V.ii.18-21)

The audience, on the other hand, has been provided with more than a mute picture. We enjoy, therefore, an advantage over the First Gentleman. He has witnessed only the astonishing resolution of an action which we have followed from the beginning. It is an advantage we have gained from the sequence of "speaking pictures" that comprise the play. We know the causes and therefore the quality of joy and sorrow figured forth in the silent figures of Camillo and Leontes. We know that the joy they reveal is attendant upon their discovery that a world which seemed to have been "destroyed" has indeed been "ransom'd" and that joy is "in the extremity" because of a "saint-like" sorrow which made the ransoming possible. Our advantage in perspective and understanding is proof of the superiority of the art of "speaking pictures" over the art of the painter.

The next section of the exposition, which begins with the Second Gentleman's announcement that the king's daughter has been found and the oracle fulfilled, affirms the superiority of the art of drama over the purely verbal arts. The implication in the First Gentleman's description of Camillo's and Leontes' discovery of Perdita that wonder eludes description is now made explicit. The emotion of wonder eludes language; wondrous events must be seen. The point is first made in the Second Gentleman's response to the report that Perdita has been found and the oracle fulfilled: "such a deal of wonder is broken out within this hour that ballad-makers cannot be able to express it" (V.ii.25-27); and it is made again in the Third Gentleman's description of the meeting of Leontes and Polixenes. When the Second Gentleman discloses that he was not present at that meeting, the Third Gentleman replies:

> Then have you lost a sight which was to be seen, cannot be spoken of
> . . . . I never heard of such another encounter, which lames report to
> follow it and undoes description to do it.   (V.ii.46-63)

Verbal accounts of wonder are no substitute for the spectacle of wonder, although merely observing it, as the First Gentleman's earlier remarks have indicated, is not enough.

Verbal accounts of wondrous events are also inadequate in another way. They are likely to be dismissed as mere fiction. The news that the oracle has been fulfilled, according to the Second Gentleman, "is so like an old tale, that the verity of it is in strong suspicion" (V. ii.30-31). The same is true of the account of the strange circumstances of Antigonus' death. It, too, is

> Like an old tale . . . which will have matter to rehearse, though credit
> be asleep and not an ear open.   (V.ii.66-68)

Such strange happenings need to be confirmed by visual proof. The Third Gentleman has witnessed such proof, for he was present at the opening of the fardel. He was also present when Paulina learned of Antigonus' death and saw the handkerchief and rings that Paulina recognized as her dead husband's. He confirms what the other Gentlemen (the audience on stage) have heard by what he has seen. He has seen the evidence that confirms the truth of what seems, when only heard, like an "old tale"; and he has witnessed the wonder which eludes description.

The Third Gentleman's likening of these extraordinary events to the contents of "an old tale" calls our attention to the credibility of the events in the play we are watching and to the advantage in perspective we have over the three Gentlemen. Again, our advantage is evidence of the superiority of the "speaking pictures" of drama in the depiction of marvelous events and the emotion of wonder. The marvelous discoveries reported by the Third Gentleman are the final events—or, to borrow a metaphor from the First Gentleman, the final "act" of a play whose "dignity . . . was worth the audience of kings and princes; for by such was it acted" (V.ii.86-88)—in an "old tale" whose actions we have followed from the start. Since we know what the fardel contains and have witnessed the sequence of events leading to the fulfilling of the oracle, we are prepared to accept as true (in terms of the play's fiction) what the First and Third Gentlemen report. We are also able to understand more fully, and therefore more deeply, the wonder which the gentlemen remark as indescribable. They know "no more but seeing." We know wonder's source and occasions; for in the "speaking pictures" of *The Winter's Tale* we have witnessed the miraculous restorative powers of love.

We enjoy no such advantage in the final revelation scene. Shakespeare has deliberately misled us. We believe that Hermione is dead, and we expect in the final scene to see a statue of Hermione created by the famous foreman of Raphael's workshop, Julio Romano. But Shakespeare's purpose should now be clear. By deceiving us he places us in the same position the gentlemen were in when they witnessed the discovery of Perdita. What we witness is astonishing—an occasion of wonder. We are as surprised (in our first encounter with the play) as the audience onstage is by Paulina's extraordinary revelation. When the curtains are drawn and the "statue" is revealed, we wonder at its verisimilitude and may note along with Leontes the very qualities of animation that he remarks. Nor can we be certain that the "statue" is truly Hermione until she speaks. We may already suspect the truth by the time Paulina informs Leontes that if he will awaken his faith, she will "make the statue move, indeed descend" (V.ii.88); but we cannot be sure. We remain uncertain even after Hermione has descended from the scaffold and has embraced Leontes. In a play so strange as *The Winter's Tale*, a play in which reality and illusion are central thematic concerns, we cannot be sure about appearances. What appears to us to be true remains to be verbally confirmed. Paulina underscores the point:

That she is living,
Were it but told you, should be hooted at
Like an old tale; but it appears she lives,
Though yet she speak not. Mark a little while.

(V.iii.115-18)

When Hermione finally speaks, we know that she lives; and as we reflect upon this astonishing revelation we recognize in it a final exemplum of love's restorative power. Furthermore, through the persuasive power of a "speaking picture," we accept as true, within the fiction of the play, what we should have "hooted at / Like an old tale," had it merely been told us.

But there is more involved in this matter of deliberate deception. By presenting us with what appears initially to be a work of art, an illusion of reality, but which, following the awakening of Leontes' faith, proves to be reality itself, Shakespeare raises for our final consideration the truth and credibility of what we have seen—the truth that is figured forth in the play itself and the act of believing that it requires of us. We have followed the fiction through its various and entertaining improbabilities and have found that it celebrates the miraculous restorative powers of love. We have discovered the *Idea* (Sidney's "fore-conceite" or "perfect patterne," *Apology*, pp. 157, 168) which gives substance to the "speaking pictures" that comprise the world of the play in performance. If we accept that *Idea* as true, as a reality in the realm of *natura naturans*, we affirm the truth that is revealed in the mirror of the play. We accept its incredible fiction as the illusion invented by a poet who, in presenting "a perfect patterne," has borrowed "nothing of what is, hath been, or shall be," and who has ranged, "only rayned with learned discretion, into the diuine consideration of what may be, and should be" (*Apology*, p. 159). A "willing suspension of disbelief" is not enough. If we are to apprehend the reality depicted in the sequence of illusions which make up the play, we, too, along with Leontes, must believe. In the absence of such belief the play is only an improbable "old tale."

In *The Tempest* Shakespeare returns to consider more fully the relationship between dramatic illusion and reality and the role of belief in the audience's apprehension of the reality figured forth in the fiction of dramatic illusion. Through the character and situation of Prospero he affirms the notion of the moral purpose of poetry subscribed to by Sidney—the notion of poetry as a means of moving men to virtuous action. Prospero, like the dramatic poet, is the creator of illusions which in deceiving reveal important truths. Those truths are recognized and believed by all the members of Prospero's on-stage audience, and all, save Sebastian and Antonio, are inspired to virtuous action. Prospero is also the means by which Shakespeare affirms the role of belief in man's attempts to discover the substantiality, and thus the meaning and purpose, beneath the surface appearances of the world in which we live out our lives. Through Prospero Shakespeare tells us that unless we believe in the "fore-conceite" of its maker, the world itself and all of its inhabitants appear to us as nothing more than an "insubstantial pageant."

NOTES

[1] The play's mode of representation has been the subject of a good deal of speculation. See, for instance, S. L. Bethell, *"The Winter's Tale": A Study* (London, 1947), pp. 71-90; J. A. Bryant, "Shakespeare's Allegory: *The Winter's Tale*," *Sewanee Review*, 43 (1955), 202-23; F. David Hoeniger, "The Meaning of *The Winter's Tale*," *University of Toronto Quarterly*, 20 (1950), 11-26.

[2] See S. L. Bethell's discussion in *"The Winter's Tale": A Study*, pp. 32-44. Northrop Frye, when discussing Shakespeare's use of primitive materials in the last plays, remarks that "the expansion of time to include the passing of a generation . . . seems, paradoxically, to have something to do with a sense of timelessness in which these romances move." *A Natural Perspective* (New York, 1956), p. 57.

[3] Robert Greene, *Pandosto, or the Triumph of Time*, ed. P. G. Thomas (London, n.d.), p. 5.

[4] Notes to the New Cambridge edition of *The Winter's Tale* (London, 1950), p. 13. See also Nevill Coghill, "Six Points of Stage-Craft in *The Winter's Tale*," *Shakespeare Quarterly*, 11 (1958), 31-41; and Roger Trienens, "The Inception of Leontes' Jealousy in *The Winter's Tale*," *Shakespeare Quarterly*, 4 (1965), 321-26.

[5] Derek Traversi erroneously assumes that the boyhood friendship of the two kings was "based on a sentimental ignoring of the reality of the temporal process." *An Approach to Shakespeare* 2nd ed. (New York, 1958), p. 264. The innocence they shared was simply the innocence of youth, the innocence of a time of life when boyhood indeed seems to be eternal.

[6] Although he does not recognize that Leontes' jealousy has its origin in an act of memory, Robert Hunter is right in insisting that it comes from within: "By refusing to give evil any objective existence outside of *humanum genus*, Shakespeare in *The Winter's Tale* insists that human nature is inherently evil—or rather 'of a mangled yarn, good and evil together,' for the same human being may prove to be capable both of monstrous crime and subsequent regeneration." *Shakespeare and The Comedy of Forgiveness* (New York, 1965), pp. 190-91.

[7] See Louis L. Martz, *The Poetry of Meditation* (New Haven, 1950). See also Douglas L. Peterson, *The English Lyric from Wyatt to Donne* (Princeton, 1967), pp. 330-48.

[8] For a different assessment of Shakespeare's replotting of *Pandosto* see Inga-Stina Eubank, "The Triumph of Time in *The Winter's Tale*," *Review of English Literature*, 5 (1964), 83-100. Miss Eubank's study is a valuable contribution to the scholarship devoted to *The Winter's Tale*. It is limited, however, by her attributing to the metaphorical figure of Time events which the play attributes to men.

[9] Ernest Schanzer, in "The Structural Pattern of *The Winter's Tale*," *Review of English Literature*, 5 (1964), 72-82, was the first critic to notice the numerous parallels between the two halves of the play: ". . . the structural pattern of *The Winter's Tale* consists not only of a series of contrasts between its two halves, but also of a series of parallels. They may be mainly structural parallels, as is the case with the brief prose scene at the beginning of each half; or mainly thematic parallels, such as the intrusion of the cruelly threatening king into a scene of happy relationships; or

mainly plot-parallels, such as Camillo's aid to the victim of the king's fury; or mainly parallels of tone and atmosphere, such as that between the description of the Delphic oracle and the statue-scene" (p. 81).

[10]For a good analysis of Leontes' sudden affliction see Hallett Smith, "Leontes' 'Affectio,' " *Shakespeare Quarterly*, 14 (1961), 163-66.

[11]See John Davies, *Mirum in Modum, The Complete Works*, ed. Alexander B. Grosart (Edinburgh, 1878), I, 7-10.

[12]See Douglas L. Peterson, " 'Wisdom Consumed in Confidence': An Examination of Shakespeare's *Julius Caesar*," *Shakespeare Quarterly*, 16 (1965), 19-28.

[13]Critics have been too ready to accept the floral act as simply a symbolic celebration of nature's powers of renewal. According to E.M.W. Tillyard, for instance, "the whole country setting stands out as the cleanest and most elegant symbol of the new life into which the old horrors are to be transmuted." *Shakespeare's Last Plays* (London, 1938), p. 45. See also Inga-Stina Eubank's discussion of the so-called "pastoral scene," "The Triumph of Time in *The Winter's Tale*," pp. 94-95.

[14]Tillyard refers to Perdita as a "symbol both of the creative powers of nature, physical fertility, and of healing and re-creation of the mind." *Shakespeare's Last Plays*, p. 46. G. Wilson Knight, when discussing the flower ceremony, suggests that one "might call Perdita herself a seed sowed in winter and flowering in summer." *The Crown of Life* (London, 1947), p. 106. Hoeniger calls her "the incarnation of spring and early summer" who as Flora "presents the principle of fertility heightened by the robe she wears...." "The Meaning of *The Winter's Tale*," pp. 20, 25. For Eubank she is "almost an image of time seen as natural growth." "The Triumph of Time in *The Winter's Tale*," p. 94.

E. K.'s gloss of Flora in the March Ecclogue of Spenser's *Shephearde's Calender* (*Spenser: Poetical Works*, ed. J. C. Smith and E. De Selincourt, London, 1912, p. 430) is a healthy corrective to easy, romantic assumptions:

Flora, the Goddesse of floweres but indede (as saith Tacitus) a famous harlot, which with the abuse of her body hauing gotten great riches, made the peple of Rome her heyre: who in remembraunce of so great beneficence, appointed a yearely feste for the memoriall of her, calling her, not as she was, nor as some doe thinke, Andronica, but Flora: making her the Goddesse of all floures, and doing yerely to her solemne sacrifice."

When Perdita dons the robes of Flora the connotations evoked by the goddess' shady reputation in Renaissance England would hardly have been missed by the play's seventeenth-century audiences. They contribute to the carefully cultivated ambiguities that pervade the entire scene.

[15]*The Winter's Tale": An Interpretation*, p. 47.

[16]*The Crown of Life*, p. 101.

[17]See C. L. Barber, *Shakespeare's Festive Comedy* (Princeton, 1959), pp. 1-11, 127.

[18]The classic discussion of the use in Renaissance drama of sub-plot as a mode of parody is William Empson's in *Some Versions of Pastoral* (London, 1935), pp. 27-86.

[19]"The Triumph of Time in *The Winter's Tale*," p. 94.

[20]For a radically different view of Autolycus' role in the play see Lee Sheridan Cox, "The Role of Autolycus in *The Winter's Tale*," *Studies in English Literature*, 9 (Spring, 1969), 283-301.

[21] G. Wilson Knight, *The Crown of Life*, p. 21. Continuing, Knight observes that "both Camillo's tortuous scheme and Autolycus' additions to it lack conviction ..." (p. 21). Bethell refers to "a patch of astonishingly awkward management" which begins "at the point where Camillo questions Florizel and learns he is determined to put to sea with Perdita." *"The Winter's Tale": An Interpretation*, p. 48.

[22] The religious overtones of Leontes' penitential experience, as well as the religious connotations of the term "grace," are unavoidable; I do not think, however, that to recognize them commits one to such theological readings of the play as Bethell's and Bryant's, *Hippolyta's View* (Lexington, Kentucky, 1961), pp. 207-25.

[23] For an especially harsh criticism of V.ii. see Sir Arthur Quiller-Couch and J. Dover Wilson, *The Winter's Tale* (Cambridge, 1931, 1950), p. xxiii.

[24] Nevill Coghill ("Six Points of Stage-Craft in *The Winter's Tale*," *Shakespeare Survey*, 11, 31-41) defends the dramatic effectiveness of the scene, pp. 38-39. See also Bertrand Evans, *Shakespeare's Comedies* (Oxford, 1960), pp. 312-13, and D. R. C. Marsh, *The Recurring Miracle* (Lincoln, Nebraska, 1962, 1969), pp. 156-57.

[25] See, for instance, S. L. Bethell, *The Winter's Tale: A Study*, pp. 102-04; and Frank Kermode, *The Winter's Tale* (New York, 1963), Introduction, xxix-xxxv.

V

The Tempest: "Remember, for That's My Business with You"

AMONG THE ROMANCES *The Tempest* has always received the most attention and the highest praise; and yet the critical consensus is that its meaning is elusive. Beyond the general agreement that the play is concerned with forgiveness, reconciliation, and renewal and moves "from initial discord and alienation to ultimate harmony"[1]—matters about which it would be difficult to raise an argument of any kind—commentary ranges widely and often impressionistically.[2] There are even those who insist that because the "vision" of the play is so "personal and delicate," it "is best left unsmutched by the rude hand of the analyzing critic, or the overearnest teacher of English Literature."[3] Nevertheless, the general feeling seems to be that further knowledge will eventually lead to a fuller understanding of the play. Such was the opinion expressed in 1954 by the New Arden editor:

> It cannot be hoped that we shall for long be content to go on saying the same things about the play. Although some critics profess indifference to scholarly investigations, they are generally much more moved

by them than it appears, and there is yet much to be *known* about the romances. The time is perhaps near when some critic will radically alter the assumptions upon which criticism of *The Tempest* is at present founded.[4]

Another editor of the play has said more recently:

> In spite of all that has been written about *The Tempest* and about Shakespeare's other romances, most of the criticism seems to be several stages removed from our experience of the works themselves. Attempts to explain the "meaning" of *The Tempest* often seem to be trivial and only vaguely connected with the play. A much more widespread and thorough understanding of the nature of romance and of the Jacobean audience's responses to it might help us to find more useful bases for discussion.[5]

Until we have that understanding, this editor concludes, "the 'meaning' of *The Tempest* must lie, ultimately, in the manner in which we respond to it."[6]

We have now perhaps reached the position in which we may begin to provide the kind of understanding of *The Tempest* and the other romances that has been lacking.

The Tempest presents two fundamental problems of interpretation which will have to be solved before discussions of the play can move beyond generalizations about harmony, reconciliation, and forgiveness. Criticism will have to establish the play's mimetic mode and identify the system of ideas in terms of which its action is conceived. Such terms as "allegory" and "symbolism" are not precise enough to be useful in describing the way in which the play gives dramatic extension to the general ideas that are its concern. I believe that what I have established in earlier chapters about the use of romance conventions in the earlier romances, particularly the tendency in each of those plays toward "emblematic narrative," and their general tendency to reveal something resembling Sidney's theory of poetry, will prove to be an instructive context in which to consider the play's mimetic mode. Equally instructive as a context in which to consider its structure and action is the time system, in all its metaphorical configurations, to which each of the earlier romances is structurally and thematically indebted.

As an imitation of an action *The Tempest* combines precept with example. It creates dramatic illusion out of the improbable events of romance to the very purpose which Prospero within the play creates illusion: it holds up to nature a mirror that reveals "truths" which in the author's view man must "see feelingly" if he is to be moved to virtuous action.

Shakespeare's subordination of representational imitation to ideological concerns is evident in the conception of character, setting, and action. Prospero, Ferdinand, and Miranda have no more substantiality than Pericles, Perdita, or Leontes; and while they may occasionally come to life in a brief episode or speech, they remain for the greater part of the play as remote from the audience as the island on which they act out their destinies. The reasons for this are not difficult to identify. They lack the particularizing detail, historical and psychological, of which memorable characters, a Brutus or a Mark Antony, are created. The substantiality of such characters is due in part to the variety of circumstances in which we see them: their responses to ever-shifting situations, their relationships with other characters in an evolving action. It is also due to the rich texture and diversity of their speeches, a diversity that includes a range of reference and allusion which, though always consistent with their character, is not always explicitly relevant to dramatic action. In contrast, what we know, or what is revealed, of Prospero, Miranda, and Ferdinand is narrowly confined to what is relevant to the ideas that the action represents. We hear nothing of Prospero's wife, and little about his life in Milan. We learn only of his negligence and the conspiracy. The same is equally true of the rest of the characters. We are provided only with the bare essentials of their personal history. Furthermore, there is remarkably little interaction during the play among the characters. The little that does occur, for instance, between Ferdinand and Miranda or between Prospero and his old enemies, is more didactic or ritualistic than representational. Its "reality" is in the ideas it is created to figure forth. Curiously, the most highly developed, and therefore most representational interaction occurs among Stephano, Trinculo, and Caliban, and among the voyagers in the opening scene on board ship. In each instance, the conversation is rich in colloquial phrase and topical detail and stands out sharply from the rest of the dialogue in the play.

Setting, too, lacks localizing detail. Prospero's island has the same curious kind of reality that settings in *The Winter's Tale* and *Cymbeline* have. In creating the fiction of the island Shakespeare exploits current rumors and reports of strange and newly discovered lands to the same purpose that he used legendary history in *Cymbeline*. Places heard of by the audience, together with the marvelous events that are reported to have taken place there, whet the imagination and even add a touch of credibility to Prospero's island. At the same time, its remoteness allows Shakespeare to present it as an island in human time where an action takes place that men throughout time are bound to repeat in one form or another. In the world of the play it is a place like rural Bohemia, the forest of Arden, and the wilds of Wales where men, although free of the encumbrances and evils of society, nevertheless encounter the consequences of fallen nature. It is a pastoral refuge where men may discover their humanity—a setting in which we expect action to be more symbolic than real. And that expectation is not disappointed. The play's action has the simplicity of emblematic narrative. It consists only of episodes that are absolutely essential to the concepts it is intended to convey. Its method of development is to reveal a moment of crisis in the lives of the principal characters through correspondences and parallels rather than through sequential action. It is a method of unfolding or of illustrating meaning through similar and contrasting examples.

The concepts that shape the play, defining the conflict out of which the action arises and the moment of final stasis that marks its temporary resolution, are those we have encountered in each of the earlier romances: the generative and destructive forces in nature which define the condition of man as mutable and precarious. They are introduced early in the play when Prospero, while accusing Ariel of ingratitude, reveals to the audience the genealogy of Caliban and the situation from which he has rescued Ariel. In the scheme of contrasting parallels that emerges, we recognize the antithetically opposed forces that determine the course of personal time, those two legacies which each generation is heir to and which give real substance to a mythical island.

The island has come under the rule first of Sycorax and then of Prospero. Both possess powers that allow them to control physical nature and to influence the lives of men. Sycorax has been banished from the community of man "For mischiefs manifold and sorceries terrible" (I.ii.264). Prospero, too, has been banished, but unjustly—the victim of an evil which his own neglect of duty had permitted to flourish. Both continue to practice their art after their arrival on the island. Sycorax had made Ariel serve her, but finding Ariel, a spirit of the fire and air, "too delicate/To act her earthly and abhorr'd commands" (I.ii.272-73), imprisoned him in a "cloven pine." Prospero, on the other hand, after freeing him, finds him a most useful servant. It is Caliban, a monstrous thing of earth and smelling like a fish, whom he finds nearly useless — able only to collect firewood under the constant threat of physical punishment—and a threat to his daughter and himself unless kept under constant surveillance. The pattern of contrasting parallels is completed by the offspring of the two practitioners of magic. Caliban is "a born devil, on whose nature/Nurture can never stick" (IV.i.188-89). His depravity is Satan's legacy by way of Sycorax, a reminder of the presence of evil on the pastoral island even before the tempest strands the Italian nobles on its shores. Miranda's innocence and compassion comprise the legacy of nobility and virtue bequeathed by her parents to the world. Unlike Caliban, she has responded beautifully to her father's nurturing. In the "blue-eyed hag" we recognize the legacy of evil and death that all men have inherited from The Fall. In Prospero and Miranda we recognize that other legacy—a love which redeems what seems to have been lost in the past, which is sustaining in the face of the tempestuous present,[7] and which promises renewal of life and the perpetuation of the lines of life into the future.

In its mode of imitation and in the ideas which shape and give meaning to its action, *The Tempest* has numerous and close affinities with *Pericles, Cymbeline,* and *The Winter's Tale;* and as we proceed to look more closely at its action, we shall see further resemblances

to those plays in its treatment of time—past, present, and future—
and in its insistence on the primacy of faith over reason and the
senses. The theory of cyclical time as potentially destroying and renewing, and of occasion as the moment of crucial choice provided
by cyclical time, is the source of the play's structure.

The play's opening scene is an extraordinary instance of the fusion
of mimetic and poetic modes. As a mirror held up to nature it simultaneously reflects (or re-creates) a dramatic event comprised of phenomenal particulars and affirms a general truth about man and the
world as a "lasting storm." The storm, the voyagers, and their reac-
tions to a catastrophe that seems inevitable, all have a substantiality
that we associate with verisimilitude. We therefore accept the actors
who appear on the bare stage as real voyagers in a "real" storm, and
we anticipate a play about the adventures of those who will survive
the shipwreck. At the same time, since we are watching or reading a
play and are familiar with tempests as *figura*, we are alert to the
scene's emblematic potentialities. As the play progresses we realize
that in addition to initiating the action of the play the scene has also
functioned as a dramatic version of the "tempest-tossed bark" emblem—as a "speaking picture" announcing the thematic significance
of the action it initiates and hinting at the ways in which the principal characters will respond to the trials they encounter.[8]

The scene also hints at the discrepancies between appearances and
reality which will prove to be a major concern throughout the play.
Appearances lead us initially to identify the Boatswain as the emblematic exemplar of constancy.[9] He goes about his business, un-
daunted by the dangers he faces, shouting encouragement to the
crew and endeavoring to keep the ship under control. He stands firm
in the face of crisis, challenging the storm with "Blow till thou burst
thy wind, if room enough!" (I.i.8-9). He orders the passengers, who
are in the way, to "keep below" (I.i.12), and when Gonzalo reminds
him of "whom thou hast aboard" (I.i.20), he responds in the spirit
recommended by the emblems:

> None that I more love than myself. You are a counsellor; if you can
> command these elements to silence, and work the peace of the present,
> we will not hand a rope more; use your authority. If you cannot, give

thanks you have liv'd so long, and make yourself ready in your cabin for the mischance of the hour, if it so hap.—Cheerly, good hearts!— Out of our way, I say. (I.i.22-29)

But at the very last, when the ship seems to be splitting up, our expectations are surprised. Gonzalo emerges as The Constant Man. While the Boatswain turns in despair to drink and Antonio and Sebastian curse their fates, he announces his readiness to accept whatever consequences the storm may bring: "The wills above be done!" (I.i.71). The Constant Man accepts whatever the gods have in store for him. It is a role from which Gonzalo never departs throughout the rest of the play.

By fusing the literal and the figurative the scene introduces simultaneously the play's action and the general truth that action will embody. Emblematically, the play we are about to witness is about constancy under the duress of tempestuous inner and outer weather. Literally, each of the principal characters will be caught in a series of events which deeply affects his future. Antonio, Sebastian, and Alonso will be confronted with the consequences of their sinful pasts; Ferdinand will fall in love at first sight and be forced to prove that love—by carrying logs; Gonzalo will have to deal with the despair and impatience of the nobles he serves; Prospero will have to resist, initially, the turbulence of his own anger and, finally, the enervating effects of ennui. The play will, in short, focus upon the tempest as crisis and occasion, upon a brief interval of less than four hours during which the future will be shaped by the way occasion is used.[10]

The sense of urgency and crisis which is so strong throughout the play is the result of the particular way in which both past and future are brought to focus upon the present. Once the audience discovers its mistake in assuming that the tempest of the opening scene originated from natural causes and that the shipwreck has been only an illusion, it views the action from the vantage point provided by Prospero's prescience and memory. We learn, along with Miranda, that the direction his future will take depends upon the present occasion, and we realize, as he proceeds to explain to her the need to "shun

delaies," that what appears to be only present time has a cosmic dimension. After years of patiently enduring exile, he has finally the
opportunity to mend his fortunes:

> Know thus far forth.
> By accident most strange, bountiful Fortune,
> Now my dear lady, hath mine enemies
> Brought to this shore; and by my prescience
> I find my zenith doth depend upon
> A most auspicious star, whose influence
> If now I court not but omit, my fortunes
> Will ever after droop. (I.ii.177-84)

The need is to act now, for the future hangs in the balance.

If the light of the future reveals the urgency of the present, it is
the perspective of the past which reveals the present as climactic:
an action initiated years earlier, on an occasion provided by Prospero's negligence as governor is now about to be resolved in one way
or another.[11] Time, by returning to "the same times," has provided
Prospero with the opportunity to reassume his authority and to settle
accounts with his old enemies.[12] There is, therefore, a literal sense
in which Antonio's remarks about the past as prologue—

> We were all sea-swallow'd, though some cast again,
> And by that destiny to perform an act
> Whereof what's past is prologue, what to come
> In yours and my discharge— (II.i.251-54)

are appropriate to the events we watch in the play. We watch the
present unfold in the light of the past, aware of the events which
have brought Prospero and Miranda to the island and that those
events have come to a head and will be resolved before the play is
over. Years before the action of the play begins, Prospero himself,
as a result of his negligence, was "sea-swallow'd" and cast up again
"to perform an act/Whereof what's past is prologue." What is to
come is in his "discharge"; and what is true for Prospero is also true
for those who had taken advantage of his negligence. His enemies
will be confronted with their involvement in the old conspiracy, and

the ways in which they respond to the consequences of that old crime will determine how Prospero finally deals with them.

The chief burden of choice, however, is Prospero's. He holds the present in his hands. The play's ending will depend upon how he construes destiny's purpose in saving him from the sea. Pericles, too, had been "sea-swallow'd" and cast up again. The action he undertakes leads to his marriage and the conceiving of an heir. He thus shapes the time to come and proves his right to his father's name. His father's noble name lives on in him and is verified in the noble actions he performs. He regains what he has seemingly lost in the tempest. Prospero's loss, unlike Pericles', was caused by his own negligence; but the sea has cast him up to give him the opportunity to regain what he has lost. Prospero has now the same chance to regain his lost nobility and its title that was given to Pericles. His control of time allows him two options, vengeance and forgiveness. The choice he makes will also depend upon the past as prologue, upon the past as Prospero remembers it.

Prospero's ultimate choice to forgive confirms his nobility as a man and at the same time his prudence as a governor. By the time he discards his mantle and staff and stands alone on the bare stage to deliver the play's epilogue, he will have considered time and put it to use in the way recommended by Peter de la Primaudaye.[13] Actions potentially tragic will finally be resolved happily by a prudent "artist" who in viewing "the past as prologue" chooses forgiveness over revenge.

Consideration of the past as memory and its influence upon the future leads to the deepest concerns of the play. As I have shown in my discussion of *The Winter's Tale*, there is in the Shakespearian view a past that is shared by all humanity and which is always manifest in the present. It is the joint legacy of self-destroying and renewing love which we have seen variously represented in each of the earlier romances. Each is latent in the personal present, a potentiality waiting to be realized through choice and action. Which of those forces will finally prevail in the lives of Prospero's old enemies will depend upon the way in which, under Prospero's influence, they remember and respond to their own sinning pasts. On this level of the play Prospero's decision to forgive is the expression of renewing love and the final confirmation of what in the Christian view would be construed as a state of grace or redemption.

The present, then, in *The Tempest*, viewed as it is from the double perspective of past and future, discloses the same levels of meaning that are present in the emblematic tempest scene. The events that take place under Prospero's controlling hand on the little island depict the archetypal situation of man, determining by his choices whether hereditary guilt or renewing love will prove prologue of what is to come.

Prospero's obligation, personally as father and brother, and publicly as the rightful governor of Milan, is to time itself. He must, in John Fox's phrase, "redeem time." The redeeming of time begins "when time and duty like those two twins, Jacob and Esau, take hold one of another, or as two loving yoak-fellows, go hand in hand. When duty attends time, as the shadow the body, or as the Maiden her Mistriss. This is to fill up time with duty, and to take opportunity by the fore-lock...."[14] When Prospero raises the tempest which strands the ship returning from Africa on the shores of his island and has his former enemies again under his authority he has the opportunity "to fill up time with duty." Here, too, Fox's discussion of "How time must be redeemed" is appropriate: "When we are truly careful to make up former negligence, with double diligence, redeeming the time, we recover our loss. Time according to this phrase, seemeth to be taken captive, and we must redeem it ... the price we redeem it with, is labour, travel, faithful and serious diligence, and greater activity and vigour in the prosecutions of our duty."[15] In the course of the play Prospero will recover what through his former negligence he has lost. He will also release time from its captivity through the vigorous prosecution of his duty.

Prospero begins in the second scene of the opening act to redeem time by assuming his paternal duties to Miranda. Although she has lived with her father on the island for twelve years, she knows nothing of his public identity, and hence nothing of her own noble lineage. In this respect her situation is something like Perdita's before she learns that she is a princess. Prospero has resisted many times in the past the inclination to inform her, as Miranda discloses:

> You have often
> Begun to tell me what I am, but stopp'd
> And left me to a bootless inquisition,
> Concluding, "Stay, not yet." (I.ii.33-36)

But now, as Prospero replies, the time is propitious, "The hour's now come;/The very minute bids thee ope thine ear" (I.ii.36-37). He has taken off the magic cloak, the symbol of the art he uses to control the elements, and speaks as the father of his daughter, informing her of her noble lineage and of the series of events that have brought them to the island and caused him to raise the tempest. But once he has made her aware of these things and recalled to her how he has used time to educate her since their arrival on the island—

> ...here
> Have I, thy schoolmaster, made thee more profit
> Than other princess can that have more time
> For vainer hours and tutors not so careful— (I.ii.171-74)

he refuses to reveal more. Miranda's future will depend upon the next three hours which, as he presently tells Ariel, "Must by us both be spent most preciously" (I.ii.241). He puts Miranda to sleep and will wake her only when the time is right. In the meantime he will turn his attention to other urgencies.

Prospero's recovery for Miranda of her past from "the dark backward and abysm of time" (I.ii.50) also marks the beginning of the lengthy exposition which takes up the rest of the scene. Along with Miranda we learn how those many years ago he had failed to use time properly. Devoting himself to his secret studies, he had allowed his brother to rule in his stead. We learn also that he holds himself responsible not only for having neglected "worldly ends" (I.ii.89) and for having found his library "dukedom large enough" (I.ii.110), but also for having awakened "an evil nature" (I.ii.93) in his brother.

But the scene has a purpose beyond the obvious one of dramatic exposition. It focuses upon memory as a shaping power of present and future. Miranda, Antonio, Caliban, Ariel, and Prospero himself are characterized by the way in which they remember and feel about the past, and their responses to the past provide us with distinctions that will be of fundamental importance throughout the rest of the play.

In his negligence as governor Prospero had allowed Antonio not only to seize power but also to *forget* his identity as brother and subordinate. Again a comparison with Pericles is illuminating. One recalls that Pericles had been taught the lesson of mortality by the tempest that isolated him in Pentapolis. Stripped of his dignities, he remembers what it means to be mortal:

> What I have been I have forgot to know,
> But what I am want teaches me to think on,
> A man throng'd up with cold. (II.i.75-77)

At the banquet following his victory in the tournament, as he looks at Simonides he remembers his father and is again reminded of mortality and man's subservience to time (II.iii.37-47). One recalls also that it is Perdita's refusal to forget who she is when she is attired as Flora that proves her innocence and natural nobility. The right use of memory in each instance leads to the knowledge of self which is prerequisite to humility and gentleness. But Antonio's memory was defective:

> He being thus lorded,
> Not only with what my revenue yielded,
> But what my power might else exact,—like one
> Who having into truth, by telling of it,
> Made such a sinner of his memory
> To credit his own lie,—he did believe
> He was indeed the Duke. (I.ii.97-103)

In the midst of his new wealth and power Antonio forgot who he was, and it will be Prospero's duty as a brother and Duke of Milan to lead him to remember properly. To that end Prospero will use his art of illusion to move his brother to virtuous action. He will endeavor to get his brother not only to see the present in the true light of past events but also to feel the sorrow that recognition of his own guilt ought to arouse.

Miranda's response to the past, in contrast to Antonio's, is exemplary. Her memory of Milan is only a dream-like recollection of "Four or five women once that tended me" (I.ii.47); but as she learns of her father's past afflictions, she responds with the same compassion with which she had responded to the illusion of the shipwreck at the outset of the scene. Learning of her father's past troubles, she cries:

> Alack, for pity!
> I, not rememb'ring how I cried out then,
> Will cry it o'er again. It is a hint
> That wrings mine eyes to't. (I.ii.132-35)

The memory of the afflictions of others is a source of the compassion that man ought to feel for others and a reminder to oneself that all men share a common burden. Miranda, lacking such memories, is nevertheless able to respond as if she had in fact experienced and remembered her father's afflictions. It is this ability to respond to the past and experience remorse and compassion for afflictions suffered by others that plays so important a part in the final moments of the play, when reconciliation and renewal are finally accomplished.

Ariel and Caliban, respectively, reveal deficiency and perversity in their responses to the past. Ariel seems initially to be guilty of the forgetfulness with which Prospero charges him.

> *Prospero:*   Dost thou forget
> From what a torment I did free thee?
> *Ariel:*   No.
> *Prospero:*   Thou dost, and think'st it much to tread the ooze
> Of the salt deep,
> To run upon the sharp wind of the north,
> To do me business in the veins o' th' earth
> When it is bak'd with frost.

Ariel: I do not, sir.
Prospero: Thou liest, malignant thing! Hast thou
 forgot
The foul witch Sycorax, who with age and envy
Was grown into a hoop? Hast thou forgot her?
Ariel: No, sir.
Prospero: Thou hast. Where was she born?
Speak; tell me.
Ariel: Sir, in Argier.
Prospero: O, was she so? I must
Once in a month recount what thou hast been,
Which thou forget'st.   (I.ii.250-63)

But Ariel has not forgotten. He is a spirit and, as we learn later (V.i. 20-24), incapable of feeling. Prospero, therefore, cannot expect him to act freely on his behalf either out of compassion or out of gratitude. He can only win his cooperation by holding out eventual freedom as a reward. He tries hard but ineffectively to stir up gratitude in Ariel by forcing him to remember the captivity from which he was rescued, but Ariel's answers continue to be confined to brief, neutral affirmations of Prospero's account of the details of Sycorax and of Ariel's imprisonment. It is only when Prospero threatens to imprison him in an oak for another twelve winters that Ariel agrees to be dutiful. We shall see eventually that the right use of human memory produces states of feeling that lead to action freely undertaken. Remorse, gratitude, compassion, and love prove to be the feelings that at least make possible the renewal of the old world, if not the birth of a "brave new world."

Caliban's memory, on the other hand, is revealed to be defective by the perversity of the passions that his recollections stir up. He remembers only to resent and, when the opportunity seems to present itself, to seek revenge upon Prospero. Love and therefore compassion and remorse are beyond him. When reminded of his attempt to rape Miranda, he is gleeful: "O ho, O ho! would 't had been done!/ Thou didst prevent me; I had peopl'd else/This isle with Calibans" (I.ii.349-51). Controlled by passions unredeemed, he is incapable of comprehending the good or of learning from the past. Despite all of

Prospero's efforts, he remains a creature "Which any print of goodness wilt not take" (I.ii.352), an intractable creature whom only
"stripes may move, not kindness" (I.ii.345). Only the fear of physical punishment and actual constraint keep Caliban under control.

Finally, there is the question of Prospero's own view of the past.
We have seen that he holds his negligence ultimately to blame for
the conspiracy and the years of exile to which it has led. We have
also learned of his intent to seize the occasion time has provided.
What we are not sure of during the play's opening action are the
feelings that his memory of old injuries has aroused. There is just
enough testiness in his demeanor to suggest that he is not above the
desire for revenge. He has raised a furious tempest as a means of
bringing his old enemies to the island; he has nagged at Miranda,
questioning her attentiveness; and when Ariel has reminded him of
the freedom he has been promised, he has angrily accused the Spirit
of ungratefulness.[16] His final decision to forgive his enemies is foreshadowed by the care he takes to save them from shipwreck, and,
later, to prevent the murder of Alonso; but his decision to forgive is
surely not a foregone conclusion. He will come to that resolution
only when he remembers that it is precisely because of the legacy of
evil, which even his art is powerless to eradicate, that man stands in
need of compassion and forgiveness.

Having begun his efforts to redeem the past, Prospero turns his
attention to Miranda's future by imposing upon Ferdinand the labor
that will try his affections for her. In the meantime the play turns to
the two groups of conspirators. Each group is also busying itself
with time, each finding in its situation the occasion for the seizure of
power.

While Alonso and Gonzalo lie sleeping under Ariel's charm, Antonio introduces the subject of regicide to Sebastian:

> Th' occasion speaks thee, and
> My strong imagination sees a crown
> Dropping upon thy head. (II.i.207-09)

This is language typical of the opportunists who so frequently appear in Shakespeare's plays—of those who misconstrue opportunity

and who are consequently destroyed by time, or who become the
fools of time or fortune. Antonio continues:

> Noble Sebastian,
> Thou let'st thy fortune sleep—die, rather—wink'st
> Whiles thou art waking.   (II.i.215-17)

One remembers Brutus' fatal miscalculation of occasion ("There is
a tide in the affairs of men . . ."). The tide metaphor, introduced by
Sebastian and picked up by Antonio, is also reminiscent of Brutus
and of the old aphorisms concerning opportunity:

> *Sebastian:*   Well, I am standing water.
> *Antonio:*   I'll teach you how to flow.
> *Sebastian:*   Do so. To ebb
> Hereditary sloth instructs me.
> *Antonio:*   O,
> If you but knew how you the purpose cherish
> Whiles thus you mock it! how, in stripping it,
> You more invest it! Ebbing men, indeed,
> Most often do so near the bottom run
> By their own fear or sloth.   (II.i.221-28)

As Antonio continues his persuasion he abuses the past by recalling
for Sebastian events that have made the time ripe for regicide. Ferdinand, the King's immediate royal successor, is surely dead; the next
heir, Clarabel, is now queen of Tunis, "Ten leagues beyond man's
life" (II.i.247). Destiny itself seems to have directed the course of
events down to the present moment. As Antonio's persuasion begins
to work, Sebastian calls upon memory to provide a supporting example—"I remember/ You did supplant your brother Prospero"
(II.i.270-71)—and he next inquires whether Antonio's conscience
has ever bothered him. The assurance he receives is another symp-
tom of an unfeeling and therefore defective memory.

> *Sebastian:*   But, for your conscience?
> *Antonio:*   Ay, sir, where lies that? If 'twere a kibe,
> 'Twould put me to my slipper; but I feel not
> This deity in my bosom. Twenty consciences,

> That stand 'twixt me and Milan, candied be they
> And melt ere they molest!   (II.i.275-80)

One more objection has been dispatched, and Antonio dismisses the final one by promising to implicate himself by killing Gonzalo (whom, incidentally, in the midst of this talk of how to seize opportunity by the forelock he contemptuously alludes to as "Sir Prudence," II.i.286) and assures him that the rest are merely time servers who will follow them without raising any questions:

> For all the rest,
> They'll take suggestion as a cat laps milk;
> They'll tell the clock to any business that
> We say befits the hour.   (II.i.287-90)

Time seems on the verge of repeating itself. Once again while a governor neglects time a brother prepares to seize his power; only Prospero's alertness, his readiness to assume the duties he had formerly neglected, prevents the conspirators from carrying out their plan. The parallels between the two occasions are underscored in the song that Ariel sings to awaken Gonzalo:

> While you here do snoring lie,
> Open-ey'd Conspiracy
>   His time doth take.
> If of life you keep a care,
> Shake off slumber, and beware;
>   Awake, awake!   (II.i.300-05)

The conspirators discover the true significance of the marvelous events that seemingly have led up to the occasion of regicide and the seizure of power in III.iii. when, after being presented with a banquet only to see it snatched away,[17] Ariel addresses them, and provides them with an accurate interpretation of the past as prologue to what is now about to be:

> You are three men of sin, whom Destiny,
> That hath to instrument this lower world
> And what is in't, the never-surfeited sea

Hath caus'd to belch up you; and on this island
Where man doth not inhabit; you 'mongst men
Being most unfit to live. I have made you mad;
And even with such-like valour men hang and drown
Their proper selves. (III.iii.53-60)

The fact that Ariel's lines echo Antonio's on the past as "prologue"
(II.i.251-54) indicates the deliberately drawn parallel between past
time misconstrued to justify a selfish end, and past time rightly construed as retribution by powers that only seem to have forgotten. As
Ariel continues he stresses that the purpose of his "business" is to
force them to remember accurately:

But remember—
For that's my business to you—that you three
From Milan did supplant good Prospero;
Expos'd unto the sea, which hath requit it,
Him and his innocent child; for which foul deed
The powers, delaying, not forgetting, have
Incens'd the seas and shores, yea, all the creatures,
Against your peace. Thee of thy son, Alonso,
They have bereft; and do pronounce by me
Lingr'ing perdition, worse than any death
Can be at once, shall step by step attend
You and your ways; whose wraths to guard you from—
Which here, in this most desolate isle, else falls
Upon your heads—is nothing but heart's sorrow
And a clear life ensuing. (III.iii.68-82)

The alternatives are clear. The future promises "ling'ring perdition"
unless they are able to remember what they have done and through
that act of remembering are able to feel "heart's sorrow." Their only
hope lies in their readiness to use the occasion to redeem time. They
must "consider," as John Fox urges in *Time and the End of Time*,
"that on the present moment of time, Eternity depends"; for if they
"let go time's opportunity," they "will certainly be ruin'd to all
Eternity."[18]

The effect upon Alonso is immediate. Prompted to remember his part in the deposition of Prospero and to reflect upon his son's death as retribution for what he himself has done, he sinks into a sorrow so desperate that he sees suicide as its only relief. The responses by Sebastian and Antonio, although more briefly revealed, are equally violent:

> *Sebastian:*   But one fiend at a time,
> I'll fight their legions o'er.
> *Antonio:*   I'll be thy second.
>
> (III.iii.103-04)

"All three," as Gonzalo observes, "are desperate."

Prospero has continued, with Ariel's help, to make good use of time. He has endeavored to get them to redeem time for themselves. The means he has used is the art of illusion. He has created a "living drollery" to serve as a mirror in which the evil doers are made to see their evil natures and the consequences they have brought upon themselves.

That other group of conspirators—Caliban, Trinculo, and Stephano—also endeavors to seize occasion. It is Caliban who encourages the other two to believe that time offers them the opportunity to satisfy their greed. He tells them that Prospero customarily sleeps in the afternoon and that all they need do is proceed to his cave, burn his books, and slay him. The island will then be theirs. The entire action in which they engage themselves gains a dimension once the fact is recognized that by agreeing to Caliban's plot, Trinculo and Stephano become time's fools. For Caliban is a fool and in accepting his proposal they allow themselves to be led by folly and thus to be made vulnerable to time—and to Prospero, who, despite a lapse during which he momentarily forgets the present, controls time.

The wretched and highly amusing end to Caliban's plotting burlesques the failure to seize opportunity. As soon as Stephano and Trinculo approach the vicinity of Prospero's cell and discover the gowns which Ariel at Prospero's instruction had hung out as a lure to trap them, they forget not only Caliban's instructions, "Remember / First to possess his books" (III.ii.99-100), but even why they have come. They can think only of the present, of the handsome gowns, forgetting their past planning and the future they had intended to gain by it. As they squabble with each other over the robes, Caliban stands helplessly by, complaining:

> We shall lose our time,
> And all be turn'd to barnacles, or to apes
> With foreheads villainous low. (IV.i.248-50)

All Prospero need do is provide their punishment, and the scene closes with his reminder to Ariel and the audience that "At this hour / Lies at my mercy all mine enemies" (IV.i.263-64). Miranda's future is not so easily managed. Ordinarily, time provides the major trial of love's authenticity. Love may occur at first sight, but it is time that tests the honor of the lover, and sometimes of the beloved.[19] The members of Navarre's academy in *Love's Labour's Lost* must wait a year to prove their constancy. Orlando in *As You Like It* must be tried by time and demonstrate that he knows how to use it well before he can marry Rosalind. But Prospero has less than four hours in which to try Ferdinand.

Miranda from her first appearance in the play is a typical heroine of Shakespearean comedy. Her virtue is assumed from the outset and never questioned. She also reveals, as we have seen, from her first appearance the passionate concern for the sufferings of others that Shakespeare repeatedly stresses as a necessary condition of genuine love. One remembers, for instance, that one of the conditions of Biron's trial in *Love's Labour's Lost* is designed to purge him of a pride that expresses itself in the mockery of the weaknesses of others. Either he must make the sick and dying laugh, or, failing that, reform himself by weeding "his fruitful brain" of "wormwood" (*LLL*, V.ii.867). Miranda in her opening speech expresses a compassion, born of a knowledge of the common humanity in which all men participate, that qualifies her for bountiful love, although how she has come by it remains a mystery, since Ferdinand is only the third man that she has ever seen (I.ii.445).

On the other hand, we know nothing of Ferdinand. He affirms the honor of his intentions, but until those intentions are tested, not even he can be sure of them. The menial duty Prospero imposes on the young Prince will determine both the authenticity of his nobility and the quality of his admiration for Miranda. Prospero, of course, has no doubts as to Ferdinand's identity when he challenges him and accuses him of deception and conspiracy. What concerns him is whether Ferdinand himself is noble and honorable, or whether his honor and nobility go no deeper than the rank he has inherited. The trial he must undergo is therefore similar in purpose to the one Pericles undergoes before Simonides accepts him as worthy of Thaisa.

It is no coincidence that the audience first sees the captive Ferdinand in the ignominious role of log gatherer just after it has watched Caliban leave the stage singing of the freedom he expects to win through his conspiracy with Trinculo and Stephano. Caliban and Ferdinand, as A. H. Gilbert noticed some years ago,[20] are presented as foils. Caliban lost his freedom when he attempted to rape Miranda, and now Ferdinand, a captive, must demonstrate that he has not confused lust with love. The contrast between the two is developed further. Caliban endures his bondage rebelliously, fetching firewood only under the constant threat of physical punishment. Ferdinand, too, labors "upon a sore injunction" (III.i.11), but he endures his bondage and labor willingly, refusing even to consider Miranda's offer to help. His opening lines (III.i.1-13) distinguish the willingness with which he performs his task in terms of motive. Some men endure painful sports for the ultimate delight they bring. Others endure baseness, knowing that to do so is proof of nobleness. Still others endure "poor matters" because they "point to rich ends." But Ferdinand's motive is to serve a lady whom he admires, a mistress who "quickens what's dead,/And makes my labours pleasures." His only weakness seems to be an inclination to sit and admire her when he should be using his time to complete his work. The point is made in terms of remembering and forgetting:

> My sweet mistress
> Weeps when she sees me work, and says such baseness
> Had never like executor. I forget;
> But these sweet thoughts do even refresh my labours,
> Most busy least when I do it.   (III.i.11-15)

As the scene progresses and the lovers finally exchange vows to marry, Prospero is delighted, although not surprised. He has evidently foreseen that his daughter and Ferdinand will fall in love at first sight. What he has not known and what he will never be able to predict is the way in which Ferdinand will manage his affections. Prospero's response is no mere rhetorical expostulation:

> Fair encounter
> Of two most rare affections! Heavens rain grace
> On that which breeds between 'em!   (III.i.74-76)

He has been able through his art to bring the two together, and he has dictated the conditions of the trial. Appearances have seemed to indicate that the prince's intentions are honorable. He has not been coerced by threats of physical punishment, the only means that prove successful with Caliban, and he has transformed his captivity into voluntary service. Nor has he undertaken his labor in anticipation of future reward, for he distinguishes, as we have seen, his own painful burden from those "poor matters" that "point to rich ends." His complete satisfaction with present time and his readiness to put it to use in the service of Miranda are the strongest proof that he is an honorable and "patient log man."

The future of love, however, can never be certain, since men are free and love, as Hermione and Imogen discover, is precarious. Prospero in his efforts on Miranda's behalf has reached the limits of his art. He has discovered occasion and raised the tempest which has brought Ferdinand and the others to the island. He has informed her of her lineage and brought Ferdinand to the cell where he meets Miranda and is tested. He has controlled the present and begun to redeem the past. Now he must consider the future, recognizing that there is nothing he can do to assure that Miranda's future will be happy and fruitful. Once he grants Ferdinand his freedom, he can only endeavor to influence the course of love through prudent counsel. The course of future time will be in the hands of the lovers. The same will be true, obviously, for all of those who are presently within his power and who eventually will regain their freedom. The state of harmony which Prospero eventually brings about through his control of time will be, as he well knows, precarious and surely temporary.

As the play moves toward its conclusion Prospero faces his most serious challenge. He must accept the fact that his art is not omnipotent. Although it has allowed him to control the present, it cannot definitively shape the future. He will finally have to be willing to surrender his power over time and the elements, and trust that those he has held captive will use their freedom well.

The fourth act opens with Prospero explaining to Ferdinand his purpose in treating him as he has:

> All thy vexations
> Were but my trials of thy love, and thou
> Hast strangely stood the test. Here, afore Heaven,
> I ratify this my rich gift. (IV.i.5-8)

It is now up to Ferdinand to use time rightly:

> If thou dost break her virgin-knot before
> All sanctimonious ceremonies may
> With full and holy rite be minist'red,
> No sweet aspersion shall the heavens let fall
> To make this contract grow; but barren Hate,
> Sour-eyed Disdain, and Discord shall bestrew
> The union of your bed with weeds so loathly
> That you shall hate it both. Therefore take heed,
> As Hymen's lamps shall light you. (IV.i.15-23)

Violation of due occasion will turn time destructive. Ferdinand can only offer his word, vowing that he will never allow his honor to melt into lust (IV.i.26-28). Prospero can only trust.

The situation in this regard is similar to the one in *The Winter's Tale* in which Leontes chooses to believe in Florizel and agrees to intercede on his behalf with Polixenes (V.i.209-32). The parallel between the two situations is strengthened by the fact that both Ferdinand and Florizel give the men who have trusted them cause for doubting their honor. Leontes catches Florizel in a lie, and Prospero,

turning to Ferdinand after speaking with Ariel, discovers something
in his behavior that causes him to warn him again:

> Look thou be true; do not give dalliance
> Too much the rein. The strongest oaths are straw
> To th' fire i' th' blood. Be more abstemious,
> Or else good night your vow!   (IV.i.51-54)

The entertainment which follows also focuses upon the future by
celebrating the rich fulfillment that love duly sanctified can anticipate. To appreciate the brilliant way Prospero's entertainment contributes to the play's thematic concerns, it is necessary to recognize,
first of all, that it is a projection of Prospero's own fancy. As he explains to Ferdinand, the actors who perform in the entertainment are

> Spirits, which by mine art
> I have from their confines call'd to enact
> My present fancies.   (IV.i.120-22)

It is not, therefore, simply a revels entertainment sponsored by an
expansive father. It is a fiction in which Prospero momentarily loses
himself, forgetting the present and the business that still requires his
attention.

Iris is appropriately the one to commence the entertainment. Goddess of the rainbow and Juno's messenger, she is at once spring's har-
binger, promising the showers that will nourish spring growth, and
visible proof of Juno's approval of Ferdinand's and Miranda's love.
She is thus the embodiment of the grace which Prospero had hoped
for in III.i. ("Heavens rain grace / On that which breeds between
'em!") and to which he again refers earlier in the present scene as
the "sweet aspersion" he hopes the heavens will "let fall / To make
this contract grow."[21] Her invocation to Ceres is a celebration of the
harvest goddess's bountiful fertility. Ceres, before accepting the invitation, expresses the same concern Prospero earlier expressed. She
wants to know whether Venus and Cupid—those deities of erotic
love, with whom since Dis's abduction of Proserpina she will have
nothing to do—intend to come to the celebration. Since the spirit
who is playing the role of Ceres is acting out Prospero's fancies, Iris'

reply bears out the view proposed earlier that Prospero finds evidence of erotic passion in Ferdinand's "dalliance." Iris has met Venus and Cupid on their way to the celebration, intending to cast "some wanton charm" on the lovers, but they turned back, perhaps when Ferdinand heeded Prospero's warning.

The entertainment continues with heavenly Juno and earthly Ceres in lovely songs blessing the coming wedding. Then Ferdinand speaks, in lines that echo Florizel's at the climax of the flower ceremony in the fourth act of *The Winter's Tale*, of his complete involvement in Prospero's illusion:

> Let me live here ever;
> So rare a wond'red father and a wise
> Makes this place Paradise.   (IV.i.122-24)

The parallel with the floral scene in *The Winter's Tale* is illuminating. Florizel is so enraptured by the charm with which Perdita plays the role of Flora that he allows himself to be drawn wholly into the illusion of the ceremony, ignoring the care with which Perdita has communicated her awareness of the fact that she is only a simple shepherdess wearing Flora's robes and acting a goddess's role. While she insists on remembering this world and the problems it presents, Florizel accepts illusion as real: Perdita is no shepherd's daughter but a goddess. He longs to live forever in the present—in what seems to be a timeless moment. Ferdinand is also caught up in illusion. In the rapturous moment he mistakes the pastoral paradise of Prospero's creation with "this place."

Prospero, too, momentarily loses himself in his own idyllic creation. The fact that this creation is an expression of his inclination to retreat into contemplation distinguishes it from the perfect commonwealth conceived by Gonzalo in II.i. Both creations in their depiction of a timeless Arcadia are, at least in terms of this world, "unreal." But Gonzalo, the exemplar of prudence and constancy, never loses sight of the present. He, too, conceives his utopia to entertain, but as a *deliberate* distraction. The contrast is surely intentional, another instance of the technique of correspondences on which Shakespeare relies so heavily in these last plays. Gonzalo points out to Antonio and Sebastian, who have been ridiculing him, that he has spoken nonsense "to minister occasion":

Alonso: Prithee, no more; thou dost talk nothing to me.
Gonzalo: I do well believe your Highness; and did it to minister *occasion* to these gentlemen, who are of such sensible and nimble lungs that they always use to laugh at nothing. (II.i.170-75)

By imagining himself king of a commonwealth in which there would be "no sovereignty" he gives the complaining nobles something to ridicule and thus succeeds, at least for a few minutes, in getting them to forget the troubled present.[22] He also succeeds, by offering himself as a scapegoat, in distracting the attention of Antonio and Sebastian away from Alonso, on whom they have bitterly turned to blame for their present miseries. Gonzalo's final speech before Ariel enters indicates that he is satisfied to have accomplished what he had intended:

You are gentlemen of brave mettle; you would lift the moon out of her sphere, if she would continue in it five weeks without changing. (II.i.182-84)

Prospero, obviously, has intended neither to distract nor deceive Ferdinand, but only to provide a suitable entertainment and thus to fulfill a promise. But he becomes so absorbed in his own fancy's creation that he actually forgets, for the first and only time in the play, the troubled present. When he suddenly remembers, the serene pastoral scene, celebrating love as a bountiful source of generation in a world in which spring comes "at the farthest / In the very end of harvest," ends in confusion and with it the hope and optimism it had expressed. In that moment of remembering, the real world of corruption and sin violates his Arcadian creation as surely as his brother's conspiracy twelve years earlier in Milan had violated his study. That world is inhabited by Calibans and Trinculos, and it is in that world that he is responsible for time. Although his conception of a timeless world of self-renewing love may be the ultimate reality to which men aspire, it is the here and now which demands his attention. He must deal with "foul conspiracy."

It is a part of the play's design that Prospero should remember Caliban just as the autumnal fruition of generative love is being celebrated by the masque. In that moment Prospero's masque is transformed by Shakespeare into a dramatic emblem of *et in Arcadia ego*. After Juno has sung her blessing of the impending marriage, the harvest goddess sings hers. It is a blessing which leaves winter out of the cycle of conception, growth, fruition, and renewal:[23]

> Earth's increase, foison plenty,
> Barns and garners never empty,
> Vines with clust'ring bunches growing,
> Plants with goodly burden bowing.
> Spring come to you at the farthest
> In the very end of harvest!
> Scarcity and want shall shun you;
> Ceres' blessing so is on you.   (IV.i.110-17)

Then, following the pause during which Ferdinand expresses the wish to "live here ever," the masque action resumes with Iris calling nymphs and reapers together to join in a dance which celebrates the union of spring and harvest time. Her first call is to the "temperate nymphs" of the spring brooks:

> You nymphs, call'd Naiads, of the wind'ring brooks,
> With your sedg'd crowns and ever-harmless looks,
> Leave your crisp channels, and on this green land
> Answer your summons; Juno does command.
> Come, temperate nymphs, and help to celebrate
> A contract of true love; be not too late.
>   (IV.i.128-33)

She next summons the "sunburnt sicklemen of August":

> Come hither from the furrow and be merry.
> Make holiday; your rye-straw hats put on
> And these fresh nymphs encounter every one
> In country footing.   (IV.i.135-38)

Just as the dance which follows nears completion—just as the cycle of growth is about to be completed and spring is again to come out of "the very end of harvest"—Prospero remembers that "the minute" of Caliban's "plot is almost come" and the illusion is dissipated. In the sequence of real time it is of course winter, the season of tempests, that follows the harvest. But the emblematic import is nevertheless clear. Death and tempestuous weather are the wages of evil, and it is the recollection of evil which destroys Prospero's pastoral.[24] Whether the intruder into Arcadia be a serpent, or death, or Caliban, it is the persistence of evil with which fathers and governors and lovers have to contend.

In the moment of Prospero's remembering Caliban, and the need once again to deal with conspiracy, the action reaches its crisis. Prospero is more deeply troubled than he has ever been at any time in the play. The lovers are alarmed:

> *Ferdinand:* This is strange. Your father's in some passion
> That works him strongly.
> *Miranda:*   Never till this day
> Saw I him touch'd with anger, so distemper'd.
>   (IV.i.143-45)

The passion that works so strongly within him is the anger of an old man forced to admit to himself the futility of an idealistic enterprise to which he has devoted nearly a lifetime. In spite of his patient efforts, evil has proved intractable. Caliban remains

> A devil, a born devil, on whose nature
> Nurture can never stick; on whom my pains,
> Humanely taken, all, all lost, quite lost; . . .
>   (IV.i.188-90)

The art to which he has devoted so many years of study is limited to externals. It does not enable him to alter the fundamental nature of things. Although it affords him a means of partially controlling the present and of constraining evil, it affords him no means of altering the round of time. Death, a legacy of the past, is a future certainty. Before spring, birth, and renewal, there must be winter; and always within the cycle of human life there will be Calibans with whom to contend, intractable in their perversity and persistent in their desire to destroy the good.

As Prospero contemplates the futility of his efforts, his anger gives way to a profound melancholy in which death, alone, appears to him to be the one reality in a world of dissolving particulars:

> Our revels now are ended. These our actors,
> As I foretold you, were all spirits, and
> Are melted into air, into thin air;
> And, like the baseless fabric of this vision,
> The cloud-capp'd towers, the gorgeous palaces,
> The solemn temples, the great globe itself,
> Yea, all which it inherit, shall dissolve
> And, like this insubstantial pageant faded,
> Leave not a rack behind. We are such stuff
> As dreams are made on, and our little life
> Is rounded with a sleep. (IV.i.148-58)

This vision of the world is not an expression of Christian resignation;[25] nor is it intended by Shakespeare to be the play's ultimate statement about the nature of reality. It is the vision of a world-weary old man whose faith in the renewing power of love and the ultimate reality of the Arcadian world it promises has been overcome by his acute awareness of evil and of the world's mortality.

Nowhere in the romances is the role of faith in Shakespeare's epistemology so movingly expressed. If Prospero's vision of a winterless world of eternally renewing love is nothing more than an idle fancy conceived as a revels entertainment, then the human history acted out upon the stage of the "globe," with its "cloud-capp'd towers," is "insubstantial"—a mere sequence of evanescent illusions in a meaningless "pageant" in which time is only the measure of ripening and rotting and change the only reality.

But Prospero's world-weariness is only a momentary aberration. Never before has he questioned the value of time or shown the slightest inclination to view the past as a mere succession of yesterdays lighting "the way to dusty death." In his use of time he has revealed his belief in a purpose and meaning in the flow of events that has taken place within it. He has endeavored to awaken the consciences of his old enemies, confronting them with the alternatives of redemption through "heart's sorrow" or "ling'ring perdition"; only moments earlier he affirmed his belief in love's power to renew, as well as to redeem, and in man's capacity to participate in nature's generative process. Now, he acknowledges his momentary weakness and reassures the lovers: "Bear with my weakness—my old brain is troubled. / Be not disturb'd with my infirmity" (IV.i.159-60). He will weather the tempestuous moment, renewing his faith in the substantiality of the human pageant and resuming his obligation to time.

Prospero's recovery is not announced. It is revealed, instead, by the final sequence of actions which he initiates by turning his attentions once again to Caliban and his accomplices and which he completes by forgiving his old enemies, discarding his magical powers, and resuming his private and public identity as a member of the human community. In the course of those actions he demonstrates his full acceptance of the conditions into which all men are born by accepting the legacy of sin and death and the public burden it imposes upon those who have public time in their keeping, and by reaffirming his faith in the legacy of renewing love.

These actions are emblematic and ceremonial rather than dramatic. Although they resolve the three hours of action upon which the play focuses, and thus the action begun twelve years earlier when Prospero neglected time, they are not depicted in the terms we ordinarily expect in drama. Prospero is not a protagonist who, after struggling to reach a decision on which to act, finally resolves uncertainties through decisive choice and action. He is, rather, a participant in an emblematic action in which Shakespeare celebrates for a final time the love which all men share as their common legacy.

In the course of this action various characters emerge as exemplars and emblematic representatives of ideas that have been important throughout the play. Their transformation is accomplished by a shift in mimetic focus. Stephano and Trinculo, for instance, are stripped of the particular attributes of character which in earlier scenes made them merely entertaining rascals. They become representative of those incorrigibles who, like Lucio and others in *Measure for*

Measure, can only be made to obey the law through physical punishment and constraint. Similar transformations are evident in Antonio and Sebastian, Ferdinand and Miranda, and Caliban. Antonio and Sebastian represent in their silence those who remain a threat, even in the moment of reconciliation and renewal, to communal harmony and the civic virtues. Ferdinand and Miranda represent the new generation who, with the untarnished innocence of youth, look forward idealistically to living happily ever after in "a brave new world." Caliban emerges as the symbolic embodiment of the evil which is transmitted from generation to generation by perverse, and therefore destructive, love and which in *Pericles* is represented by the incestuous King and Princess of Antioch and in *Cymbeline* by Cloten and his mother. Sired by a devil and conceived by the witch Sycorax, he is the legacy of evil incarnate which man must acknowledge as his own.

But the most interesting participant in this final action is Prospero. Through the choices he makes he not only confirms his own humanity and rejoins the human community as governor of Milan; he also becomes exemplar of the faith upon which the substantiality of the world's pageant depends. He retains to the end of the dramatic action his identity as exiled governor of Milan, brother to Antonio, and father to Miranda; but the particulars of which his identity within the fiction of the play is composed are subsumed by newly emerging ones which identify him as Presenter of the ceremonial final scene and Spokesman for the dramatist himself.

Prospero initiates his return to the social order, from which he has so long been an exile, by turning his attentions once again to Caliban and his accomplices and thus resuming the role that he has been given in the world's pageant. It is the duty of those who have public time in their keeping to maintain constant vigilance. There are some natures on whom "nurture can never stick." Such "natures" require of the prudent governor scrupulous surveillance and the rigorous exercise of power. He must never *forget* the evil that exists within the natural order, and he must resign himself to the fact that force and punishment are the only means of controlling those who are incapable of, or who reject, "heart's sorrow."

Having accepted the legacy of evil, Prospero proceeds to affirm, through his resolution to forgive his old enemies, his faith in that other legacy, the renewing power of love through which fallen man may redeem the past and renew the future. The readiness to forgive, as we have seen in *Cymbeline*, originates in *nosce teipsum*—in the knowledge that all men born of Adam stand in need of mercy. That Prospero has attained such knowledge is evident in his response to Ariel's account of the effects his "charm" has worked upon Gonzalo and his old enemies.

> *Ariel:*   Your charm so strongly works 'em
> That if you now beheld them, your affections
> Would become tender.
> *Prospero:*   Dost thou think so, spirit?
> *Ariel:* Mine would, sir, were I human.
> *Prospero:*   And mine shall.
> Hast thou, which art but air, a touch, a feeling
> Of their afflictions, and shall not myself,
> One of their kind, that relish all as sharply
> Passion as they, be kindlier mov'd than thou art?
> Though with their high wrongs I am struck to th' quick,
> Yet with my nobler reason 'gainst my fury
> Do I take part. The rarer action is
> In virtue than in vengeance. They being penitent,
> The sole drift of my purpose doth extend
> Not a frown further.   (V.i.17-30)

Prospero's response to Ariel's account is identical to Miranda's response in the opening act to the shipwreck she witnesses. He is compassionate. He has "a feeling" of the "afflictions" which all men suffer; and he is "mov'd" in a way that is natural to human*kind*. His readiness to "feel what wretches feel" is, in short, an expression of the love "in the nature of man" which Elyot identifies as the principal virtue of "humanity" (*The Governor*, pp. 120-21) and which, according to both Elyot and Shakespeare, finds its noblest expression in forgiving—in transcending the strict logic of retributive justice.

By choosing forgiveness as "the rarer action" Prospero not only affirms his own humanity and his faith in the humanity of others; he also proves that he has acquired the prudence he formerly lacked. "By the consideration of things past and of that which hath followed since," he has judged that "which in the like case may fall out in the time following." He has inspected the times, weighed the dangers, and recognized the occasions; and he has "boldly setteth his hand to the work."[26] He does not "forget" the "high wrongs" committed against him; nor will he, in forgiving Sebastian and Antonio, naively assume that they are now any more ready to lead morally exemplary lives than Caliban, Trinculo, and Stephano. He will maintain a measure of control over them by revealing to them his knowledge of their plan to murder Alonso. But he also remembers and trusts in that other legacy, the power, or "virtue," of love through which even a Sebastian or an Antonio may renew his fallen nature. He is now fully prepared to assume the active duties of the office which he formerly had neglected in favor of study and contemplation.

Here again, in the moment of Prospero's decision to forgive, we see figured forth the dependency of the restorative pattern upon faith; for it is Prospero's faith in the power of man to renew himself that completes the restorative pattern figured forth in the play. The proof of his faith is his readiness to give up his art. Although his magic allows him the power to control the very things which caused adversity for Pericles, Posthumus, Imogen, and Leontes—he can raise a tempest, control the elements, create compelling illusions—he, too, must finally confront the future as each of his predecessors did. He must accept gently what ungently comes, even the malice latent in the brooding silence of Antonio and Sebastian, as the legacy of fallen man—grounding his hope for the renewal of his lines of life in the fruitfulness of Ferdinand's and Miranda's love. He must also, as a governor, be ready to use force and punishment when the community that is in his keeping is threatened by the Antonios and Sebastians of the world.

Prospero's role within the play's fiction as the renewing agent who completes its restorative action is essentially over in the moment that he announces his resolution to forgive. What follows is an acting out of that decision in which we see him responding compassionately to Gonzalo, forgiving the contrite Alonso, maintaining his advantage over his brother and Sebastian in the very act of forgiving them, and acknowledging Caliban, "this thing of darkness," as his own. But, as I have indicated earlier, Prospero has in this final scene another and equally important role as presenter of a ceremonial action and as spokesman for Shakespeare. In this role he affords Shakespeare the means not only of commenting directly upon the nature of the play's denouement but also of affirming once again the vital role of faith in the epistemological and ethical systems articulated in *The Tempest* and in each of the earlier romances.

Prospero's identification with Shakespeare in the final act is carefully prepared. From the moment Prospero raises the tempest which initiates the action by casting up the voyagers on his island until he delivers the play's epilogue, he is depicted as Stage Director and Surrogate Dramatist. The action over which he presides as Dramatist and Director is, in turn, identified metaphorically with the action of a play—first, by Antonio's speech on the past as "prologue" and again, by Prospero's melancholy reflection on the "insubstantial pageant" of the world. There is also the fact that Prospero in his other role as principal participant in the play's action exercises his powers as illusionist to create dramatic fictions. In this role he is depicted as an artist who, like Sidney's Poet and Shakespeare himself, uses his powers of illusion to teach, to delight, and to persuade. He endeavors to move his old enemies to virtuous action by holding up a mirror to their fallen natures, and he entertains Miranda and Ferdinand with a revels masque which figures forth and celebrates the Idea of renewing love and the ultimate reality of a winterless world which it alone promises.

In both of his roles, then, Prospero is identified as a dramatist, and thus, implicitly, with Shakespeare. As surrogate playwright he plots the action, creating and controlling the situations in which the characters find themselves and finally deciding the denouement; as protagonist he is an artist who uses his skills as an illusionist to the same ends that Shakespeare has used his own skills in creating the fictional worlds of *Pericles, Cymbeline, The Winter's Tale,* and *The Tempest* itself.

Prospero's identification with Shakespeare is completed in the final act when, after reminding us that his "project" gathers "to a head," he announces that he intends to resolve the play's action by forgiving his old enemies. From that moment on until the play is over, our attention is focused upon his role as "author" and "director" of the action. His resemblance in that role to the author not only of *The Tempest* but of the earlier romances as well, is striking. During the play he has confronted its characters with the same kinds of trials that Shakespeare has devised for the principal characters of the earlier romances. He has raised a tempest and separated a king from his only heir. He has tested the readiness of wrong-doers to repent, and he has tried the constancy of youthful love. Now, in the play's final moments he steps forward to affirm his faith in the restorative power of love by providing the play with a conclusion that differs only in its incidental particulars from the conclusions that Shakespeare has provided the earlier romances. Alonso, like Leontes, recovers, through the right use of memory, the heir he has lost; Ferdinand, like Pericles and Florizel, wins the maiden he loves after proving to a man of winter the authenticity of his love; Gonzalo, the prudent counsellor—like his predecessors Helicanus, Pisanio, and Camillo—is reunited with his master. The communities of Naples and Milan, like Cymbeline's Britain and Leontes' Sicilia, have been purged of long-standing disorders and the lineal succession of their ruling houses has been reassured. Through his readiness to forgive, Prospero affirms his faith in man's power to renew himself and he thus completes the restorative action of the play.

We see, then, in this final scene a celebration of the theme of restoring, sustaining, and renewing power of love—the theme that Shakespeare has celebrated in *Pericles, Cymbeline,* and *The Winter's Tale;* and it has been presented to us by a master of illusion who in his role as surrogate dramatist strongly resembles Shakespeare himself. But the resemblance between Prospero and Shakespeare does not stop there. When the play is over, Prospero and the dramatist face the future as all men must. They are supported only by their trust in the "mutual concord and love in the nature of man." The only alternative to trust is the despair of a Timon. All men is their imperfection stand in need of forgiveness; and it is only through their forgiving of one another that they may affirm their "humanity." Love alone in this view is the sustaining force of human institutions as well as of humanity itself. It is the generative principle in the universe by which genera and species are sustained within the mutable order and which assures the substantiality of the world's pageant, even though the pageant itself seems to consist only of dissolving particulars.

Time, Tide, and Tempest

Notes

[1]Herbert R. Coursen, Jr., "Prospero and the Drama of the Soul," *Shakespeare Studies*, 4 (1968), 316-33.

[2]See, for example, Colin Still, *Shakespeare's Mystery Play* (London, 1921); G. Wilson Knight, *The Shakespearean Tempest* (London, 3rd ed., 1953); Derek Traversi, *Shakespeare: The Last Phase* (New York, 1954); Northrop Frye, *A Natural Perspective* (New York, 1965); and A. D. Nuttall, *Two Concepts of Allegory* (London, 1967).

[3]G. B. Harrison, "*The Tempest*," in *Stratford Papers on Shakespeare*, No. 848 (1962), 212-38.

[4]Frank Kermode, ed., in *The Tempest* in *The Arden Edition of The Works of William Shakespeare* (London, 1954), p. lxxxvii.

[5]David Galloway in *Shakespeare Series*, II of College Classics in English (New York, 1969), 240.

[6]*Ibid.*, 241.

[7]The infant Miranda provides Prospero with the will and strength to endure the raging seas. Compare the following passage with *Pericles*, III.i.15-27:

> *Prospero:*   O, a cherubin
> Thou wast that did preserve me. Thou didst smile,
> Infused with a fortitude from heaven,
> When I have deck'd the sea with drops full salt,
> Under my burden groan'd; which rais'd in me
> An undergoing stomach, to bear up
> Against what should ensue.   (I.ii.152-58)

[8]Philip Brockbank, in "*The Tempest*: Conventions of Art and Empire," *Stratford-Upon-Avon Studies*, VIII (London, 1966), suggests that the storm raised by Prospero may have its source in Sylvester Jourdain's account of Sir Thomas Gates' and Sir George Summers' discovery of the Bermudas. The survival of Gates and Sir George Summers "had something of the miraculous, and it invited as much comment on the ways of Providence as the skill and resourcefulness of English sailors . . . . Shakespeare, with the storms of *Othello* and *The Winter's Tale* freshly accomplished for the theatre, would recognize occasion enough for a play on the story of the Bermudas wreck. And the material offers itself most invitingly to a playwright whose interest in the ways of Providence, and in the conversion and salvation of man, had matured through long practice in allegoric, romantic comedy" (p. 185). The passages Brockbank cites from *A Discovery* do indeed suggest that *The Tempest* is in some measure indebted to it. But, given the pervasiveness of the tempest, throughout the literature of the sixteenth century and throughout Shakespeare from his earliest work on, as emblematic of adversity directed by providence, it is impossible to accept the tempest in Jourdain's narrative as the only source for Prospero's storm. The emblematic tempest was available to both Jourdain and Shakespeare in a variety of visual and verbal expressions.

[9]Shakespeare's earliest use of the tempest emblem occurs in *3 Henry VI*. Queen Margaret speaks to the beleaguered loyalist forces on the plains near Tewkesbury, attempting to fortify their hopes and thus strengthen their will to resist.

> Great lords, wise men ne'er sit and wail their loss,
> But cheerly seek how to redress their harms.
> What though the mast be now blown overboard,
> The cable broke, the holding-anchor lost,
> And half our sailors swallow'd in the flood?
> Yet lives our pilot still. Is't meet that he
> Should leave the helm and like a fearful lad
> With tearful eyes add water to the sea
> And give more strength to that which hath too much,
> Whiles, in his moan, the ship splits on the rock,
> Which industry and courage might have sav'd?
> Ah, what a shame! ah, what a fault were this!
> Say Warwick was our anchor; what of that?
> And Montague our topmast; what of him?
> Our slaught'red friends the tackles; what of these?
> Why, is not Oxford here another anchor?
> And Somerset another goodly mast?
> The friends of France our shrouds and tacklings?
> And, though unskillful, why not Ned and I
> For once allow'd the skillful pilot's charge?
> We will not from the helm to sit and weep,
> But keep our course, though the rough wind say no,
> From shelves and rocks that threaten us with wreck.
> As good to chide the waves as speak them fair.
> . . . .
> This speak I, lords, to let you understand,
> If case some one of you would fly from us,
> That there's no hop'd-for mercy with the brothers
> More than with ruthless waves, with sands and rocks.
> Why, courage then! What cannot be avoided
> 'Twere childish weakness to lament or fear.   (V.iv.1-38)

Friar Lawrence in Arthur Brooke's *Romeus and Juliet* finds the same figure appropriate when confronted by a Romeus who is so deeply distraught by the news of his exile that he threatens suicide. Similarities of phrasing suggest that the Friar's speech is a source for Margaret's:

> A wise man in the midst of troubles and distres,
> Still standes not wayling present harme, but seeks his harmes redres,
> As when the winter flawes with dredfull noyse arise,
> And heave the fomy swelling waves up to the starry skies,
> So that the broosed barke in cruell seas betost,
> Dispayreth of the happy haven in daunger to be lost.
> The pylate bold a helme, cryes, mates strike now your sayle
> And turnes her stemme into the waves, that strongly her assayle,
> Then, driven hard upon the bare and wrackfull shore,
> In greater daunger to be wract, then he had been before
> He seeth his ship full right against the rocke to ronne,
> But yet he dooth what lyeth in him the perilous rocke to shonne.

Sometimes the beaten boate, by cunning government,
The ancors lost, the cables broke, and all the tackle spent,
The roder smitten of and over boord the mast,
Doth win the long desyred porte, the stormy daunger past.
But if the master dread, and overprest with woe,
Begin to wring his handes, and lets the gyding rodder goe
The ship rents on the rocke, or sinketh in the deepe,
And eke the coward drenched is.   (ll. 1358-78)

[10]Two studies of *The Tempest* have recently appeared in which the importance of the dramatic present is accurately assessed: Ernest Gohn's "*The Tempest:* Theme and Structure," *English Studies*, 45 (1964), 116-25, and James E. Robinson's "Time and *The Tempest*," *Journal of English and Germanic Philology*, 63 (1964), 255-67. Gohn, noting how often in the play the word *now* occurs, goes on to comment on the play's structure: "The episodes of the play are usually conceived in a present which is a crucial nexus uniting the past to the future: the past is relevant only as it affects the present" (p. 117). Robinson finds that the structure of *The Tempest* "involves a movement that defines a present crisis as it has evolved from the past and reaches resolution only when all are aware of the relation of the past to the present" (p. 256). It is a "circular structure" which he suggests derives from the medieval and Renaissance commentaries on Terence: "In Terence the one day (two days in one play) of dramatic action becomes, as Donatus and the Renaissance commentators realized, the day wherein a whole history is revealed and resolved, and 'order and circle' of life brought to happy consummation" (p. 258). Robinson does not discuss the concepts of cyclical time and recurrent occasion that I have stressed throughout this study, but his reading of *The Tempest* indicates that he is aware of their presence in the play. He observes, for instance, that the time spanned in the play is "an embodiment of the transient course of the world and the intense demands on life that the swift force of time effects." He sees time as Prospero's "most pressing protagonist" (p. 259). Time, in this play as in those I have already discussed, is simply neutral, with its value determined by the purposes to which it is used.

Robinson's discussion is valuable and persuasive and generally supportive of my own reading of the play. I would add to his conclusions that if Shakespeare found the "circular structure" of Terentian comedy suitable to his own purposes in *The Tempest*, it was because he had long been interested in concepts of cyclical and tempestuous time, of occasion and of renewal.

[11]Robinson notes (p. 261) that "Time comes full circle in the last act of the play . . . when the relation of past and present is explained to all the characters."

[12]F. D. Hoeniger notices certain of these parallels: "The real significance of the intrigue of Antonio and Sebastian is that it parallels the events which caused Prospero's exile, and which he is about to rectify. Antonio can be said to re-enact his past evil deed. Thus to a degree, the past and present are combined not only in the characterization of Prospero, but also in that of his enemies." "Prospero's Storm and Miracle," *Shakespeare Quarterly*, 7 (1956), 33-38.

[13]See Chapter I, p. 17.

[14]*Time and the End of Time* (London, 1664), p. 4.

[15]*Time and the End of Time*, p. 5.

[16]Some critics have interpreted Prospero's testiness here and elsewhere in the play as evidence of his desire for revenge. See, for example, Kenneth Muir, *Last Periods of Shakespeare, Racine, and Ibsen* (Detroit, 1961), p. 52.

[17]The symbolic significance of the disappearing banquet scene has been the occasion of a good deal of critical speculation. See Frank Kermode's notes to III.iii.17 in the New Arden edition of the play in which he observes that the illusory banquet "is' conceivably related to allegorical interpretations of Scripture. Eve was tempted with an apple, and Christ with an illusory banquet; the former temptation successful, as with the 'men of sin,' the latter a failure, as with the pure Gonzalo." Northrop Frye in *A Natural Perspective* suggests that "the disappearing banquet stands for the deceitful and illusory status" of what the court group has assumed to be reality (i.e. "whatever their greed can clutch"), p. 157. Robert G. Hunter in *Shakespeare and the Comedy of Forgiveness* (New York, 1965), pp. 227-41, argues that the banquet is "the commonest of all symbolic banquets: the communion table" (p. 234). Hunter's reading seems to me to be the more persuasive, perhaps only because it is consistent with my own view that the illusion, itself, is a mirror created by Prospero in which the evil doers are made to see themselves and what they have brought upon themselves.

[18]p. 53.

[19]Helena, for instance, in *All's Well that Ends Well*.

[20]"*The Tempest:* Parallelism in Characters and Situations," *Journal of English and Germanic Philology*, 14 (1915), 63-74.

[21]Northrop Frye (*A Natural Perspective*, pp. 157-58) suggests that the symbolism within the entertainment is Christian: "What the wedding masque presents is the meeting of earth and heaven under the rainbow, the symbol of Noah's new-washed world, after the tempest and flood had receded, and when it was promised that springtime and harvest would not cease. There is in fact a definite recall of the biblical scene:

> Spring come to you at the farthest
> In the very end of harvest."

The Christian meanings are surely there, though I would insist that they are deliberately submerged, as I believe similar Christian meanings are deliberately submerged in each of the earlier romances and in *King Lear*.

There is, incidentally, in Jean Seznec's *The Survival of the Pagan Gods* (New York, 1953) a discussion of a medieval allegorization of Juno as memory which suggests an iconographical tradition that might throw further light on Prospero's "entertainment." Seznec's subject is a mythological treatise by John Ridewall (*Fulgentius metaforalis*) in which "the chapter sequence is determined by the identification of gods with Virtues. Saturn is Prudence, and since Prudence is made up of Memory, Intelligence, and Foresight, Ridewall next treats of Saturn's children: Juno-Memoria, Neptune-Intelligencia, Pluto-Providencia; and finally of Jupiter-Benevolencia, who sums up Prudentia, Sapientia, and Intelligencia." The working out of the allegory, Seznec continues, "is carried out to fantastic extremes . . . Juno, as we have seen, is identified with Memory, and therefore has the following attributes: she is veiled, crowned with a rainbow, and perfumed; she holds a scepter, is bound by a golden chain, surrounded by peacocks, etc. . . . All these details are explained by the very fact that the goddess represents memory.

"Memory does, of course, keep alive the recollection of sin: hence the veil behind which Juno may hide her shame. The recollection of sin leads to repentance, and thus to reconciliation with God: this explains the rainbow, sign of divine forgiveness. Reconciliation gives birth to spiritual consolation, which fills the soul with rapture: hence the perfumes. And having, by virtue of Memory, attained repentance and reconciliation, the soul in its new state of blessedness regains that mastery of itself which sin had caused it to lose: hence the scepter, etc." (p. 94).

The connections between Prospero's Juno and Ridewall's are elusive but, when considered in the light of the importance attributed to memory and "heart's sorrow" throughout the play, extremely suggestive.

[22]G. C. Waterston in "Shakespeare and Montaigne: A Footnote to *The Tempest*," *The Romanic Review*, 40 (1949), 165-72, suggests that to Gonzalo Shakespeare gave Montaigne's own habit of meeting adversity with intellectual diversion. Waterston misses the point that Gonzalo is diverting the rest of the royal party, who have been unable to accept their adversity in the spirit of gentle resignation which Gonzalo's own behavior exemplifies.

[23]The point is noted by Richard J. Quinones in "Views of Time in Shakespeare," *The Journal of the History of Ideas*, 26 (1965), 327-52. "Through the 'vanity of his art' Prospero seeks to lend a permanence and continuance to the passing things of this world. . . . In the masque that he creates for the newly-pledged lovers, Miranda and Ferdinand, Love is granted extension in a majestic vision of bounty and grace. Heaven and Earth unite to enrich this Prayer for a Daughter. Even Nature, in this idealized picture, seeks to avoid the wintry season of decline . . ." (p. 351).

[24]Caliban interrupts Prospero's "revels" as Marcade in *Love's Labour's Lost* (V.ii. 723-29) and Polixenes in *The Winter's Tale* (IV.ii.427-34) interrupt festive time.

[25]For a radically different interpretation of this speech see S. L. Bethell, "Planes of Reality," from *Shakespeare and the Popular Dramatic Tradition* (London, 1944). Reprinted in *Modern Shakespearean Criticism*, ed. Alvin B. Kernan (New York, 1970), pp. 21-22.

[26]Peter de la Primaudaye, *The French Academy*. I have quoted the full text of Primaudaye's definition of prudence in Chapter I, p. 17.

INDEX

91; compared with *Pericles*, 60-61; "distancing" in, 63-64; Perdita and Marina compared, 81; compared with *Cymbeline*, 118, 124-25, 151-52; seeing, dependency on faith, 149 *n*18; source of Leontes' jealousy, 152-60 *passim;* Shakespeare's replotting of *Pandosto*, 153-59; destructive action, 161-67; renewing action, 167-209; Autolycus' role, 170-71, 175, 182, 183-85, 188-91, 199-202, 212 *n*20; the play as "speaking picture," 205-09; Florizel and Ferdinand compared, 236-38; mentioned, 3, 9, 10, 18, 36, 68 *n*40, 104 *n*1, 112, 113, 216, 217, 222, 225, 247, 248, 250 *n*8, 254 *n*24. *See also* Appearance and reality, Emblems, Emblematic mode, Emblematic scenes, Memory, Mimesis, Occasion, Time

Wither, George: emblem of occasion, 43-44; emblem of constancy, 49-50; emblem of patience, 69 *n*47; mentioned, 68 *n*39, 69 *n*49

Woodhouse, A. S. P., 65 *n*21

Wrednot, William, 64 *n*12

Wriosthesly, Henry, 69 *n*46

Wyatt, Thomas: Eros as pilot, 55